CW01023979

Few in Europe doubt that climate change repres
lenge. But less obvious is the extent to which cli
a subject and tool of global diplomacy in recer
well-researched book, Ingrid Boas sheds light o
pean states—notably the UK—have constructed
threat, and their unsuccessful efforts to persuade major emerging developing
countries—notably India—that this threat is significant. Her analysis tells us
much about the misunderstandings and mistrust that beset international diplomacy in the twenty-first century.

—*Richard Black, Professor, SOAS, University of London*

Threats of 'climate wars' and floods of 'climate refugees' have been central
in the climate-change discourse for years, especially in the richer countries in
the North. But does such 'securitisation' of climate policy really help? Who
pushes discourses of 'environmental security', and who benefits? Ingrid Boas'
outstanding analysis reveals in great detail the complex politics around recent
attempts at a 'securitisation' of climate politics. Her book is a must-read for
scholars as well as policy makers in this field, who will find in this remarkable
study an important insight: 'scare stories' are not the best means to convince
an already sceptical audience.

—*Frank Biermann, VU University Amsterdam*
and Lund University

Climate Migration and Security

Climate migration, as an image of people moving due to sea-level rise and increased drought, has been presented as one of the main security risks of global warming. The rationale is that climate change will cause a mass movement of climate refugees, causing tensions and even violent conflict. Through the lens of climate change politics and securitisation theory, Ingrid Boas examines how and why climate migration has been presented in terms of security and reviews the political consequences of such framing exercises.

This study is done through a macro–micro analysis and concentrates on the period of the early 2000s until the end of September 2014. The macro-level analysis provides an overview of the coalitions of states that favour or oppose security framings on climate migration. It shows how European and small island states have been key actors to present climate migration as a matter of security, while the emerging developing countries have actively opposed such a framing. The book argues that much of the division between these state alliances can be traced back to climate change politics. As a next step, the book delves into UK–India interactions to provide an in-depth analysis of these security framings and their connection with climate change politics. This micro-level analysis demonstrates how the UK has strategically used security framings on climate migration to persuade India to commit to binding targets to reduce their greenhouse gas emissions. The book examines how and why such a strategy has emerged, and most importantly, to what extent it has been successful.

Climate Migration and Security is the first book of its kind to examine the strategic use of security arguments on climate migration as a political tool in climate change politics. Original theoretical, empirical, and policy-related insights will provide students, scholars, and policy makers with the necessary tools to review the effectiveness of these framing strategies for the purpose of climate change diplomacy and delve into the wider implications of these framing strategies for the governance of climate change.

Ingrid Boas is Assistant Professor in Climate Governance at the Environmental Policy Group at Wageningen University, the Netherlands. Her research particularly focusses on the topic of climate change-induced migration and climate security.

Environmental Politics/Routledge Research in Environmental Politics
Edited by Steve Vanderheiden
University of Colorado at Boulder

Over recent years environmental politics has moved from a peripheral interest to a central concern within the discipline of politics. This series aims to rein-force this trend through the publication of books that investigate the nature of contemporary environmental politics and show the centrality of environmental politics to the study of politics per se. The series understands politics in a broad sense and books will focus on mainstream issues such as the policy process and new social movements as well as emerging areas such as cultural politics and political economy. Books in the series will analyse contemporary political practices with regards to the environment and/or explore possible future direc-tions for the 'greening' of contemporary politics. The series will be of interest not only to academics and students working in the environmental field, but will also demand to be read within the broader discipline.

The series consists of two strands:

Environmental Politics addresses the needs of students and teachers, and the titles will be published in paperback and hardback. Titles include:

Global Warming and Global Politics
Matthew Paterson

Politics and the Environment
James Connelly and Graham Smith

International Relations Theory and Ecological Thought
Towards synthesis
Eric Laferrière and Peter Stoett

Planning Sustainability
Edited by Michael Kenny and James Meadowcroft

Deliberative Democracy and the Environment
Graham Smith

EU Enlargement and the Environment
Institutional change and environmental policy in Central
and Eastern Europe
Edited by JoAnn Carmin and Stacy D. VanDeveer

The Crisis of Global Environmental Governance
Towards a new political economy of sustainability
Edited by Jacob Park, Ken Conca and Matthias Finger

Routledge Research in Environmental Politics presents innovative new research intended for high-level specialist readership. These titles are published in hardback only and include:

Climate Migration and Security
Securitisation as a Strategy in Climate Change Politics

Ingrid Boas

Routledge
Taylor & Francis Group

LONDON AND NEW YORK

First published 2015
by Routledge

2 Park Square, Milton Park, Abingdon, Oxon OX14 4RN
711 Third Avenue, New York, NY 10017, USA

Routledge is an imprint of the Taylor & Francis Group, an informa business

First issued in paperback 2017

Library of Congress Cataloging-in-Publication Data
A catalog record has been requested

ISBN: 978-1-138-81151-5 (hbk)
ISBN: 978-1-138-06668-7 (pbk)

Typeset in Times New Roman
by Apex CoVantage, LLC

Contents

Figures

Tables

Acknowledgements

This book originates from my PhD research conducted at the University of Kent, which was funded by the UK Economic Social Research Council. Above all, I am indebted to Anne Hammerstad and Frank Biermann, my supervisors, for all their advice and support they have given me throughout this period. I would also like to thank Richard Black and Feargal Cochrane, who served as external examiners to my PhD thesis, for their valuable feedback and encouragements to turn my thesis into a book.

To achieve that goal, I again have numerous people to thank. First of all, my colleagues at the Environmental Policy Group at Wageningen University, who supported my journey to write this book. With particular thanks to Megan Bailey, Jan van Tatenhove, and Jennifer Lenhart who I could always turn to for advice. I would also like to thank Giovanni Bettini, Delf Rothe, and Chris Methmann who all gave valuable feedback to earlier versions of my work. I am indebted to Delf Rothe who told me about the Discourse Network Analyser software I used to extend the analysis conducted for this book.

I am grateful to all people who agreed to be interviewed for this analysis. I know their time is precious and therefore much appreciate the time they have made available to speak to me. I thank them all. With special thanks to Joel Watson and Sarah Cullum of the FCO. I found it inspiring how both Joel and Sarah were open in sharing their experiences with academics, and have been actively engaged in dialogues around the issue of climate change and security. I am indebted to Ranjit Gupta and Madhukar Gupta for introducing me to so many relevant interviewees in India. I very much appreciate all they have done for me. My field research in India was an incredible experience that I will never forget. For that reason, I am again grateful to Anne Hammerstad and her family who made this possible.

Last but not least, I would like to thank my friends and family for all the support they have given me the past few years. With special thanks to my father and Freek for making so much time available for reading and discussing my work. Writing a PhD, and on top of that a book, is a real journey, and I am grateful they wanted to share it with me.

1   Introduction

The Securitisation of Climate Migration

Climate change-induced migration (in short, climate migration), as an image of people moving due to sea-level rise, increased drought, and flooding, has been presented as one of the main security risks of global warming. In 2007, for instance, *The Guardian* opened an article with the headline: 'Climate wars threaten billions. More than 100 countries face political chaos and mass migration in global warming catastrophe' (McKie 2007). Alarming statements were made by non-governmental organisations (NGOs), such as Christian Aid, who warned that 'without urgent action, climate change will make the forced displacement crisis the biggest threat facing developing countries over the next 50 years' (Christian Aid 2007: 5). Margaret Beckett, the UK Foreign Secretary who served from 2006 to 2007, also discussed the matter through security lenses:

> Take immigration. If people find their homes permanently flooded they will have to up sticks and move. Simple as that. . . . By tackling climate change we can lessen the push factors driving immigration. If we don't tackle it, we have to brace ourselves for populations shifts on a scale we have never seen before.
>
> (Beckett 2006)

These quotes suggest that climate migration has become the subject of a process called *securitisation*, broadly defined as the process through which non-traditional security issues (such as climate change or migration) are discussed and/or acted upon in terms of security and thereby drawn into the security domain. This finding raises a number of questions: Has climate migration been securitised? To what degree, and by whom? What are the reasons for actors to present or deal with climate migration in terms of security? Does it benefit their political agenda, their bureaucratic interests, or do they regard climate migration as a serious threat harming their national or human security? How is security defined? Do actors present climate migration in terms of national security or in terms of human security and risk? What measures do actors seek to promote? Does securitisation result in extraordinary security measures in the form of strict border controls and military responses to deal with climate change and migration? Or does it help to raise awareness of action preventing climate change and thereby preventing scenarios of climate migration? To what extent is it successful to engage in securitisation to achieve certain policy goals? Does it produce counterproductive outcomes? Who loses and who gains from the securitisation process?

This book tackles these questions by examining the securitisation of climate migration in the context of climate change politics. This is where security frames on climate migration have emerged and most actively play out (see Brown et al. 2007; Trombetta 2008; Methmann and Rothe 2012; Rothe 2012).[1] As argued by Brown et al. (2007: 1144): 'it is part of a clear process to invest the international debate with a greater sense of urgency'. This book delves into that aspect of the securitisation of climate migration. It asks: What is the role of the securitisation of climate migration in climate politics? How does securitisation function as a diplomatic technique to push climate change negotiations forward? Who is driving such a strategy and what arguments do they make; and above all, does it work? By climate politics, I do not just refer to the negotiations in the United Nations Framework Convention on Climate Change (UNFCCC). Most securitisation attempts (called *securitising moves*) take place in the wider context of the actual negotiations: for example, in diplomatic encounters between states, in the media, or in other UN forums seeking to influence the UNFCCC (such as the UN Security Council or the UN General Assembly). The analysis will therefore centre on the broader field of climate politics, and not just on the UNFCCC negotiations.

This study is done by means of a macro–micro analysis, and focusses on the period of the early 2000s until the end of September 2014, when the New York UN Climate Summit took place. The macro-level analysis provides an overview of the coalitions of states that favour or oppose securitising moves on climate migration, and examines how this intersects with climate politics. This overview is provided through the help of discourse network analysis software (Leifeld 2013), which visualises the relations between actors through the arguments they make. The analysis centres on the 2007 and 2011 debate on the security implications of climate change held in the UN Security Council, in which over 50 countries participated (UNSC 2007, 2011). The debate of 2007 was the first-ever UN Security Council debate on the effects of climate change on world peace and security, and focussed on issues such as food insecurity, water insecurity, conflicts, and also climate migration (Sindico 2007; UNSC 2007; Scott 2008; Detraz and Betsill 2009). The issue of environmental degradation had once before been referred to by the UN Security Council. On 31 January 1992 the Council had issued a statement that '[t]he non-military sources of instability in the economic, social, humanitarian and ecological fields have become threats to peace and security' (UNSC 1992). But never before had there been a UN Security Council debate focussed solely on the issue of climate change and its consequences (such as climate migration). The debate in 2007 triggered follow-ups in the UN General Assembly in 2009, and in the UN Security Council in 2011 under Germany's presidency. During this latter debate, the UN Secretary General spoke of 'environmental refugees' as 'reshaping the human geography of the planet' (UN Secretary General 2011). These UN Security Council debates are key settings where many securitising moves on climate migration have been made. Climate migration 'serves as an argumentative shortcut that substantiates claims about the security impacts of global warming' (Methmann and Rothe 2014: 162).

The micro-level analysis zooms in on the activities and views of specific actors in this field. The actors analysed in the micro-level analysis are the UK's Foreign and Commonwealth Office (FCO) and the climate change and security community in the Government of India. The FCO is amongst the key securitisers of climate migration (securitiser being the promoter of securitising moves). It initiated the first-ever debate on climate change (including climate migration) in the UN Security Council (see chapter 4 for details). According to Brauch (2009), this UN Security Council debate represented a primary momentum for notions of security to come into prominence in debates on climate change (including climate migration). It is therefore valuable to gain more insight into the origin of the FCO's securitising move, its activities, and motivations. As I will demonstrate, the FCO's securitising move on climate migration emerged to promote greater action on climate change amongst the emerging developing countries and the United States (US); specifically, binding measures to reduce greenhouse gas (GHG) emissions under the UNFCCC. In order to promote such action, the FCO raised the issue of climate migration to demonstrate that inaction can create dire circumstances.[2] India, being an emerging economy not yet subjected to binding mitigation targets under the UN Climate Convention, acts as a key audience to such securitisation attempts. The analysis zooms in on the interactions between the FCO and the Government of India, and will examine whether the FCO's attempt to influence India's position on climate change has been successful.

Despite climate politics being a primary context for the securitisation of climate migration, there are risks for it producing aversive policies in the domain of immigration and military policy. A number of academics have warned that security framings of climate migration can lead to the militarisation of climate change or to increased border controls to stop so-called 'climate refugees' (Smith 2007; Hartmann 2010; White 2011; Trombetta 2014). For instance, White (2011) demonstrates how Morocco draws on a discourse on climate migration to promote its role of a transit state in the management of migration towards the European Union (EU). Along similar lines, the argument has been made that the reframing of Bangladeshi migrants as climate refugees provides India with an additional reason to reinforce and justify its border controls (see e.g., German Advisory Council on Global Change 2007: 123; Friedman 2009; White 2011: 71–72). To engage with, and add to, that debate, I will delve into that aspect of the securitisation of climate migration in the micro-level analysis of India.

The micro-level analysis conducted in the UK and India is based on in-depth interviews and on a textual analysis of range of primary documents relevant to the debate on climate change, migration, and security (media articles, policy documents, departmental reports, etc.). A total of 51 in-depth interviews have been conducted with key actors in the Indian and UK government between 2011 and 2012. Some of the people interviewed were Margaret Beckett (the UK's Foreign Secretary most active in promoting a security discourse on climate migration); the FCO's Climate Security Team; John Ashton (the FCO's Special Representative for Climate Change from June 2006–June 2012); Shyam Saran (the Indian Prime Minister's Special Envoy on Climate Change from 2007 to March 2010 and in this period India's chief climate change negotiator); high-ranked (active and retired) Indian officials working on border management and immigration; and two members of India's Prime Minister Council on Climate Change. In addition, 33 interviews have been conducted with non-state actors in the UK and India, such as non-governmental organisations working on climate migration and climate change, security-based think tanks, journalists, and researchers. See the appendix to this book, for a full list of interviewees.

The book places itself in, and seeks to contribute to, securitisation theory. I adopt a relatively broad understanding of securitisation. The aim is to encompass the various theoretical insights on securitisation as provided by the four schools on this subject: the Copenhagen School, the Paris School, Critical Security Studies, and the Risk School. This is relevant since each of these schools provide a relatively restricted, yet valuable, understanding of securitisation. They rely on a narrow concept of security and assume that securitisation has a certain set of outcomes. For instance, the Copenhagen School assumes that the concept of security is about existential danger, urgency, and survival (Wæver 1995; Buzan et al. 1998). In contrast, Critical Security Studies emphasises positive and progressive ways in which issues can become securitised through the notion of human security (see e.g., McSweeney 1999; Wyn Jones 1999; Booth 2007).[3] To take another example, the Copenhagen School assumes that securitisation induces a state of exception in which the issue under securitisation can be dealt with through emergency measures (Buzan et al. 1998). In contrast, the Paris School points towards more subtle security measures that can emerge in a securitisation process, such as surveillance measures to control immigration (Bigo 2002; Huysmans 2006; see chapter 2 for a detailed and comprehensive analysis of the different schools).

In contrast to a more narrow view on securitisation, this book argues that the securitisation of climate migration takes on various forms and meanings. These meanings and understandings are shaped by the context in which the securitisation process is situated and can be affected by interaction processes between the actors involved (the securitiser and the audience). A narrow understanding of securitisation, as provided by the individual schools, does not allow for an in-depth analysis of securitisation processes in which different concepts of security and security practices can be traced. In order to analyse a complex and dynamic process of securitisation, this book develops a new pragmatic framework for analysis, while recognising the existing theoretical insights on securitisation. This framework integrates the four main schools on securitisation:

the Copenhagen School, the Paris School, Critical Security Studies, and the Risk School. It provides a practical approach to the study of securitisation by creating a structure that allows for a flexible use of their theoretical insights. It thus does not aim to propose a new theory on securitisation, but instead creates a framework in which all insights on securitisation as provided by the four schools can play a role, and can interact, in the analysis of securitisation. The applicability of these insights depends on their fit with the case under study; each informed by a particular context. The aim is to understand how a securitisation process unfolds, with all its meanings and complexity, instead of trying to prove the explanatory value of a certain school on securitisation.

The framework for analysis is divided into three stages to allow for an interactive analysis of a securitisation process: Stage one is the securitising move by the securitiser (the starting point of the securitisation process); Stage two is the response to this move by the audience(s); Stage three is the outcome of the examined securitisation process. I apply this framework in the empirical analysis of the securitisation of climate migration. Attention is given to the audience's reaction to the securitising move and to the manner in which its response affects the final outcome of the securitisation process. Securitisation is treated as a dynamic process in which different actors (and not just the securitiser) can influence its course.

Some Background: The Climate–Migration–Security Nexus

In the 1980s, the debate on the climate change, migration, and security nexus emerged with a focus on *environmental* migration; environmental migration being a broader category than climate migration by encompassing migrations caused by a wider range of environmental impacts than just climate change. The concept of *environmental refugees* was popularised in the 1980s in a report by the UN Environment Programme (El-Hinnawi 1985); a term which was also used in the 1987 Brundtland report, 'Our Common Future' (World Commission on Environment and Development 1987, chapter 11, points 6 and 8) and in 'Agenda 21, the Programme of Action for Sustainable Development', adopted in 1992 at the Rio Summit (UN 1992, chapter 12, paragraphs 12.4, 12.46, and 12.47). But it was not until the 2000s that *climate change*-induced migration received serious attention (in short, climate migration). Climate migration became actively discussed in terms of security. This coincided with developments of the early 2000s when climate change prominently entered the political spectrum as a new security issue. Climate change had long been marginalised by political elites as a peripheral environmental concern (Brown et al. 2007; Trombetta 2008). But in the early 2000s, there were multiple attempts to place it on the security agenda. David King, at the time chief scientific advisor to the UK government, for instance argued that climate change represented 'a far greater threat to the world's stability than international terrorism' (quoted in BBC 2004). In that same period, the media also got hold of the secret Pentagon Report on climate change and its implication for US national security. This led to alarming news headings both in the US and Europe, such as 'Now the Pentagon tells Bush: climate change will destroy us' (Townsend and Harris 2004). The image of the threat of climate change was further strengthened by popular movies like *The Day After Tomorrow* (2004) and former Vice President Al Gore's documentary *An Inconvenient Truth* (2006). Even the Intergovernmental Panel on Climate Change (IPCC) has connected climate change and security. Its summary for policy makers of the latest Working Group II report warns that 'climate change can indirectly increase risks of violent conflicts' (IPCC 2014a: 20). The full report, however, adopts a more nuanced tone. It argues that some studies 'find a weak relationship, some find no relationship, and collectively the research does not conclude that there is a strong positive relationship between warming and armed conflict' (IPCC 2014b: chapter 12, p. 16).

Climate migration was presented as one of the main risks of global warming. As discussed above, the issue was widely debated in the UN Security Council in both 2007 and 2011. In 2013, the UK, together with Pakistan, proposed another UN Security Council debate on climate change (including climate migration). Russia and China, however, have blocked this initiative and only allowed for a closed-door informal debate on the issue (King 2013; Krause-Jackson 2013; for more details, see chapter 4). Small island states have also played an important role in connecting climate change, migration, and security. They were central in all UN Security Council debates on the topic and even led the drafting of a resolution on climate change and security that was discussed and accepted by the UN General Assembly in 2009 (UNGA 2009). The United Nations High Commissioner for Refugees (UNHCR) also developed an interest in the links between climate change, refugee movements, and security, seeing climate change as one of the 'biggest drivers' of future displacement (UNHCR 2009; see also Borger 2008). Moreover, climate migration is discussed in the many reports produced on climate change and security by governments, the European Union, think tanks, and NGOs (see e.g., Schwartz and Randall 2003; CNA 2007, 2014; DCDC 2007, 2010, 2014; German Advisory Council on Global Change 2007; Smith and Vivekanada 2007; Council of the European Union 2008; Cabinet Office 2009). For instance, in a high-profile report by a group of retired US generals and admirals (the Military Advisory Board) climate-induced immigration 'from neighbor states' was referred to as one of the key security risks of global warming (CNA 2007: 32). Last but not least, President Obama has warned of 'more severe storms, more famine and floods, new waves of refugees, coastlines that vanish, oceans that rise' (Obama 2013).

As the spectre of climate migration directly relates to ideas on a Malthusian crisis and Fortress Europe (Hartmann 2010; Trombetta 2014), it represents one of the impacts of climate change that seems easily susceptible to ideas and narratives on insecurity. Independent from the debate on climate change, the general issue of migration has already been subject of securitisation processes (see e.g., Huysmans 2006; Trombetta 2014). Certain immigrant groups, such as people from Eastern Europe or from Africa moving to Western Europe in search of better economic opportunities, have become associated with a language of risk and threat and with fears for identity and sovereignty loss. In that context, climate migration is an issue that has often been played on to raise alarm and fears about climate change.

Assumptions, Definitions, and the Scholarly Debate over Scientific Evidence

The issue of climate migration has been a contentious one in academic debate (Gemenne 2009). The most famous and influential publication on the topic is by Norman Myers (Myers and Kent 1995; Myers 2002). He argues that there will be 212 million environmental refugees by 2015, 162 million of which will be sea level–rise refugees (Myers 2002: 609 and 611). His work triggered much scepticism. The number of environmental refugees estimated by Myers has often been described as guess work. Myers simply assumes that a certain percentage of a population will be forced to flee due to sea-level rise, without providing persuasive empirical evidence to support such assumptions (see e.g., discussion Castles 2002; Black et al. 2011). Academics furthermore criticised notions of climate (or environmental) migrants or refugees as these concepts seem to imply a direct causal relationship between migration and climate change, for which, they argue, there is little proof (Black 2001; Castles 2002). As commented by Castles (2002: 5): 'the notion of the "environmental refugee" is misleading and does little to help us understand the complex processes at work in specific situations of impoverishment, conflict and displacement'. Instead, these scholars highlight that migration takes place in a multi-causal setting. Migration is dependent on a range of factors, such as the political situation, the amount of adaptation measures taken, economic push factors, and the personal situation of the migrant. Climate change is only one factor adding to migratory processes; even though some do acknowledge that the links between sea-level rise and migration may be clearer and more direct (see e.g., Black 2001: 7). Building on such criticism, current scholarly work on the environment, climate change, and migration nexus increasingly tends to emphasise the complex and multi-causal relationships associated with these issues (see e.g., Warner et al. 2010; Black et al. 2011; The UK Government Office for Science 2011). At the same time, however, many scholars continue to put more and explicit emphasis on the impact of climate change (or of the environment more generally) on migration compared to other push factors (see e.g., Williams 2008; Jäger et al. 2009; Biermann and Boas 2010; Warner 2010; for a critical discussion on this see Nicholson 2012). While acknowledging the multi-causal nature of migration, these scholars seek to enhance insight into the climate change–migration nexus or try to find solutions for specific problems associated with migration caused by climate change (such as displacement due to sea-level rise). Moreover, it is emphasised that the impact of climate change on migration increases when climate change events become more structural and severe (Biermann and Boas 2010).

A related debate has been on the consequences of climate migration. Particularly in the 1990s but also in the course of the 2000s, academics have highlighted that climate migration (or environmental migration more generally) may be a cross-border phenomenon, taking place in the form of mass movements causing conflicts. In the 1990s, Homer-Dixon's work fuelled alarmist ideas about environmental migration. He presented it as one of the root causes of conflict (Homer-Dixon 1991, 1994, 1999). He argues it could cause conflict between different ethnic groups but possibly also create threats to international security. With respect to international security implications, Homer-Dixon concluded in his 1991 article that:

> environmental stress and its attendant social disruption will so debilitate the economies of developing countries that they will be unable to amass sizeable armed forces. . . . But the North would surely be unwise to rely on impoverishment and disorder in the South for its Security.
>
> (Homer-Dixon 1991: 113–114)

These ideas on threats to national and international security were further disseminated by the journalist Robert Kaplan (1994) in his piece 'The Coming Anarchy'. Kaplan (1994) drew a looming picture of migration movements, environmental degradation, conflicts, and human despair in the Global South, leading to serious security implications for the Global North. In the 2000s, such ideas became connected to the notion of climate conflicts (Burke et al. 2009; for a critical discussion see Barnett 2003; Nordås and Gleditsch 2007), fuelled by projections of drastic climate change (Warren et al. 2006; Lenton et al. 2008; Burke et al. 2009). The aforementioned study by Norman Myers has only added to such an alarmist imagining of climate migration.

The presentation of climate migration in terms of mass displacement and conflict has increasingly been contested (see e.g. Black et al. 2011). Many scholars highlight that climate migration is largely an internal phenomenon, always standing in interaction with other factors, and they approach it as a development, human rights, or adaptation issue instead of being about great danger and insecurity. For instance, a high-profile report on the issue, called the Foresight Report on Migration and Global Environmental Change (chaired by Richard Black), emphasises that environmental migration (including climate migration) can act as an adaptation strategy, through which people can improve their livelihoods (e.g., by enhancing employment opportunities) (The UK Government Office for Science 2011; see also Warner 2010; McSweeney and Coomes 2011 on windows of opportunity that follow a climate-related disaster). Related to that, the scholarly debate moved towards a more nuanced perception of the relationship between climate change, conflict, and migration (Gleditsch, Nordås and Salehyan 2007; Hendrix and Glaser 2007; Nordås and Gleditsch 2007; Raleigh and Urdal 2007; Buhaug, Gleditsch and Theisen 2008; Salehyan 2008; Theisen 2010; Gleditsch 2012). Generally speaking, it is argued that the role of climate change impacts should not be ignored, especially with regards to its increasing future risk. Even so, it is emphasised that direct relationships between climate change, migration, and conflict are hard to prove and that other socioeconomic, political, and ethnic factors often have a stronger influence on conflict in comparison to climate change impacts. As argued by Gleditsch (2012: 7): 'it seems fair to say that so far there is not yet much evidence for climate change as an important driver of conflict'.

While these debates show that the dominant trend is moving towards a less alarmist perception of climate migration (Baldwin et al. 2014; Bettini 2014), it is clear that the issue has been controversial and that there is no clear-cut answer as to the relationship between climate change and migration or regarding its consequences. A problem is that climate migration is in many respects a future issue of which political and environmental contexts may drastically change:

> [T]he debate about climate-induced migration has been dominated by its futurology. It has led to the question of whether or not predictions about climate-induced migration are try, how many climate-induced migrants will have to be expected and how the consequences of climate change will interest with other drivers of flight and migration.
>
> (Baldwin et al. 2014: 121)

Precisely because there is much uncertainty associated with the issue of climate migration, even in academic circles, it is interesting to examine how it is perceived and played on by political actors. This uncertainty gives political actors much leeway to present and approach the issue of climate migration as they see fit. Moreover, this uncertainty allows for actors to form various perceptions and understandings of the issue. Since much ambiguity about the nature and consequences of climate migration remains, people can associate the issue with a wide range of ideas; ranging from more alarmist images of mass migration to more positive notions of human security.

In this book, I do not specifically define climate migration; even though I do limit the analysis to the securitisation of the climate change–migration–security nexus. Instead of specifically defining climate migration, the analysis focusses on how the actors perceive, present, or play on the issue: for instance, whether they perceive it as a mass phenomenon or as an issue affecting the livelihood security of local populations, and if so, why and how this affects policy making or political debate.

Organisation of the Chapters

The book is organised as follows: after this general introduction to the theme of climate migration and securitisation, chapter 2 provides an accessible overview and review of the four schools on securitisation: the Copenhagen School, the Paris School, Critical Security Studies, and the Risk School. I outline, analyse, and compare the schools, and discuss on which grounds their insights can be improved. The overall argument is that each school provides a valuable, but relatively narrow, understanding of securitisation. This does not allow for an in-depth analysis of securitisation processes in which different concepts of security and security practices can be traced.

Chapter 3 develops a new pragmatic framework for analysis to broaden the scope of securitisation analysis. I integrate all four schools into this framework to allow for their interplay and for a flexible application of their various theoretical insights on securitisation. The aim is to understand how a securitisation process unfolds, with all its meanings and complexity, instead of trying to prove the explanatory value of a certain school on securitisation. The framework for analysis assumes that the context in which a securitisation process is embedded and the interaction processes between the securitiser and the audience (the securitiser being the initiator of the process and the audience the receiver) inform which insights of the four schools are relevant to analyse the securitisation process under study. The framework outlines three stages of a securitisation process: the securitising move, the audience's response, and the outcome. These stages form the basis of the analysis in the remainder of the book.

As a next step, the book provides the macro–micro analysis of the securitisation process of climate migration. Chapter 4 delves into securitising moves on climate migration and asks how these connect with climate politics. Through a macro-level analysis of the UN Security Council debates on climate change (including climate migration), I map the coalition of states performing securitising moves. I demonstrate that European and small island states are the main securitisers, but I also review the (at times fluctuating) support from some African and Latin American countries, and from the US. In the micro-level analysis, I zoom in on the endeavours by one of the key actors: the UK's Foreign and Commonwealth Office (FCO). The analysis reveals how a securitising move on climate migration was strategically developed in the FCO's climate change diplomacy. I examine the rationale driving this securitising move, review the climate action being promoted, and examine what audience it intends to reach.

Chapter 5 centres on the key audience to securitising moves on climate migration: the emerging developing countries. The chapter starts with a macro-level analysis of their positioning in the 2007 and 2011 UN Security Council debates on climate change (including climate migration). This shows on what grounds these states have opposed securitising moves on climate migration. As a next step, the chapter zooms in on India's reaction to the FCO's securitising move, with a focus on the perspective of the Government of India's climate change and security community. The analysis shows that the securitisation process has been unsuccessful and even counterproductive in the Indian context. I demonstrate that much of India's opposition to security arguments on climate migration can be explained when understanding its position in UNFCCC negotiations and its colonial history. In addition, I review whether the discourse on climate migration has had an impact on India's border security policy towards

Bangladeshi immigrants. Researchers and journalists have often expressed fears that the climate refugee discourse may provide Bangladeshi immigrants with a negative and threatening image, which can spark stricter border controls (see e.g., German Advisory Council on Global Change 2007: 123; Friedman 2009; White 2011: 71–72). To obtain more insights into this risk, I will examine whether the FCO's securitising move has had such an unintended effect on India's immigration policy.

Chapter 6 reviews the outcome of this securitisation process. In the case of India and the UK, it only worsened their relationship on climate change and added to an environment of mistrust. Moreover, this process can add to divisions in climate change negotiations, in particular between the EU (including the UK) and powerful emerging economies, in particular China and India. The securitisation process did, however, attract South Africa and strengthen the alliance on climate change between the EU, the Alliance of Small Island States, and the Least Developed Countries. But this alliance has not been able to substantially change India's position in the negotiations. Finally, I discuss that the popularity of alarmist security arguments on climate migration has been decreasing in recent years. The FCO has adjusted its arguments to achieve greater support from its audience and to meet changing priorities within the UK government.

The concluding chapter outlines the key findings of the analysis and discusses their wider relevance. Most importantly, the book demonstrates: (1) how the securitisation of climate migration and climate politics are deeply connected through strategy and diverse understandings; (2) how the alarmist nature of security framings on climate migration can make them unsuccessful amongst their audiences; (3) that there is no simple and direct relationship between the securitisation of climate migration and border security politics, as this depends on the contextual environment in which the securitising move is situated.

Notes

1. These scholars examined the broader security discourse on climate change (including, but not specific to, climate migration) in relation to climate governance.
2. The analysis takes into account wider policy developments in the UK Government that relate to the FCO's securitising move, but the primary focus is on analysing the FCO.
3. In its original form, Critical Security Studies provides a normative theory of security. As discussed in further detail in chapter 2, I treat this school as another account of securitisation that can offer empirical insights.

References

Baldwin, A., C. Methmann, and D. Rothe (2014) 'Securitizing "climate refugees"': the futurology of climate-induced migration', *Critical Studies on Security*, 2(2): 121–130.
Barnett, J. (2003) 'Security and climate change', *Global Environmental Change*, 13(1): 7–17.

BBC (2004) 'Global warming "biggest threat"', *BBC*, 9 January. Available at: http://news.bbc.co.uk/1/hi/3381425.stm (last visit 19 September 2014).

Beckett, M. (2006) *Beckett: Berlin speech on climate change and security*. Speech at British Embassy, Berlin, 24 October. Available at: http://ukingermany.fco.gov.uk/en/newsroom/?view=Speech&id=4616005 (last visit 22 March 2013). This speech is no longer available online.

Bettini, G. (2014) 'Climate migration as an adaptation strategy: de-securitizing climate-induced migration or making the unruly governable?', *Critical Studies on Security*, 2(2): 180–195.

Biermann, F. and I. Boas (2010) 'Preparing for a warmer world. Towards a global governance system to protect climate refugees', *Global Environmental Politics*, 10(1): 60–88.

Bigo, D. (2002) 'Security and immigration: Towards a critique of the governmentality of unease', *Alternatives*, 27(1): 63–92.

Black, R. (2001) *Environmental refugees: myth or reality?* New issues in refugee research working paper 34. Geneva: United Nations High Commissioner for Refugees.

Black, R., W. N. Adger, N. W. Arnell, S. Dercon, A. Geddes, and D.S.G. Thomas (2011) 'The effect of environmental change on human migration', *Global Environmental Change*, 21S: S3–S11.

Booth, K. (2007) *Theory of world security*. Cambridge: Cambridge University Press.

Borger, J. (2008) 'Conflicts fuelled by climate change causing new refugee crisis, warns UN', *The Guardian*, 17 June. Available at: www.guardian.co.uk/environment/2008/jun/17/climatechange.food (last visit 19 September 2014).

Brauch, H.-G. (2009) 'Securitizing global environmental change'. In: H.-G. Brauch, U. Oswald Spring, C. Mesjasz, J. Grin, P. Dunay, N. C. Behera, B. Chourou, P. Kameri-Mbote, and P. H. Liotta (eds.), *Globalization and environmental challenges. Reconceptualizing security in the 21st century*. Hexagon series on human and environmental security and peace, Volume 3. Heidelberg, Germany: Springer-Verlag: 65–102.

Brown, O., A. Hammill, and R. McLeman (2007) 'Climate change as the "new" security threat: implications for Africa', *International Affairs*, 83(6): 1141–1154.

Buhaug, H., N. P. Gleditsch, and O. M. Theisen (2008) *Implications of climate change for armed conflict*. Paper presented at World Bank workshop on social dimensions of climate change. The World Bank, Washington DC, 5–6 March 2008.

Burke, M. B., E. Miguel, S. Satyanath, J. A. Dykema, and D. B. Lobell (2009) 'Warming increases the risk of civil war in Africa', *Proceedings of the National Academy of Sciences*, 106(49): 20670–20674.

Buzan, B., O. Wæver, and J. de Wilde (1998) *Security: a new framework for analysis*. Boulder, CO: Lynne Rienner.

Cabinet Office (2009) *Security for the next generation: national security strategy update*. London: Crown Copyright/Cabinet Office.

Castles, S. (2002) *Environmental change and forced migration: making sense of the debate*. New issues in refugee research working paper 70. Geneva: United Nations High Commissioner for Refugees.

Christian Aid (2007) *Human tide: the real migration crisis*. London: Christian Aid.

Council of the European Union (2008) *Climate change and international security*. Doc: 7249/08, 3 March, 2003. Brussels: Council of the European Union.

CNA, Military Advisory Board (2007) *National security and the threat of climate change*. Alexandria, VA: The CNA Corporation.

CNA, Military Advisory Board (2014) *National security and the accelerating risks of climate change*. Alexandria, VA: The CNA Corporation.

Detraz, N. and M. Betsill (2009) 'Climate change and environmental security: for whom the discourse shifts', *International Studies Perspectives*, 10: 303–320.

Development, Concepts and Doctrine Centre (DCDC) (2007) *The DCDC Global Strategic Trends Programme 2007–2036*. London: Crown Copyright/MOD 2007 (3rd edition).

Development, Concepts and Doctrine Centre (DCDC) (2010) *Strategic Trends Programme. Global Strategic Trends—Out to 2040*. London: MOD (4th edition).

Development, Concepts and Doctrine Centre (DCDC) (2014) *Strategic trends programme. Global strategic trends—Out to 2045*. London: MOD (5th edition).

El-Hinnawi, E. (1985) *Environmental refugees*. Nairobi: United Nations Environment Programme.

Friedman L. (2009) 'A global "national security" issue lurks at Bangladesh border', *The New York Times*, 23 March. Available at: www.nytimes.com/cwire/2009/03/23/23 climatewire-a-global-national-security-issue-lurks-at-ba-10247.html?pagewanted= all (last visit 19 September 2014).

Gemenne, F. (2009) *Environmental changes and migration flows. Normative frameworks and policy responses*. Paris, Liège: Institut d'Estudes Politiques de Paris, University of Liège.

German Advisory Council on Global Change (2007) *World in transition: climate change as a security risk*. Berlin: German Advisory Council on Global Change.

Gleditsch, N. P. (2012) 'Whither the weather? Climate change and conflict', *Journal of Peace Research*, 49(3): 3–9.

Gleditsch, N. P., R. Nordås, and I. Salehyan (2007) *Climate change and conflict: the migration link*. Coping with Crisis Series. New York: International Peace Academy.

Hartmann, B. (2010) 'Policy arena. Rethinking climate refugees and climate conflict: rhetoric, reality and the process of policy discourse', *Journal of International Development*, 22(2): 233–246.

Hendrix, C. S. and S. M. Glaser (2007) 'Trends and triggers: climate, climate change and civil conflict in Sub-Saharan Africa', *Political Geography*, 26(6): 695–715.

Homer-Dixon, T. (1991) 'On the threshold: environmental changes as causes of acute conflict', *International Security*, 16(2): 76–116.

Homer-Dixon, T. (1994) 'Environmental scarcities and violent conflict: evidence from cases', *International Security*, 19(1): 5–40.

Homer-Dixon, T. (1999) *Environment, scarcity and violence*. Princeton, NJ: Princeton University Press.

Huysmans, J. (2006) *The politics of insecurity. Fear, migration and asylum in the EU*. London: Routledge.

Intergovernmental Panel on Climate Change (IPCC) (2014a) *Climate change 2014: impacts, adaptation, and vulnerability. Summary for policymakers*. Available at: http://ipcc-wg2.gov/AR5/images/uploads/IPCC_WG2AR5_SPM_Approved.pdf (last visit 10 October 2014).

Intergovernmental Panel on Climate Change (IPCC) (2014b) *Climate change 2014: impacts, adaptation, and vulnerability*. Available at: http://ipcc-wg2.gov/AR5/report/final-drafts/ (last visit 10 October 2014).

Jäger, J., J. Frühmann, S. Grünberger, and A. Vag (2009) *Environmental change and forced migration scenarios*. Synthesis Report. Bonn: EACH-FOR project.

Kaplan, R. (1994) *The coming anarchy. Shattering the dreams of the post Cold War.* New York: Vintage Books, a division of Random House.

King, E. (2013) 'China and Russia block UN Security Council climate change action', *Responding to Climate Change (RTCC)*, 19 February. Available at: www.rtcc.org/2013/02/18/china-and-russia-block-un-security-council-climate-change-action/ (last visit 30 September 2014).

Krause-Jackson, F. (2013) 'Climate change's links to conflict draws UN attention', *Bloomberg*, 15 February. Available at: www.bloomberg.com/news/2013–02–15/climate-change-s-links-to-conflict-draws-un-attention.html (last visit 30 September 2014).

Leifeld. P. (2013) *Discourse network analyzer.* Available at: https://github.com/leifeld/dna/releases (last visit 27 September 2014).

Lenton, T., H. Held, E. Kriegler, J. Hall, W. Lucht, S. Rahmstorf, and H.-J. Schellnhuber (2008) 'Tipping elements in the earth's climate system', *Proceedings of the National Academy of Sciences*, 105(6): 1786–1793.

McKie, R. (2007) 'Climate change to force mass migration', *The Guardian*, 13 May. Available at: www.guardian.co.uk/environment/2007/nov/04/climatechange.scienceofclimatechange (last visit 22 September 2014).

McSweeney, B. (1999) *Security, identity and interests. A sociology of international relations.* Cambridge: Cambridge University Press.

McSweeney, K. and O.T. Coomes (2011) 'Climate-related disaster opens a window of opportunity for rural poor in northeastern Honduras', *PNAS*, 108(13): 5203–5208.

Methmann, C. and D. Rothe (2012) 'Politics for the day after tomorrow: the political effect of apocalyptic imageries in global climate governance', *Security Dialogue*, 43(4): 323–344.

Methmann, C. and D. Rothe (2014) 'Tracing the spectre that haunts Europe: the visual construction of climate-induced migration in the MENA region', *Critical Studies on Security*, 2(2): 162–179.

Myers, N. (2002) 'Environmental refugees: a growing phenomenon of the 21st century', *Philosophical Transactions: Biological Sciences*, 357(1420): 609–613.

Myers, N. and J. Kent (1995) *Environmental exodus. An emergent crisis in the global arena.* Washington, DC: Climate Institute.

Nicholson, C.T.M. (2012) *The environmental change, migration and displacement debate: distinguishing analytic and normative frameworks and gaining critical distance.* Paper presented at the COST Workshop on human rights legal frameworks in the climate change regime, 6–7 September.

Nordås, R. and N.P. Gleditsch (2007) 'Climate change and conflict', *Political Geography*, 25(6): 627–638.

Obama, B. (2013) *Remarks by President Obama at the Brandenburg Gate—Germany.* Speech at the Brandenburg Gate, Berlin, Germany, 19 June. Available at: www.whitehouse.gov/the-press-office/2013/06/19/remarks-president-obama-brandenburg-gate-berlin-germany (last visit 27 September 2014).

Raleigh, C. and H. Urdal (2007) 'Climate change, environmental degradation and armed conflict', *Political Geography*, 26(6): 674–694.

Rothe, D. (2012) 'Security as a weapon: how cataclysm discourses frame international climate negotiations'. In: J. Scheffran, M. Brozska, H. G. Brauch, P. M. Link, and J. Scheilling (eds.), *Climate Change, Human Security and Violent Conflict.* Hexagon series on human and environmental security and peace, Volume 8. Berlin Heidelberg: Springer-Verlag: 243–258.

Salehyan, I. (2008) 'From climate change to conflict? No consensus yet', *Journal of Peace Research*, 45(3): 315–326.

Schwartz, P, and D. Randall (2003) *An abrupt climate change scenario and its implications for United States national security*. Washington, DC: Global Business Network.

Scott, S.V. (2008) 'Securitizing climate change: international legal implications and obstacles', *Cambridge Review of International Affairs*, 21(4): 603–619.

Sindico, F. (2007) 'Climate change: a Security (Council) issue?', *The Carbon and Climate Law Review*, 1(1): 29–44.

Smith, D. and J. Vivekananda (2007) *A climate of conflict: the links between climate change, peace and war*. London: International Alert.

Smith, P.J. (2007) 'Climate change, mass migration and the military response', *Orbis*, 51(4): 617–633.

The UK Government Office for Science (2011) *Foresight: migration and global environmental change. Future challenges and opportunities*. Final Project Report. London: Crown Copyright/The Government Office for Science.

Theisen, O.M. (2010) *Scarcity and organized violence in Kenya, 1989–2004. A 'fitting' or a 'mis-fitting' case of environmental security theory?* Paper presented at climate change and security conference, on the occasion of the 250th anniversary conference of The Royal Norwegian Society of Sciences and Letters, Trondheim, Norway, 21–24.

Townsend, M. and P. Harris (2004) 'Now the Pentagon tells Bush: climate change will destroy us', *The Guardian/The Observer*, 22 February. Available at: www.guardian.co.uk/environment/2004/feb/22/usnews.theobserver (last visit 23 September 2014).

Trombetta, M.J. (2008) 'Environmental security and climate change: analysing the discourse', *Cambridge Review of International Affairs*, 21(4): 585–602.

Trombetta, M.J. (2014) 'Linking climate-induced migration and security in the EU: insights from the securitization debate', *Critical Studies on Security*, 2(2): 131–147.

United Nations (UN) (1992) *Agenda 21: the United Nations programme of action from Rio*. Available at: http://sustainabledevelopment.un.org/content/documents/Agenda21.pdf (last visit 23 September 2014).

United Nations General Assembly (UNGA) (2009) *Climate change and its possible security implications*. 85th plenary meeting, 3 June.

United Nations High Commissioner for Refugees (UNHCR) (2009). *Climate change could become the biggest driver of displacement: UNHCR chief*. Available at: www.unhcr.org/4b2910239.html (last visit 23 September 2014).

United Nations (UN) Secretary General (2011) *With environmental refugees reshaping human geography, Security Council has unique duty to mobilize action to confront climate change threat, says Secretary-General*. Speech at UN Security Council debate on Maintenance of Peace and International Security. 6587th meeting, 20 July, New York. Available at: www.un.org/News/Press/docs/2011/sgsm13712.doc.htm (last visit 24 September 2014).

United Nations Security Council (UNSC) (1992) *Statement by the Council President on behalf of the Members*. 3046th meeting of 31 January. Available at: www.un.org/en/sc/repertoire/89–92/Chapter%208/GENERAL%20ISSUES/Item%2028_SC%20respons%20in%20maint%20IPS.pdf (last visit 24 September 2014).

United Nations Security Council (UNSC) (2007) *Security Council holds first-ever debate on impact of climate change on peace, security, hearing over 50 speakers*. 5663rd meeting, 17 April, New York. Available at: www.un.org/News/Press/docs/2007/sc9000.doc.htm (last visit 24 September 2014).

United Nations Security Council (UNSC) (2011) *Security Council, in statement, says 'contextual information' on possible security implications of climate change important when climate impacts drive conflict.* Press release of the 6587th meeting, 20 July, New York. Available at: www.un.org/News/Press/docs/2011/sc10332.doc.htm (last visit 24 September 2014).

Wæver, O. (1995) 'Securitization and desecuritization'. In: R. D. Lipschutz (ed.), *On security*. New York: Colombia University Press.

Warner, K. (2010) 'Global environmental change and migration: governance challenges', *Global Environmental Change*, 20: 402–413.

Warner, K., M. Hamza, A. Oliver-Smith, F. Renaud, and A. Julca (2010) 'Climate change, environmental degradation, and migration', *Natural Hazards*, 55(3): 689–715.

Warren, R., N. Arnell, R. Nicholls, P. Levy, and J. Price (2006) *Understanding the regional impacts of climate change*. Research Report prepared for the Stern Review on the Economics of Climate Change. Tyndall Centre working paper 90. Norwich: Tyndall Centre for Climate Change Research.

White, H. (2011) *Climate change and migration*. Oxford: Oxford University Press.

Williams, A. (2008) 'Turning the tide: recognizing climate change refugees in international law', *Law & Policy*, 30(4): 502–529.

World Commission on Environment and Development (1987) *Our common future*. New York: United Nations. Available at: www.un-documents.net/wced-ocf.htm (last visit 24 September 2014).

Wyn Jones, R. (1999) *Security, strategy, and critical theory*. London: Lynne Rienner Publishers.

2 Comparing the Schools on Securitisation

Research on securitisation emerged following the end of the Cold War. That historic event created an impetus for academia to explain why international politics was increasingly occupied with new types of threats, such as environmental or societal issues. The traditional focus on military threats was losing its dominance, as many organisations, such as NATO, broadened their activities to include a range of issues traditionally classified as 'low politics' (see e.g., discussion Trombetta 2008). While Russia's interventions in Ukraine have put traditional security interests back to the forefront, attention to non-traditional security issues continues to evolve. For instance, in September 2014, the UN Security Council declared the Ebola virus, which has affected thousands of people in West Africa, to be a threat to international peace and security (BBC 2014).

To account for the broadening of the security agenda, Buzan et al. (1998) coined the term 'securitisation' in their publication 'Security: a new framework for analysis'. Securitisation here describes the process through which new issues become exposed to the language of traditional security and subsequently drawn into the security domain. It has become a popular term, as it is used in many different studies (see e.g., Abrahamsen 2005; Buzan 2006; Doty 2007; Floyd 2007; Wilkinson 2007; Huysmans and Buonfino 2008; Trombetta 2008; Neal 2009; Emmers 2010; Balzacq 2011a; Hammerstad 2012).

The meaning of the term *securitisation* has widened over the years. There is no longer one perspective on securitisation: it has obtained different meanings and has come to describe various types of processes. For example, Buzan et al. (1998) examine how securitisation draws an issue into the traditional domain of security, and thus associates it with notions of exceptionality, fear, survival, and emergency responses. Meanwhile, Trombetta (2008) shows how the concept of security can obtain a softer meaning, characterised by notions of human security and collaboration, when discussed in the discursive context of non-traditional security, such as the environment.

This chapter provides an accessible and systematic overview of the main schools of thought on securitisation. The outline provides the basis of chapter 3, in which I develop a pragmatic framework for analysis on securitisation. This framework for analysis sets up an approach to the study of securitisation processes in which various theoretical insights on securitisation can be applied in a flexible manner.

The Schools on Securitisation

The work by Buzan et al. (1998) is probably the most well-known attempt to understand and explain securitisation. Their work has set the grounds for the securitisation theory that we now refer to as the Copenhagen School. From their perspective, a new issue can enter the security domain by means of a speech act presenting the issue as a security threat. They assume that the concept of security revolves around traditional key terms such as survival, exceptionality, urgency, and war. The speech act therefore presents an issue as an existential threat. This conceptualisation of security evokes a logic of confrontation, competition, and defence, which allows for extraordinary measures when combating the security threat.

Albeit the first, the Copenhagen School does not provide the only theoretical perspective on securitisation. Broadly speaking, there are three other schools of thought on securitisation: the Paris School, Critical Security Studies, and the Risk School. Wæver (2008) refers to the 'triangle of CSS [Critical Security Studies], Copenhagen and Paris' (Wæver 2008: 111) and discusses the new focus on risk in security studies (Wæver 2008: 108–109; see also C.A.S.E. Collective 2006). The Paris School has provided an alternative account to the Copenhagen School by highlighting that securitisation may emerge through everyday routine and technocratic practices. Such a securitisation attempt is presented as part of daily and regular practice, in contrast to an exceptional act that receives much public and political attention. Critical Security Studies and the Risk School also provide alternative accounts on securitisation. Critical Security Studies, and risk scholars drawing on Ulrich Beck's insights, emphasise that a securitisation process can be based on more positive notions of security. Such a conceptualisation of security endorses alternative security measures with more positive connotations of cooperation, progressive human security, emancipation, and prevention.

In this chapter, I provide an overview of how the Copenhagen School, the Paris School, Critical Security Studies, and the Risk School view securitisation. These four schools can be considered theoretical perspectives on securitisation. They are considered part of 'theory development for the use in security studies' (Wæver 2004: 3) and build on theoretical assumptions as to the nature and functioning of securitisation. The Risk School, however, is a more recent theoretical perspective and therefore in relative terms less well established. In many respects it builds on the assumptions provided by the Copenhagen School and the Paris School (for details, see the Risk School section). Part of the aim of this chapter is therefore to trace the main novelty provided by this school of thought and to demonstrate how it adds to the analysis of securitisation.

Critical Security Studies has also not provided a theory on securitisation equally to the level of the Copenhagen School and the Paris School. In contrast to these schools, its original aim is not to empirically assess how a securitisation process takes place. Instead, it provides a normative theory on security, based on a belief in a progressive future. Critical Security Studies' scholars do, however, refer to empirical developments in the area of human security when discussing their vision of an ultimate state of security (see e.g., McSweeney 1999; Wyn Jones 1999; Booth 2007). Related to that, one of their key scholars, Wyn Jones (1999: 145), has argued that theory and practice need to become better connected in their work as the aim of Critical Security Studies is to induce change. For these reasons, I argue that this school of thought provides more than just a normative theory and can be of use when trying to empirically understand securitisation processes in terms of human security.

Assessing Six Components of Securitisation

Through a careful reading of securitisation literature, I distilled six components, which as a whole provide a coherent overview of a school's perspective on securitisation. I structure the analysis of the four schools around these six components in order to provide in-depth insight into their assumptions and to demonstrate on what aspects the four schools differ from one another.

The first component focuses on the *mechanism(s)* at work in a securitisation process; it seeks to explain how an issue becomes securitised. This mechanism could, for instance, be a speech act through which an issue is presented as a security threat, or routine and technocratic processes that gradually integrate an issue in everyday security practice, or other mechanisms may be at work.

The second component is about the actors involved in securitisation processes. These are the *securitiser*, the actor that employs the securitisation mechanism (e.g., a speech act), and the *audience*, the actor that receives the message of the securitiser. I will examine what types of actors the four schools assume to be the securitiser and the audience: are these elite actors, local communities, social movements, or other types of actors? How do they interact?

The third component revolves around the *level of politics* where securitisation takes place; the level where securitisation mechanisms can be traced and examined. Securitisation may, for instance, take place at the level of high politics, or at an administrative level of politics.

The fourth component focusses on the *conceptualisation of security*. Each school outlines a set of specific key notions, such as survival and war, or one comprehensive concept, such as risk, that determines the character and meaning of the term security. The manner in which a school defines security is crucial for the type of security environment it envisages.

The fifth component is the *logic of security measures*. This logic determines the types of security measures induced or endorsed by the securitisation process, such as war activities or preventive strategies, put in place to address the security threat. The logic of security measures thus suggests how to handle a security issue.

To further facilitate comparison between the four Schools, I examine whether a school's assumptions and views on securitisation processes is based on *a negative or positive understanding of securitisation*. Such a classification of the four schools draws on McSweeney's definition of the negative and positive 'dimension[s] of security' (McSweeney 1999: 92). The negative dimension refers to 'human fears', and to the protection from an objective threat to one's 'physical security' (McSweeney 1999: 92). It describes the more conventional definitions of security, such as those building on notions of confrontation, survival, enemy, unease, and otherness. A negative understanding of securitisation has a pessimistic outlook that revolves around conflictive and/or exclusionary understandings of security, based on a friend–enemy or insider–outsider dichotomy. The positive dimension of securitisation focusses on 'human *needs*' and refers to the 'overall quality of life' that requires protection (McSweeney 1999: 92, emphasis in the original, see also 13–16, 81). It describes schools on securitisation that focus on alternative definitions of security and on security measures associated with more positive connotations, such as cooperation or human security.

These six components of securitisation can be divided into two types: the analytical tool components and the content components. The first three components (mechanism(s), securitisers and the audience(s), and level of politics) represent a school's understanding of how, by whom and where securitisation unfolds. These components inform how to empirically research a securitisation process. The latter three components are focussed on the content of a securitisation process; what is a school's conceptualisation of security, what kind of logic of security measures does the securitisation process endorse, and is it based on a negative or positive understanding of securitisation? For instance, the conceptualisation of security can be based on an alarmist and negative notion of security. This tells you something about the content, the nature, of a securitisation process.

To compare the different schools, I have made each component explicit for each school to the extent possible. As an exception, I only specifically discuss the Risk School's content components. The content components give the Risk School its originality, while in terms of analytical tool components it mostly relies on insights provided by the Copenhagen School and the Paris School. A summary of this overview of the four schools is provided in the table placed at the end of this chapter.

Copenhagen School

In brief, the Copenhagen School assumes that securitisation revolves around a negative conceptualisation of security that evokes extraordinary measures to deal with the identified threat (Buzan et al. 1998). This theory of securitisation is probably the most influential one of the four schools. The fact that its assumptions are often criticised is evidence of its influence. In the remainder of this section, I will describe the Copenhagen School's understanding of securitisation by means of the six components outlined in the introduction.[1]

Mechanism(s)

The Copenhagen School maintains that securitisation is triggered by a speech act; a discursive practice in which an issue is staged as a security threat. As argued by Buzan et al. (1998: 5), new issues 'have to be staged as existential threats to a referent object by a securitizing actor who thereby generates endorsement of emergency measures'. The argument is that through a speech act on security, a certain perception of reality is produced which allows for a particular course of action to emerge. As explained by Balzacq (2011b: 1): 'these utterances [speech acts] realize specific action; they "do" things: they are "performatives"'. The speech act is a highly visible act. In the words of Buzan et al. (1998: 177): 'it is against its nature to be hidden'.

The Copenhagen School's account of speech acts has been criticised (Balzacq 2005, 2011b; Stritzel 2007). According to Balzacq (2011b:1), the Copenhagen School 'believes in a "social magic" power of language, a magic in which the conditions of possibility of threats are internal to the act of saying "security"'. Scholars argue that the Copenhagen School fails to effectively theorise how structural factors may affect a securitisation process and why a securitisation may emerge in the first place (see discussion in: Balzacq 2005, 2011b; Stritzel 2007, 2011a; McDonald 2008: 564, 571–572; Hammerstad 2012: 5; Watson 2012: 387). The Copenhagen School, for instance, largely overlooks the social (contextual) embeddedness of a speech act (Stritzel 2007: 365–367; McDonald 2008: 576). As argued by Hammerstad (2012: 5), 'certain securitisations are promoted by bureaucracies if they confirm institutional values, advance institutional goals or confirm existing power relations'. Related to that, the Copenhagen School has been criticised for not sufficiently taking into account how the success of a speech act depends on its level of resonance in the receiving context. As argued by Balzacq (2005: 182), the success of a securitisation attempt 'is contingent upon a perceptive environment' and is no simple consequence of the act of saying security. The speech act needs to resonate with its audience's understandings and experiences in order to find acceptance (Balzacq 2005; Stritzel 2007: 370; see discussion McDonald 2008: 564, 573; for more detail on the importance of contextual resonance see chapter 3). As will be discussed below, the Copenhagen School does acknowledge that an audience needs to accept a speech act. But it does not sufficiently theorise how or why such an acceptance takes place.

Securitisers and the Audience

The Copenhagen School perceives securitisers, those who execute the speech act, to be elites that hold some form of authority. These could be political leaders or 'bureaucracies, governments, lobbyist, and pressure groups' (Buzan et al. 1998: 40). This category of elite actors is somewhat abstract, as it is not specified which actors in a pressure group or the government should be perceived as an elite actor. To make this concept more specific, Huysmans (2006: 91) suggests that discursive approaches, such as the one by the Copenhagen School, focus on 'the top of the political and bureaucratic hierarchy'. An elite actor can then best be understood as an agent who has a relatively high position in the hierarchy of a particular organisation or institution and is therefore capable of influencing a securitisation process by means of high profile speech acts. But where lies the border between an elite and a regular member? A senior government official can act as a bureaucrat; a professional executing a certain policy. At the same time, a senior government official is part of the government elite; for instance, when informing politicians in high-level debates and when engaged with important economic and security state interests. As a result, the identification of an elite actor is not always clear-cut.

According to the Copenhagen School, the level of authority of a securitiser is important. This increases the chances that the speech acts are accepted by its audience. Without the acceptance of the audience, the speech act remains no more than a securitising move. Only in case of acceptance, can the issue be elevated beyond the boundaries of ordinary politics and be dealt with through extraordinary means (Buzan et al. 1998: 25); at least, in democratic settings.

Much ambiguity regarding the role of an audience remains. First of all, it is often unclear who this significant audience may be (Stritzel 2007: 363; Neal 2009: 336–337). Secondly, it has not been specified when an audience has accepted the speech act, nor what level of authority is required to persuade an audience. Thirdly, the Copenhagen School provides a strict 'speaker-audience model' (Stritzel 2007: 363), which does not do justice to the more dynamic and interactive processes that are at play in the securitisation process. As argued by Stritzel (2007: 365), the Copenhagen School 'reduce[s] the speaker-audience relationship to the securitizing attempt: "the likelihood of the audience accepting the claims made in a securitizing attempt"'. Meanwhile, an audience may have an active role in influencing the nature and outcome of the securitisation process (Balzacq 2005; Stritzel 2007, 2011a; McDonald 2008: 572, 575; Hammerstad 2012; Watson 2012: 298–299) by being receptive to certain elements of the speech act while ignoring or contesting others (Balzacq 2005: 182; McDonald 2008: 572, 575). For that reason, many of these scholars have argued that the audience should have a more central place in the analysis of securitisation processes (Balzacq 2005, 2011b; Stritzel 2007; see chapter 3 for more detail).

Level of Politics

The Copenhagen School assumes that a securitisation process takes place at the level of high politics. The very act of securitisation can be traced in important debates, diplomatic agreements, and in high-level reports. Buzan et al. therefore argue that analysis should be directed to '*texts that are central*' (1998: 177, emphasis in the original).

In practice it is, however, often not that clear-cut which texts are central and which texts are not. What if the report does not receive a high amount of media attention as the topic of the report is not considered of high interest at the time, yet uses a particular language that gradually become more widely adopted? In such a case, it may at first instance not be fully clear that the report should be considered a central text, but it turns out to be one over time. Moreover, it is open to discussion to what extent diplomatic agreements and negotiations neatly fall under the rubric of elite and high politics. The Copenhagen School focuses on public texts (Wæver 2002: 26) and on visible and high-profile acts taking place at the level of high politics. But diplomacy is not always publicly traceable or is enacted upon in more mundane everyday communication with other state parties. At the same time, in line with the Copenhagen School's focus, diplomacy is about status and about high-level state interests. This shows that in practice it remains challenging to neatly apply the Copenhagen School's insights on elite-level and high profile acts of securitisation.

Conceptualisation of Security

From the Copenhagen School's perspective, the concept of security revolves around notions of exceptionality, priority, survival, competition, and confrontation. By a security threat the Copenhagen School refers to an existential threat that puts one's survival in danger (Buzan et al. 1998: 21–23).

The Copenhagen School's conceptualisation of security is said to rely on the concept of the political as developed by the realist Carl Schmitt, which places the friend–enemy dichotomy at its core (Williams 2003, see also Trombetta 2008; and discussion Huysmans 1998a, 1998b). It allows for a state of exception to emerge, implying 'the suspension of the normal rules of politics' (McDonald 2008: 578). In this line, Buzan (2006: 1103) describes how the United States (US) created a state of exception following 9/11. It provided a discursive environment in which the US was staged as willing to do anything in its power to save 'western civilization' from its enemy Al-Qaeda and the threat of terrorism (Buzan 2006: 1101, 1103).

The Copenhagen School aimed to 'rethink the concept "security" in a way that is true to the classical discussion [on security]' (Wæver 1995); a discussion that can be traced back to realist thought that focusses on issues of survival, war, and zero-sum thinking (Williams 2003). The Copenhagen School maintains that when a new issue is securitised, it will be considered in these terms of security. Wæver (1995) argues that if this classical inheritance is ignored, the analyst can be charged to be ignorant or naïve with respect to the powerful connotations associated with security, and becomes 'an innocent contributor to the reproduction—and even expansion—of securitization'.

Many have criticised the Copenhagen School's move to provide such a narrow meaning of security. Stritzel (2007: 366), for instance, argues that securitisation theory should rather focus on the dynamic ways in which issues are securitised. By adopting a static conception of security, the Copenhagen School seems to limit its constructivist basis of the securitisation theory (see discussion Williams 2003). It puts much emphasis on one perception of security, rooted in realist thought, instead of being open to a wider social construction of security based on notions of cooperation or the quality of life. As noted by Williams (2003: 514–515):

> For the Copenhagen School, "security" is not just any kind of speech-act, not just any form of social construction or accomplishment. It is a specific kind of act. . . . Indeed its roots lie not in contemporary constructivism, but in a much older Realist tradition, a tradition emanating from the thinking of the German jurist and political theorist Carl Schmitt.

Even though Williams (2003) and Stritzel (2007) make a strong and convincing argument, it could equally be argued that the Copenhagen School is actually quite receptive to the social construction of the concept of security. The Copenhagen School directs its attention to the long-term, historically informed social construction of security instead of focussing on short-term social construction processes. In the Copenhagen School's understanding, the social construction of concepts does not happen overnight. Instead, concepts, such as security, often carry a significant amount of historical baggage. From this perspective, it can equally be argued that an analyst should be cautious when focussing on the effects of short-term social construction processes. As argued by Conca (1994: 108):

> . . . redefining security does not mean automatically renegotiating prevailing metaphorical understandings of security. Even if they were to be renegotiated, this would not automatically convert the institutions of the national security state.

For these reasons, the Copenhagen School's insights should not be too easily dismissed, as they do represent the dominant way in which the concept of security has developed over the past centuries.

But even when taking this into consideration, the analysis does not have to be closed off to alternative conceptualisations of security. As argued by Wyn Jones (1999: 112): '[I]t is [not] easy to challenge the traditions that are attached to a particular concept . . . [b]ut argumentation and disputation can have—and have had—profound effects even on the practice of security'.

Logic of Security Measures

The logic of security measures that is evoked is the logic of exceptionality, confrontation, competition, and defence. It allows for zero-sum thinking, rivalry, and for legitimate 'actions outside the normal bounds of political procedure' (Buzan et al. 1998: 24) when combating the security threat (see also Wæver 1995, 2008: 102; see Behnke 2000: 91). As stated by Buzan et al. (1998: 21): 'by stating "security," a state representative declares an emergency condition, thus claiming a right to use whatever means are necessary to block a threatening development'.

Buzan (2006: 1103, 1108, 1110) argues that the rhetoric of 'global war on terrorism' legitimised the war in Afghanistan against the Taliban and Al-Qaeda, and created room for emergency actions to emerge. It led to the torture of prisoners and unilateralist behaviour; even though these actions did not go without a substantial amount of criticism. Smith (2007) similarly argued that a national security rhetoric allows for the usage of military means to deter illegal immigration. He refers to a case in 1994, when the US employed naval ships to intercept migrants from Haiti and Cuba. This defensive attitude by the US towards Cuban immigrants was mainly triggered by the 1980 Mariel boatlift. During this boatlift, Fidel Castro allowed many Cubans to leave the island, which led to an exodus of Cubans into the US (see discussion in Scanlan and Loescher 1983 on the US's changing attitude towards Cuban immigrants). According to Dowty and Loescher (1996: 50), a White House official regarded these immigrants as '"bullets aimed at the United States"' (quoted in Dowty and Loescher 1996: 50), as Fidel Castro put so-called criminals and psychotics on the Mariel Boatlift as well.

But what is a state of exception? Can it be pre-determined whether a security measure can be defined as a state of exception? As will be discussed in more detail throughout the book, there can be different perceptions of what constitutes something confrontational and something that surpasses the boundaries of normal politics. For instance, for one country unilateralist action on climate change may seem like normal politics. But for another country (e.g., one isolated between bigger powers or fearing for its survival) such action represents great danger. The limit of what represents something exceptional is not fixed, but may differ per actor. Related to that, it is important to note that the Copenhagen School's logic of security measures does not only apply to security practices in terms of violence or military action. A state of exception can entail that citizens of a big city are not allowed to leave their homes because of possible health threats, such as when there is a certain contagious virus.

Positive or Negative Understanding of Securitisation

The Copenhagen School's account is based on a negative understanding of securitisation. It assumes that when an issue becomes securitised a more tense and potentially dangerous political climate is created. Imagine a situation where a certain minority group is presented as a security threat to the larger society. From the Copenhagen School's perspective, this could lead to harsh and exclusive policies harming the rights of this minority group (e.g., by denying them access to certain public places). This shows that a securitisation process is seen as endorsing confrontational situations, in which securitisers act on the basis of fear and self-protection. Even if such policies would provide one group (the larger society in this case) with a greater sense of safety, the policy remains driven by negative feelings of exclusion to protect oneself from a so-called threatening other.

For this very reason, Buzan et al. (1998) are cautious of securitising moves. As argued by Buzan et al. (1998: 4): 'Security should not be thought of too easily as always a good thing. It is better . . . to aim for desecuritization: the shifting of issues out of emergency mode and into the normal bargaining processes of the political sphere'.

In sum, the Copenhagen School's analytical tool components revolve around the speech act mechanism, executed by elite actors of an organisation, aiming to convince an audience of a securitising move. These speech acts can be traced at the level of high politics.

The content components centre on a negative understanding of securitisation. The Copenhagen School argues that a speech act on security provides an issue with a threatening connotation. This evokes exceptional security measures driven by a sense of emergency, survival, and rivalry.

The Paris School

The work of the Paris School on securitisation has largely revolved around the 'governmentality of unease', as developed by Didier Bigo (2002) and followed by many others, such as Huysmans (2006), Huysmans and Buonfino (2008), Salter (2008a), Neal (2009), and Oels (2012).

The Paris School largely bases its theory on securitisation around Foucault's concept of governmentality. Governmentality should be understood as the act of government, or another authority, to regulate society. It concentrates on the 'instruments of government' (Foucault 1991a [1980]: 95). These instruments, or techniques, of government should be understood as the 'everyday enactment of procedures, routines, regulations and devices' that govern society, including security (Huysmans 2006: 97). Foucault (1977 [1975]) has applied this concept of governmentality to describe how discipline is being regulated within society, particularly through techniques of punishment and imprisonment (Foucault 1977 [1975]).

Bigo (2002) has connected this governmentality approach to the notion of 'unease'. This concept can be understood as a 'worry' or a feeling of disturbance about a deviating aspect within the societal order that securitisers seek to govern and regulate (Bigo 2002, 2008a, 2008b). Such a deviating aspect could be a certain group of migrants that has a substantially different culture to the society it wants to enter or is likely to make extensive use of the country's social welfare system, or shares some characteristics with defined risk groups, such as terrorists. Bigo (2002) argues that authorities attempt to regulate this level of unease through techniques of security to reaffirm and preserve the normal societal order. These techniques include the usage of visas, or detention and expulsion measures (Schuster 2003; Huysmans 2006: 95).

To further clarify this perspective, it is useful to briefly discuss Huysmans' (2006) analysis of the creation and effects of the European Union (EU)'s internal market. In his analysis, the internal market functions as a secure, normal, order which allows for the free movement of EU citizens and goods within the EU. Simultaneously, however, 'The construction of a space of free movement will facilitate criminal and illegal activity . . .', which triggers a sense of unease about the functioning of the internal market (Huysmans 2006: 87). 'Free movement needs thus to be protected from its abusive and dangerous use' (Huysmans 2006: 87). In order to do so, authorities employ techniques of security, such as external border control activities to regulate and maintain the normal state of the EU's internal market.

Mechanism(s)

As the mechanism of securitisation, the Paris School concentrates on the everyday and routine technologies of security: the 'everyday enactment of procedures, routines, regulations and devices' of security (Huysmans 2006: 97). Think of surveillance mechanisms or border control regulations attempting to govern border insecurity. As argued by Huysmans (2011: 375):

> Securitizing in contemporary world politics develops significantly through unspectacular processes of technologically driven surveillance, risk management and precautionary governance. These processes are less about declaring a territorialized enemy and threat of war than about dispersing techniques of administering uncertainty and 'mapping' dangers.

Not only do such techniques address levels of unease, but they also produce levels of unease within society on a gradual and continuous basis. According to Bigo (2002), routine measures and everyday practices detect groups as possible dangers or risks to society, and in that manner securitises them. 'Securitization . . . is the result and not the cause of the development of technologies' (Bigo 2002: 73).

Securitisation may also take place through a technological spillover of the everyday technologies of security into other issue areas (Huysmans and Buonfino 2008), or through technological exchange between institutions. For instance, border control techniques (such as identity cards) for the regulation of immigration, are increasingly being employed to contain possible terrorist threats (Huysmans and Buonfino 2008: 783). As a consequence, these different social problems of migration and terrorism become connected as a source of unease made governable by means of the same technology.

This focus on routine practices and techniques of security does not mean that the Paris School denies the role of discourse. Actually, everyday discourse is entrenched within routine techniques of government (see discussion Huysmans 2006: 91–94), which is precisely what makes these techniques so powerful. As argued by Foucault (1991b [1980]: 79): 'discourses . . . serve to found, justify and provide reasons and principles for ways of doing things'. However, in contrast to the speech act mechanism as outlined by the Copenhagen School, these discursive processes are more deeply embedded assumptions about the ways in which an organisation deals with certain issues.

Securitisers and the Audience

The securitisers are professionals of unease who deal with the daily management of risk and threats (Bigo 2002: 63–64, 73; Huysmans 2006: 8–9). The definition of a professional remains, however, somewhat unspecified. Bigo (2002: 63–64) refers to a wide range of actors, such as policy organisations, intelligence services, bank analysts, customs officers, judges, etc. He refers to actors that actually employ and/or develop these techniques of security. Professionals can act in different parts of an institutional or organisational hierarchy; for instance, at the level of research and policy development where techniques of security are created and further enhanced, and/or at the executive side where the measures are actually being employed.

The Paris School argues that professionals of unease constantly try to maintain or increase feelings of disturbance through securitisation techniques, as this legitimises the normal state of affairs, and simultaneously their 'capacity to govern' (Huysmans and Buonfino 2008: 783). As argued by Bigo (2002), their intent is 'to play with the unease, or to encourage it if it does not yet exists, so as to affirm their role as providers of protection and security and to mask some of their failures' (Bigo 2002: 65). As a result of such endeavours, the authority of the professionals is maintained and reassured (Bigo 2002: 63–65), while deviating groups or aspects of society are being securitised.

It has to be noted that professionals do not necessarily have to be conscious of this calculating behaviour (see discussion Balzacq et al. 2010). When they are part of a routinised system of border controls it becomes regular practice to further develop these control measures through technological innovation and regulations. Therefore, 'players are not always conscious of the game they are playing' (C.A.S.E. Collective 2006: 458). Securitisation works as a technological or routine development, triggered by technological spill-over or exchange that are 'unspectacular, unexceptional, continuous and repetitive' (Huysmans 2011: 376). These securitisation techniques may gradually expand, or may even have unintended securitisation effects, without this necessarily representing a conscious act by the professionals.

Interestingly, the group of professionals also acts as the primary audience in the Paris School's framework. By drawing on insights from Pierre Bourdieu (see 1990 [1980]), Bigo pays attention to processes of socialisation and practice that result in a particular (or more heterogeneous) mode of governmentality. He examines how certain instruments of security are shared or come to be shared by means of practice (e.g., through institutional struggles, networks, technological exchange between professionals operating in a certain social field [see Bigo 2002; Bigo 2008a: 14; see discussion C.A.S.E. Collective 2006: 458, in the governance field] of the environment, or of border security). Therefore, the focus of interaction in such securitisation processes is between the various professionals. For instance, the securitisers are those professionals introducing an innovation in citizen-alert systems of the government aimed to notify citizens about certain risks or threats. The audience is the other professionals in the field who need to be socialised to adopt and further expand on these practices for these to become routinised techniques of security.

The Paris School does not give much insight into the role of audiences outside the field of professionalism, or at least does not actively theorise this. How do citizens, politicians, or targeted immigrant groups react to certain regulations, policy procedures, or control techniques? And do these actor groups also react by means of routine techniques of security or do they engage in speech acts or in other mechanisms in their responses? As argued by C.A.S.E. Collective (a group of leading securitisation scholars) (2006: 459), the Paris School ignores 'the multiple and complex ways in which "the dangerous" themselves resist practices of security'.

Level of Politics

In the Paris School's account, securitisation processes take place at the level of daily and routine management. This is the administrative level of politics that is 'less spectacular and transparent' than the highly visible political realm (Huysmans 2006: 92).

But what is exactly implied by the administrative level of politics? I would argue that the administrative level does not strictly refer to everyday levels of politics that take place beyond the public eye. Securitisation can be traced in ordinary policy documents or even in parliamentary debates that do not have a highly significant status (see Huysmans and Buonfino 2008). For instance, they discuss the updates and development of certain regulations, instruments, and procedures.

Conceptualisation of Security

The Paris School's conceptualisation of security predominantly revolves around the concept of unease. A situation of unease can be understood as a state of insecurity that needs to be addressed to reaffirm and maintain the normal, secure societal order. Evoking a sense of unease is not necessarily aimed to securitise certain groups or deviating aspects of society; rather it seeks to legitimise and reaffirm the dominant perception of what is perceived as a normal society or a normal state of affairs (Bigo 2002; Bigo 2008b). This legitimisation process is achieved through securitisation; securitisation is therefore rather a means to an end rather than the end itself. It is through everyday techniques of security (securitisation mechanisms), such as profiling techniques defining certain groups or forms of behaviour as deviant, by which the standard for the accepted and the normal is being set. For instance, someone walking around the airport with a backpack, on his own, who comes from a risk country such as Afghanistan, and is flying to the US, is automatically detected as a possible risk. The techniques of security will then intend to '"normalize" the behaviours of target individuals' (Balzacq et al. 2010). If a person does not follow this description, he or she is considered to fit the category of normal behaviour; unless the person would meet characteristics of another risk category. This securitisation process reinforces and reaffirms perceptions of deviating behaviour on the one hand and normal behaviour on the other hand.

It is important to note that this conceptualisation of security differs substantially from the conceptualisation of security as developed by the Copenhagen School (Bigo 2002: 73). Bigo describes unease as a '*worry*' citizens may feel about some uncertain or deviant aspects in society (Bigo 2002: 65, emphasis added), instead of an extreme and extraordinary feeling of danger. As argued by Bigo and Tsoukala (2008: 3), the conceptualisation of security 'insists on a different way of conceptualizing the (in)securitization process, far from freedom from fear and terror, but concerned with insecurity as risk and unease'. In this respect, the notion of risk also plays a vital role in this conceptualisation of security. The term risk is similar to the notion of worry and unease associated with a more subtle feeling of insecurity.

Logic of Security Measures

The security measures that follow the securitisation process largely revolve around the logic of proactivity, exclusion, management, and control. This logic consists of a combination of control technologies, such as 'population profiling, risk assessment, statistical calculation, category creation, proactive preparation . . .' (Bigo 2002: 65), with exclusionary practices such as border controls 'that discriminate between those who can and cannot enter' (Huysmans 2006: 95). The border control measures can be relatively mild, through the form of tourist visas, for instance (Huysmans 2006: 95). These visa techniques may add to securitisation if a certain group is denied access because it forms a risk category. Border control techniques can have strong exclusionary effects, through techniques of expulsion and detention (Huysmans 2006: 95; Schuster 2003). These control activities have a proactive outlook (Bigo 2008b: 35–36). The aim is to manage risk before it even exists, by creating risk groups, by extending border controls, etc. As argued by Bigo (2008: 36):

> The logic of proactivity aims to act before an offence is committed, by collecting information oriented towards repressive action and by anticipating the behaviour of dangerous individuals or groups. . . . [I]t consists above all of managing movement and flux, of managing groups of people in advance, analysing their potential future, in order to normalize them.

Bigo (2002) suggests that the usage of control techniques, such as categorisation measures, automatically triggers exclusionary activities based on an insider–outsider dichotomy. Control measures define certain groups as defiant, and thereby render them a threat to the so-called normal society. Bigo (2002: 67) argues:

> The activation of the term *migrant* in *im-migrant* is by definition seen as something destructive. The metaphor of the body politic embedded in the sovereignty myth . . . creates an image of immigration associated with an outsider coming inside, as a danger to the homogeneity of the state, the society, and the polity.

Such control techniques can, however, also define certain groups of immigrants as being useful and beneficial to society (Huysmans 2006: 98–99). They are still separately categorised as being different than the population of the receiving society, but they are not connected to notions of unease. As argued by Huysmans (2006: 96), control techniques trigger no simple insider–outsider dichotomy. Instead, the immigrant group is differentiated into sub-groups, of which some are being denied full access or are even detained, while others are granted some temporary access or are even actively recruited. However, those actively recruited can also become securitised. For instance, labour immigrants in the Netherlands recruited from Morocco in the 1960s are currently seen (by some societal groups at least) as deviant elements of the Dutch society, harming the Dutch culture (see e.g., Hogenhuis 2012; Wijblijvenhier 2013).

It has to be noted that these exclusionary and control practices do not come across as exceptional and extraordinary. Instead, in such situations of securitisation, it is considered normal to regulate deviating aspects of society and therefore to exclude certain risk groups. In a similar vein, it is considered normal to put thieves in jail in order to keep society running. As argued by Bigo and Tsoukala (2008: 5): 'some (in)security moves . . . performed by bureaucracies, the media, or private agents are so embedded in these routines that they are never discussed and presented as an exception but, on the contrary, as the continuation of routines.'

Positive or Negative Understanding of Securitisation

The Paris School's understanding of securitisation can largely be described as a negative one. The securitisation process sustains forms of exclusion and negative feelings of unease. For instance, monitoring of immigrant groups maintains a sense of worry in society about the possible risk that immigrants form. When people become subjected to subtle mechanisms of the management of unease, there are no obvious means to free oneself from this system of regulation.

In sum, the Paris School's account of securitisation centres on the governmentality of unease. The analytical tool components consist of everyday and routine techniques of security as a securitisation mechanism, executed by professionals of unease. The securitiser–audience relation also centres on interactions between professionals. This securitisation process can be traced on an administrative (routine) level of politics. The content components include a negative understanding of securitisation that builds on the concept of unease and on a logic of proactive exclusion, management, and control.

Critical Security Studies

Critical Security Studies did not intend to assess empirically how a securitisation process unfolds. Instead, its aim is to develop a normative account of what security should ideally mean and entail. Driven by Enlightenment ideals, it centres on oppressive structures, such as capitalism, from which human beings should free themselves in order to create a world that is more responsive to basic human needs such as health and the freedom to make one's own choices.

Central values are freedom to develop one's own life, tolerance, and equality of rights.

But many of the original Critical Security Studies' scholars have tried to connect this normative theory to empirical developments in current security politics on human or common security (McSweeney 1999; Wyn Jones 1999; Booth 2007). Some Critical Security Studies' scholars have furthermore attempted to put more emphasis on the relation between theory and practice, in the hope to induce change in the current world order (Wyn Jones 1999: 145, 151). For those reasons, I treat Critical Security Studies as one of the schools on securitisation.

But since Critical Security Studies is by origin not an empirical securitisation theory, most of its scholars have not explicitly tried to develop analytical tool components of securitisation that can be used to assess empirical processes. Nonetheless, some Critical Security Studies' scholars, and in particular Wyn Jones (1999), have attempted to develop such analytical tool components while connecting them to the overall normative theoretical framework of Critical Security Studies. Analytical tool components that fit the Critical Security Studies' framework can furthermore be drawn from recent accounts on securitisation, such as those by Wilkinson (2007) and Hansen (2000). These scholars try to stretch the analysis of securitisation beyond 'Westphalian straitjackets' that build on 'Eurocentric assumptions' (Wilkinson 2007: 11). They aim to show how less-powerful actors play a role in securitisation processes (see Hansen 2000; Wilkinson 2007; Hammerstad 2012). In line with Critical Security Studies, they perceive securitisation as a process that can induce change to improve insecure situations. Therefore, when outlining the analytical tool components, these insights are taking into account and connected to the theoretical and normative assumptions of Critical Security Studies.

Mechanism(s)

Human choice works as an essential mechanism within Critical Security Studies. Through human choice, people can be liberated from oppressive modern structures that subordinate vulnerable groups to the rights of the powerful and the rich (for more detail on these structures, see discussion on 'conceptualisation of security'). From that understanding, human choice creates room for progress and can achieve true human security (Booth 2007; see also McSweeney 1999: 208–219).

But how does an oppressed group articulate human choice? Some refer to emancipatory discursive acts, by building on the Copenhagen School's speech act mechanism (see discussion McDonald 2008: 575). For instance, a political dissident can engage in public and private speech acts to challenge its opponents. But many scholars emphasise that not all actors, especially the more vulnerable ones, have the means or the ability to speak in wider circles for their arguments to be heard (Hansen 2000; Wilkinson 2007; Hammerstad 2012). Therefore, it is important to consider more physical articulations of human choice (Wilkinson 2007: 12; Hammerstad 2012), such as protest marches or strikes, in addition to speech acts. Wilkinson (2007: 12) argues that displacement could also be considered a form of protest, as forced migrants may send out a signal that they are in need of more security and that things need to change. Along similar lines, Hansen (2000) speaks of silence as a form of expression. Some actors might be in such a dire situation that they are afraid to speak, such as in Pakistan, where women's lives are threatened by honour killings. These women are afraid to report a rape out of fear of persecution for having sexual intercourse outside their marriage (Hansen 2000). As a result, the women remain silent, which shows there is an insecure situation and that progressive change is needed (Hansen 2000).

Securitisers and the Audience

In Critical Security Studies' account of securitisation, securitisers can be elite actors and social movements. Elite actors are more likely to employ speech acts, while social movements are more likely to use physical securitisation acts.

Elite actors can be political dissidents (see discussion Wilkinson 2007: 16–17), intellectuals (including academics and even critical theorists themselves) (Wyn Jones 1999: ch. 6), charismatic leaders, an NGO (see McDonald 2008: 575 on the role of Amnesty International in the securitisation of human rights), or even elite members of an (inter)governmental organisation who try to empower vulnerable groups.

Social movements are civil society groups that promote social change and human progress. These could be peace movements, or other types of civil society groups, including NGOs. These social movements could also consist of vulnerable communities that decide to take action. As argued by Nyers (2006), vulnerable groups, such as refugees, also have the determination to induce change and should not be considered as helpless victims. Therefore, vulnerable groups should not be excluded as securitisers. Moreover, notion of social movements and elite actors may overlap. For instance, NGOs could participate as elite actors in important debates and at the same time be involved in street protests, and therefore act as a social movement.

In the work of Critical Security Studies, the whole of humanity represents the audience, which includes both the oppressed and the oppressors (Booth 2007; see discussion Wyn Jones 1999: 151). The ideal is that the whole of humanity realises that change is needed and embraces a fairer and more tolerant world order. Change can first be promoted by certain elite actors and social movements, as outlined above, but the ultimate aim is to induce a wider and more encompassing change among mankind to eliminate all oppressive structures.

It remains very abstract, however, how such an ideal can be obtained through securitiser–audience interaction. Critical Security Studies assumes that progress is possible but has not theorised extensively how such progress can be obtained (on this, see critique by Wyn Jones 1999: 151). How can change promoted by one social movement convince others? How can social groups or individuals ensure that common goals gradually come to be valued over matters of self-interest, so that a better world society can be obtained? As argued by Wyn Jones (1999: 151– 153), it is of key importance that Critical Security Studies puts in more effort to linking theory and practice to obtain their progressive ideals: 'Indeed, without a more convincing conceptualization of the theory–practice nexus, one can argue that critical international theory, by its own terms, has no way of redeeming some of its central epistemological and methodological claims and thus that it is a fatally flawed enterprise' (Wyn Jones 1999: 152).

Level of Politics

The level of politics has not been explicitly defined by Critical Security Studies. Based on the above discussions it can be assumed that securitisation will take place predominantly at the level of high politics and on the grassroots level. The elite political actors are likely to be involved in important debates and express their views through high-profile reports that receive a high amount of media attention. McDonald (2008: 575, emphasis in the original) for instance refers to a high-profile report released by Amnesty International, '*Turkey: No Security Without Human Rights*', in which emancipatory change was being promoted. The securitising acts of civil society groups can best be traced on the grassroots level of politics, as this involves street protests, local actors, or even whole local communities.

In addition, such securitisation processes may unfold, in more mundane levels of policy making. Imagine the development of a tolerant immigration policy that does not have an immediate widespread effect. First, small steps are taken to lessen exclusive policies towards immigrants (e.g., by ensuring that asylum seekers obtain better provisions when waiting for the decision whether they can enter the receiving state). This can trigger more protests protecting the rights of asylum seekers and of illegal immigrants, which leads to a further softening of immigration policies. Gradually, this can evolve into a more wide-spread and more structural change, and ideally to a more cosmopolitan society.

Conceptualisation of Security

Critical Security Studies' conceptualisation of security revolves around the notion of human security in a progressive understanding. In this conception, the concept of security is directed to 'human *needs*, not just human fears' (McSweeney 1999: 92, emphasis in the original). A focus on human needs implies 'more than the physical survival and the threats to it' (McSweeney 1999: 92). From this understanding, security is about improving the 'qual-ity of life' (McSweeney 1999: 92) and is based on the Enlightenment ideal that progress is possible. In a similar vein, Booth understands security 'as an instrumental value concerned to promote security *reciprocally*, as part of the invention of a more inclusive humanity' (2007: 2, emphasis in the original). From this perspective, security should be perceived in the form of common, human, or world security (Booth 2007: 109), where the self and the other are no longer seen as opposites, but as part of one common humanity (Booth 2007: 142). Booth (2007: 102) has proposed the concept 'survival-plus', as a means to grasp this widened and progressive conception of security. Booth perceives survival as 'an existential condition: it means continuing to exist' (Booth 2007: 102). This protection of one's existence is, however, not equal to 'living tolerably well' (Booth 2007: 102), and to having the ability to make choices about one's social and political life (2007: 107). To obtain these goals, more is required than survival, namely '*survival-plus*' (Booth 2007: 102, emphasis in the original), or in other words 'security' (Booth 2007: 102).

To make this conception of security somewhat more specific, many scholars, such as McSweeney (1999: 81), Wyn Jones (1999: 110, 156–158), and Booth (2007: 321–322, 381) have referred to current political developments on human, or common, security that have taken place since the 1980s and especially in the 1990s (see e.g., UNDP report 1994). These political developments have aimed to improve livelihoods and to create greater freedom from oppressive structures. It gives more attention to the needs and security of the individual and of vulnerable communities. Even though it is acknowledged by Critical Security Studies that still much more needs to be done to achieve a true form of human security, these political developments do pave the way for a world order based on a notion of security, as envisaged by Critical Security Studies.

A key characteristic of Critical Security Studies is its focus on the oppressive and unequal effects of modern politics and economics (McSweeney 1999; Wyn Jones 1999; Nyers 2006; Booth 2007; for a gender perspective see Enloe 1989; Tickner 1992; McSweeney 1999: 93, 96, 98; for accounts in Critical Theory see Linklater 1982; Walker 1997). The common endeavour is to criticise, problematise, and expose oppressive structures, instead of adding to their legitimacy (see Cox 1981). It is for instance argued that current political structures based on an international system of nation-states, create inside–outside, citizen–refugee, friend–enemy dichotomies (Linklater 1982; Walker 1997; Nyers 2006; Booth 2007). The intent is to critically expose the present order for relying on these dichotomies.

The critical analysis of modern political structures and the belief in a potentially emancipated world does raise some questions. It remains unclear why Critical Security Studies perceives most modern structures, such as capitalism and the nation-state system, as oppressive ones that inherently create dichotomies between the poor and the rich, or between oppressed and the powerful, while it at the same time perceives the progressive future as liberated from such inherent contradictories. By looking into human history, as Critical Security Studies does, it could very well be expected that in any future political system, certain dichotomies and oppressive structures are going to be developed.

This does not mean that no progress is possible. But the question remains: to what degree can it be obtained?

It can be questioned, furthermore, to what extent the emphasis on a world or common security, which overcomes inside–outside dichotomies, can actually provide liberty, freedom, and equality in the manner people would ultimately seek. For instance, it can be argued that the current nation-state system, which produces inside–outside dichotomies (Linklater 1982), does actually provide positive forms of security. Some scholars that work in the field of political justice and ethics argue that it is a human right to establish a distinct political unit, as it allows for self-governance, political freedom, and cultural membership and identity (see e.g., Kymlicka 1995). To account for this, some scholars drawing on Critical Security Studies' insights have emphasised the right to establish collective social groups as an important value of life (see e.g., Barnett, Matthew and O'Brien 2010: 19). The creation of distinct political units can be essential to allow for human diversity and for political life and freedom. But for such a world order to work from the understanding of Critical Security Studies, the political communities should allow one another to flourish, to share resources, and security needs to be guaranteed for the whole of humanity (see e.g., Booth 2007).

Logic of Security Measures

The logic of security measures developed by Critical Security Studies revolves around a human security approach (McSweeney 1999: 99–100; see Booth 2007: 322). It combines both top-down *and* bottom-up measures.

Top-down measures focus on the protection and providence of basic human needs. These are activities that help to establish a basic income level for poor communities, that guarantee a healthy work environment, or that provide certain agricultural techniques, information, infrastructure, and local adaptation measures.

In addition, the human security approach as envisaged by Critical Security Studies puts much emphasis on bottom-up measures through which communities themselves try to change and improve their living situation. These vulnerable groups are often very active and have substantial local knowledge about how to survive and cope in their living circumstances (Sen 1999; Nyers 2006). They subsequently have a key role in the development and execution of human security measures.

The active role of local communities and of bottom-up approaches is accentuated by Critical Security Studies. Its core normative goal is that all human beings obtain the means to improve their own lives and to choose their own living situations. This emphasis on empowerment and self-governance is therefore the key characteristic of the envisaged human security measures.

It is important not to simply conflate measures of human security with general humanitarian and development cooperation. As argued by Huysmans and

Squire (2009: 6–7), in many forms of humanitarianism, local communities are often perceived as victims and not as agents capable of inducing change. This does not correspond with the Critical Security Studies' focus on the role for affected groups who, by means of bottom-up processes, try to empower themselves, with the goal to live a more 'secure' life.

Moreover, it should be noted that the term *human security* is often co-opted for strategic considerations and used to justify border control practices, humanitarian intervention, socioeconomic reform, or even the war against terrorism (Liotta 2002; Duffield and Waddell 2006; Huysmans and Squire 2009). This is partly a result of the broadness of the term *human security*. It has been criticised for becoming 'a loose synonym for "bad things that can happen," and it then loses all utility to policymakers—and incidentally to analysts' (Krause 2004: 367–368). Human security can mean many things and therefore can easily 'be tailored to fit a government's foreign policy mandate' (Burgess and Owen 2004: 345), be mobilised to promote a strict immigration policy in the name of the well-being (human security) of the receiving population, or be used to legitimise any type of humanitarian intervention. Therefore, when assessing human security measures, it is important to carefully examine whether these truly represent a human security approach as envisaged by Critical Security Studies or whether and to what extent they have departed from it.

Positive or Negative Understanding of Securitisation

Critical Security Studies emphasises positive dimensions of securitisation; even though it does not deny or ignore the negative dimension of security (McSweeney 1999: 92–93; Booth 2007). It is precisely by means of the envisaged enlightened world order that Critical Security Studies aims to address and challenge the negative dimensions of security, such as wars and forms of exclusion.

But overall, Critical Security Studies puts the emphasis on achieving a positive conceptualisation of security based on notions of human needs, cooperation, solidarity, and a belief in progress. Scholars such as Booth (2007: 109, 16) and Wyn Jones (1999: 109, 110) for that reason criticise theoretical perspectives on securitisation, in particular the Copenhagen School, that solely rely on a negative concept of security.

In sum, for Critical Security Studies securitisation is about the emancipatory quest for human security. Its analytical tool components focus on human choice that is articulated through speech or physical securitisation acts, of which the first is mainly executed by elite actors and the latter by social movements. The aim is to emancipate subordinate groups from oppressive establishments. The content components centre on a positive understanding of securitisation that relies on the concept of human security and on a human-security approach as its logic of security measures.

The Risk School

In recent years a fast-growing group of scholars has highlighted a shift within the politics of security from threat deterrence to risk management; a shift which, according to these scholars, was set into motion with the end of the Cold War (see e.g., Rasmussen 2001, 2004; Coker 2004; Van Munster 2005; Aradau, Lobo-Guerrero and Van Munster 2008; Elbe 2008; Mythen and Walklate 2008; Trombetta 2008; Williams 2008; Corry 2012). They argue that the concept and practices of security increasingly revolve around notions of risk, potentiality, risk-management, preparedness, pro-active action, and prevention, rather than around the more traditional security repertoire set out by the Copenhagen School (Corry 2012). The many articles published in the past decade that adopt a risk perspective, demonstrate the popularity of this emerging school of thought (see e.g., Rasmussen 2001; 2004; Coker 2004; Van Munster 2005; Aradau and Van Munster 2007; Aradau, Lobo-Guerrero and Van Munster 2008; Trombetta 2008; Williams 2008; Corry 2012).

The concept of risk was popularised by Ulrich Beck's Risk Society thesis (1992, 1997, 1999, 2006). The Risk Society thesis asserts that the present society is confronted with side-effects, the so-called risks, produced by the age of industrialisation (Beck 1999: 2), and by current forms of globalisation (Beck 2006). Think of climate change as an unintended side effect of industrialisation. Even though risk scholars still use Beck's insights (see in particular Rasmussen 2001, 2004; Coker 2004; Trombetta 2008; Williams 2008), his arguments have proven to be inadequate to the understanding and explaining of securitisation as it adopts a relatively positivistic outlook (Aradau and Van Munster 2007: 95; Dillon 2008: 322–323). While Beck takes risks as given, many securitisation scholars are interested in processes of social construction that make risk and risk management central in modern security politics. Most risk scholars working on securitisation have therefore moved away from this original thesis by Beck and adopted a more social constructivist approach. One group of scholars has done so by analysing risk through a Foucauldian lens of governmentality (see e.g., Van Munster 2005; Elbe 2008; Mythen and Walklate 2008; see section on the Paris School for details about governmentality). Another group of scholars continues to heavily rely on Beck's insights but combines the study of risk with discourse theory (see e.g., Trombetta 2008; Corry 2012).

The Risk School, in the field of securitisation, thus compromises two groups of scholars (Corry 2012).[2] These groups of scholars provide different accounts of securitisation. Those drawing on a Foucauldian framework largely adopt a negative view on securitisation. They argue that notions and practices of risk management result in control mechanisms that can exclude certain social groups (such as immigrants) from other parts of society, or even in pre-emptive strikes to prevent a potential threat. In contrast, those who take forward Beck's insights, provide a more positively oriented understanding of risk, with a focus on prevention of harm and on collaborative action.

In this section, I will predominantly discuss the Risk School through the lens of the latter group of scholars providing a more positive conceptualisation of risk. This understanding of risk gives the Risk School something unique that cannot easily be incorporated by the remaining schools, while the negative conceptualisation of risk is in line with the Copenhagen School and the Paris School (see discussions below for more details). By concentrating on the contribution by this group of scholars, this section aims to trace the main novelty provided by this school of thought.

In terms of the analytical tool components, the risk scholars rely on the insights on the analytical tool components as provided by the Copenhagen School and the Paris School. Risk scholars combining Beck's insights with a constructivist approach, rely on the Copenhagen School's speech act theory to examine how notions and practices of risk emerge (see e.g., Trombetta 2008; Corry 2012). Corry (2012) analyses language of risk in debates on climate change and security by reviewing high-level statements, such as those by Al Gore in his Nobel Prize lecture. Those risk scholars developing their risk argument around a Foucauldian framework rely on the analytical tool components as developed by the Paris School (see e.g., Van Munster 2005; Elbe 2008; Mythen and Walklate 2008; see also discussion in Corry 2010: 2, 7–8). They focus their analysis on the everyday technologies of security and routine practices (such as profiling and surveillance techniques) when analysing the ways through which issues become securitised (see discussion in Van Munster 2005; Aradau, Lobo-Guerrero and Van Munster 2008). Since these insights on the analytical tools of securitisation are not that different from those outlined by the Copenhagen School and the Paris School, these will not be discussed in further depth.

Conceptualisation of Security

As the analytical tool components of the Risk School rely on the Copenhagen School's and Paris School's insights, the novelty will have to come from the content components. This is also precisely where most risk scholars claim their originality. As argued by Corry (2010: 10), 'risk-security writers are not suggesting an adjustment to the conventional notion of security but a radical configuration of the concept itself'. What constitutes this radical configuration?

I argue that the Risk School's originality lies in its ability to provide a more subtle conceptualisation of security that allows for a more positive approach to address insecurity. As will be clarified in more detail below, the notion of risk tends to be more subtle than security as defined by the Copenhagen School (Corry 2012). Risk is about *potential* threats, possibilities, future issues, uncertainties, and puts less emphasis on insider–outsider, friend–enemy dichotomies. Plus, the Risk School assumes that the notion of risk can transform 'security politics away from confrontation and conflict' (Hammerstad and Boas 2014: 5), by seeing opportunities for collaboration, dialogue, improvement of governance capacity, and positive prevention. This somewhat more positive conceptualisation of risk has most affinities with those risk scholars who provide a speech act (discursive) analysis while engaging with the insights of Ulrich Beck (see e.g., Trombetta 2008; Corry 2012).

So, what constitutes this more subtle and positive conceptualisation of security? First of all, an increasing usage of the term *risk* as opposed to *threat* could make the notion of security less negative and confrontational. As argued by Neal (2009), some securitisers rely on the term *risk*, as it is less associated with notions of emergency and urgency, and may therefore be used in more subtle ways to legitimise a need for security governance. To some degree, this conceptualisation of risk fits within the Paris School's politics of unease (as argued by Neal [2009] himself) aiming to legitimise dominant forms of governance. However, the term *risk*, depending on its usage, can also have a less negative connotation than the concept of *unease*. Imagine a case in which a politician draws on a language of risk to make people aware of certain health risks (such as malaria) in order to make the issue governable in a positive and preventive manner. Such a conceptualisation of risk may suggest something new and different that has not been theorised by the Copenhagen School and the Paris School.

Second, risk writers, such as Corry (2012) and Van Munster (2005: 6), highlight that the notion of risk is about *potential* threats. This provides an additional reason why the Risk School allows for a more subtle and positive view of security. It is less concerned with existential threats, urgency, destructive danger, and survival compared to the notion of security as defined by the Copenhagen School. The concept of risk is about potential threats that may pose harm but at the present time can be managed with political tools of cooperation, capacity building, mitigation, surveillance mechanisms, etc. As argued by Corry (2010: 11), 'The infusion of risk-thinking into the security field has in other words softened up the question of survival'. That does not mean, however, that the notion of potentiality is unique to the Risk School. The notion of potentiality can for instance be traced in situations where traditional forms of security were at stake. In the Cold War, for instance, both the US and the Soviet Union continued the nuclear arms race just in case either of them would start an attack. It is even fair to say that traditional warfare in general is based on continuous preparation, as both parties must always be ready for a potential attack. What makes the notion of potentiality different in the conceptualisation of risk, however, is its explicit presence. As argued by Corry (2010: 10, emphasis in the original): 'identifying an existential *threat* would no longer be a necessary part of securitization in a global risk society where potentialities rather than actualities dominate the political security imagination'. The concept of risk is less about the here and now; it is about intangible and uncertain threats that may possibly occur in the near or far future. As mentioned above, traditional security politics similarly revolves around the notion of potentiality and can be forward looking as well. But actualities and urgency remain its key focus, while notions of potentiality, uncertainty and future are central within the conceptualisation of risk.

Third, what allows for a more subtle and positive conceptualisation of security is the lesser emphasis on threats posed by a particular group, and on issues of intent and agency (Van Munster 2005: 7; Aradau, Lobo-Guerrero and Van Munster 2008; Trombetta 2008; Corry 2010: 12; Corry 2012: 244). Instead attention is directed to risk factors, system characteristics of the governance object, and statistical relations (Van Munster 2005: 7; Aradau, Lobo-Guerrero and Van Munster 2008; Elbe 2008; Corry 2010: 12). As carefully summarised by Corry: 'Whereas securitization tends to personalize [by designing an enemy], risk-thinking objectifies' (Corry 2010: 12). For instance, airport screening is in first instance directed to potential dangerous objects rather than possible dangerous passengers (Salter 2008a: 251). Some even go a step further by saying that the friend–enemy distinction no longer underlies risk thinking (see e.g., Aradau, Lobo-Guerrero and Van Munster 2008: 151), as the population at large is at risk. There is no clear enemy when so many aspects of society are defined in terms of risk and rendered governable.

This lesser emphasis on notions of otherness and enemy allows for a more positively oriented view on securitisation. As argued by Trombetta (2008: 597): 'A focus on emissions [as a solution to manage the risk of climate change] has the merit of involving industrialized countries' and helps to avoid a focus on 'the global south, its inadequacy and responsibility'. A more positive conceptualisation of security may thus overcome friend–enemy dichotomies, and instead benefit opportunities for greater multilateral action and collaboration.

It is important to note, however, that a range of risk scholars do not necessarily regard these developments as positive. These scholars examine how the objectification of risk makes whole societies subject to control mechanisms such as surveillance and monitoring techniques and border security controls (see e.g., Van Munster 2005; Aradau and Van Munster 2007). And through these control mechanisms, new inequalities and exclusion are created (see e.g., Mythen and Walklate 2008). For instance, some risk groups, such as undocumented immigrants or a certain ethnic group, may become exposed to higher levels of surveillance than the rest of the population. These arguments are aligned with the Paris School's focus on control and pro-active exclusion.

Fourth, the concept of risk revolves around the notion of prevention, also known as the precautionary principle. Prevention is argued to be central, as risks are there to be mitigated and prevented (see e.g., discussion William 2008: 72–74; Trombetta 2008; Corry 2012). In adopting a positive understanding of prevention, risk scholars associate it with notions of multilateralism, collaboration, management, resilience, and adaptation to new environments (see Trombetta 2008; Corry 2010, 2012). Again, not all risk arguments on prevention fit this more positive and subtle conceptualisation. Van Munster (2005) perceives prevention in quite negative and destructive terms (see also Coker 2004; Williams 2008; see also Aradau and Van Munster 2007). Van Munster provides an example of the War on Terror to support this argument:

[T]he United States can no longer solely rely on a reactive posture as we have in the past. The inability to deter a potential attacker, the immediacy of today's threats, and the magnitude of potential harm that could be unleashed by our adversaries' choice of weapons, do not permit that option. We cannot let our enemies strike first.

(White House 2002: 15 in Van Munster 2005: 9)

This statement, however, shows the traditional security-deterrence language rather than the language of risk-prevention. The term *potential*, or the preventive focus, does not make the concept of security as defined by the Copenhagen School any less central in this statement. The following statement says it all: 'We must deter and defend against the threat *before* it is unleashed' (White House 2002: 14 cited in Van Munster 2005: 9). The term *before* may be highlighted, but the same sentence also uses terms *deter* and *defend*. Therefore, as similarly argued by Corry (2010: 28), aggressive and confrontational precautionary language easily fits within the Copenhagen School's repertoire. Buzan (2006), for instance, examined pre-emptive security measures in his analysis of the War on Terror where he draws on the Copenhagen School's framework for analysis.

Logic of Security Measures

What is different and original for the Risk School is the logic of positive prevention and positive risk management.[3] Measures of positive prevention and positive risk management include more top-down multilateral and diplomatic preventive activities in the realm of foreign policy possibly in combination with more operational plans, such as adaptation and resilience measures taken in the area of climate change (Trombetta 2008: 593, 595, 597–599; Corry 2012: 255). As argued by Corry (2012: 255) in analysing the field of climate change: 'long-term societal engineering through innovation, governance and cooperation is promoted'.

It is important to note that this logic of security measures is different to the one envisaged by Critical Security Studies. While Critical Security Studies is about emancipation and progress in line with Critical Theory, the Risk School as outlined here belongs to the group of 'problem-solving' theories (Cox 1981). It does not challenge dominant structures but tends to work within them in order to prevent future risks through management, early-warning systems, calculation, cooperation, dialogue, adaptation, etc. Moreover, the focus is more top-down, while Critical Security Studies emphasises bottom-up measures led by affected and local groups.

Positive or Negative Understanding of Securitisation

As discussed, the Risk School in the field of securitisation compromises two groups of scholars (Corry 2012): those who draw on a Foucauldian framework and those further built on Beck's insights. This second group provides a more positive conceptualisation of risk, which gives the Risk School something unique that cannot easily be incorporated by the remaining schools. An emphasis on risk, potentialities, and management may appear less threatening to politicians and the public, and subsequently allows for a somewhat more hopeful and constructive outlook on security.

In sum, Risk School's novelty primarily resides in its somewhat more subtle conceptualisation of security combined with a more positive outlook. It conceptualises security in terms of risk, based on notions of potentiality and uncertainty, and argues that securitisation can result in the logic of positive prevention and positive risk management.

Concluding Discussion

The above analysis has reviewed the schools on securitisation by means of the following six components: mechanism(s), securitisers and the audience, level of politics, conceptualisation of security, logic of security measures, and a negative or positive understanding of securitisation. The first three components represent the analytical tools to empirically examine a securitisation process. The latter three are the content components. These focus on the nature of a securitisation process. An overview of the similarities and differences between the four schools is provided in Table 2.1.

The review shows that each single school builds on a relatively narrow view on securitisation: each draws on a particular concept of security and defines securitisation by a particular set of outcomes. For example, while the Risk School conceptualises security in terms of potentiality and risk, the Copenhagen School focusses on securitisation in terms of existential threats. This book will not build on any particular school, but will instead make use of the various insights on securitisation in order to grasp the complexity and dynamism of securitisation processes you find in reality (see chapter 3 for more details). In order to do so, the next chapter develops a pragmatic framework for analysis what allows for a flexible application of the insights as provided by all four schools. The framework for analysis will not merge the different schools into a new theory. It allows for their separate and distinct insights to persist, each having its added value, while enabling these insights to be applied in an interactive and pragmatic manner. Each of the school's insights says something specific about securitisation that could be of interest in a particular study of securitisation and should be recognised.

In addition to providing a more flexible and pragmatic approach to the analysis of securitisation, the framework for analysis aims to provide more insight into the role of securitiser–audience relations in securitisation processes. None of the four schools offers a comprehensive account of securitiser-audience interactions. The focus tends to be on a particular group of actors, or it remains unclear how audiences can respond to securitising moves and how this may affect the concept of security or the security measures promoted. Scholars have therefore argued that the role of the audience requires further theorising and attention (see e.g., Balzacq 2005, 2011b; Roe 2008; Salter 2008b).

Table 2.1 Overview of the Schools on Securitisation, Per Component (Including Analytical Tool and Content Components)

Components	The Copenhagen School	The Paris School	Critical Security Studies	The Risk School
Mechanism(s) (Analytical tool component)	Speech act	Everyday techniques of security (routine and technocratic processes)	Speech act and physical act to articulate human choice	See Copenhagen School and Paris School
Securitisers and audience (Analytical tool component)	Elite actors as securitisers. The audience's role is under-theorised	Professionals (acting both as securitisers and audience, it examines their relations)	Elite actors and social movements, aiming to convince the oppressed and the oppressors that change is needed	See Copenhagen School and Paris School
Level of politics (Analytical tool component)	Level of high politics	Administrative level of politics	In particular, the level of high politics (for the speech acts) and the grassroots level (for the physical acts)	See Copenhagen School and Paris School
Conceptualisation of security (Content component)	Revolves around notions of exceptionality, confrontation, priority, competition, and survival	Revolves around the notion of unease, and related concepts of worry and disturbance	Revolves around the notion of human security in terms of progress and emancipation	Revolves around the notion of risk, and related concepts of potentiality, uncertainty, and positive prevention as its main innovation
Logic of security measures (Content component)	Logic of exceptionality, competition, confrontation, and defence	Logic of proactivity, management, control, and exclusion	A human security approach	Logic of positive prevention and risk management as its main innovation
Positive or negative understanding (Content component)	Negative	Negative	Positive	Positive, as its main innovation

Another aspect that requires further improvement in the four theoretical perspectives on securitisation is the level of engagement with the context in which a securitisation process is embedded. In that light, scholars have argued that context should be granted a more prominent role in the analysis of securitisation (see e.g., Balzacq 2005, 2011b; Stritzel 2007, 2011a, 2011b); context in the form of relations of power, institutional or political interests, institutional remits, cultural heritage, or even material circumstances (e.g., the actual weather circumstances influencing perceptions of climate change). Such criticism has largely concentrated on the Copenhagen School's formulation of securitisation. As argued by Wilkinson (2011: 94), the Copenhagen School's framework for analysis risks representing '*selective* abstracts of all the different acts and narratives that contributed to a successful securitization, stripped of reference to any internal dynamics and local context that are not directly related to the final securitization'. The Paris School most actively engages with contextual factors. But it tends to concentrate on questions of bureaucratic interests, technology, institutional remits, and institutional experiences, while putting less emphasis on the contextual influence of high-profile political debates, high-level political agendas and policy discourse, local cultures, etc. Through the use of the fast-emerging insights of the more contextualised securitisation scholars (see e.g., Balzacq 2005; 2011b; Stritzel 2007, 2011a; 2011b), the framework for analysis will discuss how context informs the manner in which a securitisation process unfolds.

Notes

1. When I speak of the Copenhagen School, I refer to its original and most famous formulation, as particularly developed in the 1998 book, *Security. A new framework for analysis*, by Buzan et al. This is similar to most academics drawing on the Copenhagen School's insights or critiquing them (see e.g., Balzaqc 2011b; Wilkinson 2011; Hammerstad 2012).
2. According to Petersen (2012), there is a third group of scholars, from political risk studies. This group is, however, not included in this analysis. Political risk scholars do not aim to understand or expose securitisation processes, but instead seek to classify risks and propose ways to manage and assess them. In that regard, one can even argue that this group of scholars can rather be seen as securitisers themselves, by framing and addressing issues in terms of risk.
3. As mentioned above, the notion of destructive (negative) prevention is not persuasively different from the Copenhagen School. Plus, the focus on pro-active exclusion and on negatively orientated control mechanisms fits within the Paris School's framework.

References

Abrahamsen, R. (2005) 'Blair's Africa: the politics of securitization and fear', *Alternatives*, 30(1): 55–80.
Aradau, C., L. Lobo-Guerrero, and R. Van Munster (2008) 'Security, technologies of risk, and the political: guest editors' introduction', *Security Dialogue*, 39(2–3): 147–154.

Aradau, C. and R. Van Munster (2007) 'Governing terrorism through risk: taking pre-cautions, (un)knowing the future', *European Journal of International Relations*, 13(1): 89–115.

Balzacq, T. (2005) 'The three faces of securitization: political agency, audience and context', *European Journal of International Relations*, 11(2): 171–201.

Balzacq, T., T. Basaran, D. Bigo, E.-P. Guittet, and C. Olsson (2010) 'Security practices'. In: R.A. Denmark (ed.), *International Studies Encyclopaedia Online*. Available at: www.didierbigo.com/documents/SecurityPractices2010.pdf (last visit 19 September 2014).

Balzacq, T. (ed.) (2011a) *Securitization theory. How security problems emerge and dissolve*. London: Routledge.

Balzacq, T. (2011b) 'A theory of securitization: origins, core assumptions, and variants'. In: T. Balzacq (ed.), *Securitization Theory. How security problems emerge and dissolve*. London: Routledge: 1–30.

Barnett, J., R.A. Matthew, and K.L. O'Brien (2010) 'Global environmental change and human security: an introduction'. In: R.A. Matthew, J. Barnett, B. McDonald, and K.L. O'Brien (eds.), *Global environmental change and human security*. Cambridge: The MIT Press: 3–32.

BBC (2014) 'Ebola "threat to world security" — UN Security Council', *BBC*, 19 September. Available at: www.bbc.com/news/world-africa-29262968 (last visit 27 September 2014).

Beck, U. (1992) *Risk society. Towards a new modernity*. London: Sage Publications.

Beck, U. (1997) *The reinvention of politics. Rethinking modernity in the global social order*. Cambridge: Polity Press.

Beck, U. (1999) *World risk society*. Cambridge: Polity Press.

Beck, U. (2006) 'Living in a world risk society', *Economy and Society*, 35(3): 329–345.

Behnke, A. (2000) 'The message or the messenger?: Reflections on the role of security experts and the securitization of political issues', *Cooperation and Conflict*, 35(1): 89–105.

Bigo, D. (2002) 'Security and immigration: towards a critique of the governmentality of unease', *Alternatives*, 27(1): 63–92.

Bigo, D. (2008a) 'Globalized (in)security. The field and the ban-opticon'. In: D. Bigo and A. Tsoukala (eds.), *Terror, insecurity and liberty. Illiberal practices of liberal regimes after 9/11*. London: Routledge: 10–48.

Bigo, D. (2008b) 'Security: a field left fallow'. In: M. Dillon and A.W. Neal (eds.), *Foucault on politics, security and war*. Hampshire: Palgrave Macmillan: 93–114.

Bigo, D. and A. Tsoukala (2008) 'Understanding (in)security'. In: D. Bigo and A. Tsoukala, *Terror, insecurity and liberty. Illiberal practices of liberal regimes after 9/11*. London: Routledge: 1–9.

Booth, K. (2007) *Theory of world security*. Cambridge: Cambridge University Press.

Bourdieu, P. (1990[1980]) *The logic of practice*. Cambridge: Polity Press, translated by R. Nice.

Burgess, P. and T. Owen (2004) 'Editors' note: special section: what is "human security"?', *Security Dialogue*, 35(4): 345–346.

Buzan, B. (2006) 'Will the 'global war on terrorism' be the new Cold War?', *International Affairs*, 82(6): 1101–1118.

Buzan, B., O. Wæver, and J. de Wilde (1998) *Security: a new framework for analysis*. Boulder, CO: Lynne Rienner.

C.A.S.E. Collective (2006) 'Critical approaches to security in Europe: a networked manifesto', *Security Dialogue*, 37(4): 443–487.

Coker, C. (2004) *Globalization and insecurity in the twenty-first century: NATO and the management of risk*. London: International Institute of Strategic Studies.

Conca, K. (1994) 'In the name of sustainability: peace studies and environmental discourse', *Peace & Change*, 19(2): 91–113.

Corry, O. (2010) *Securitization and 'riskization': two Grammars of security*. Working paper prepared for Standing Group on International Relations, 7th Pan-European International Relations Conference, 9–11 September, Stockholm.

Corry, O. (2012) 'Securitisation and "riskification": second-order security and the politics of climate change', *Millennium: Journal of International Studies*, 40(2): 235–258.

Cox, R. W. (1981) 'Social forces, states and world orders: beyond international relations theory', *Millennium: Journal of International Studies*, 10(2): 127–155.

Dillon, M. (2008) 'Underwriting security', *Security Dialogue*, 39(2–3): 309–332.

Doty, R. L. (2007) 'States of exception on the Mexico–U.S. border: security, "Decisions," and civilian border patrols', *International Political Sociology*, 1(2): 113–137.

Dowty, A. and G. Loescher (1996) 'Refugee flows as grounds for international action', *International Security*, 21(1): 43–71.

Duffield, M. and N. Waddell (2006) 'Securing humans in a dangerous world', *International Politics*, 43(1): 1–23.

Elbe, S. (2008) 'Risking lives: aids, security and three concepts of risk', *Security Dialogue*, 39(2–3): 177–198.

Emmers, R. (2010) 'ASEAN and the securitization of transnational crime in Southeast Asia', *The Pacific Review*, 16(3): 419–438.

Enloe, C. (1989) *Bananas, beaches and bases. Making feminist sense of international politics*. Berkeley: University of California Press.

Floyd, R. (2007) 'Towards a consequentialist evaluation of security: bringing together the Copenhagen and the Welsh Schools of security studies', *Review of International Studies*, 33(2): 327–350.

Foucault, M. (1977 [1975]) *Discipline and punish. The birth of the prison*. Translated by A. Sheridan. London: Penguin Books.

Foucault, M. (1991a [1980]) 'Questions of method'. In: G. Burchell, C. Gordon, and P. Miller (eds.), *The Foucault effect. Studies in governmentality*. London: Harvester Wheatsheaf: 73–87.

Hammerstad, A. (2012) 'Securitization from below: the relationship between immigration and foreign policy in South Africa's approach to the Zimbabwe crisis', *Conflict, Security & Development*, 12(1): 1–30.

Hammerstad, A. and I. Boas (2014) 'National security risks? Uncertainty, austerity and other logics of risk in the UK government's national security strategy', *Cooperation and Conflict*, online first: 1–17.

Hansen, L. (2000) 'The little mermaid's silent security dilemma and the absence of gender in the Copenhagen School', *Millennium: Journal of International Studies*, 29(2): 285–306.

Hogenhuis, C. (2012) 'Was Nederland voor de komst van de Marokkanen nu echt zoveel prettiger', *Volkskrant*, 11 December (only available in Dutch). Available at: www.volkskrant.nl/vk/nl/3184/opinie/article/detail/3361706/2012/12/11/Was-Nederland-voor-de-komst-van-de-Marokkanen-nu-echt-zoveel-prettiger.dhtml (last visit 19 September 2014).

Huysmans, J. (1998a) 'Security! What do you mean? From concept to thick signifier', *European Journal of International Relations*, 4(2): 226–255.

Huysmans, J. (1998b) 'The question of the limit: desecuritisation and the aesthetics of horror in political realism', *Millennium: Journal of International Studies*, 27(3): 569–689.

Huysmans, J. (2006) *The politics of insecurity. Fear, migration and asylum in the EU.* London: Routledge.

Huysmans, J. (2011) 'What's in an act? On security speech acts and little security nothings', *Security Dialogue, Special Issue on the Politics of Securitization,* 42(4–5): 371–383.

Huysmans, J. and A. Buonfino (2008) 'Politics of exception and unease: immigration, asylum and terrorism in parliamentary debates in the UK', *Political Studies,* 56(4): 766–788.

Huysmans, J. and V. Squire (2009) 'Migration and security'. In: M. Dunn Cavelty and V. Mauer (eds.), *Handbook of security studies.* London: Routledge.

Krause, K. (2004) 'The key to a powerful agenda, if properly delimited', *Security Dialogue,* 35(3): 367–368.

Kymlicka, W. (1995) *Multicultural citizenship.* Oxford: Oxford University Press.

Linklater, A. (1982) *Men and citizens in the theory of international relations.* London: The Macmillan Press.

Liotta, P. H. (2002) 'Boomerang effect: the convergence of national and human security', *Security Dialogue,* 33(4): 473–488.

McDonald, M. (2008) 'Securitisation and the construction of security', *European Journal of International Relations,* 14(4): 563–587.

McSweeney, B. (1999) *Security, identity and interests. A sociology of international relations.* Cambridge: Cambridge University Press.

Mythen, G. and S. Walklate (2008) 'Terrorism, risk and international security: the perils of asking "what if"?', *Security Dialogue,* 39(2–3): 221–242.

Neal, A. W. (2009) 'Securitisation and risk at the EU border: the origins of FRONTEX', *Journal of Common Market Studies,* 47(2): 333–356.

Nyers, P. (2006) *Rethinking refugees. Beyond states of emergency.* London: Routledge.

Oels, A. (2012) 'From the 'securitization' of climate change to the 'climatization' of the security field: comparing three theoretical perspectives'. In: J. Scheffran, M. Brzoska, H. G. Brauch, M. Link, and J. P. Schilling (eds.), *Climate change, human security and violent conflict. Challenges for societal stability.* Berlin: Springer: 185–205.

Petersen, K. L. (2012) 'Risk: a field within security studies', *European Journal of International Relations,* 18(4): 693–717.

Rasmussen, M. V. (2001) 'Reflexive security: NATO and international risk society', *Millennium: Journal of International Studies,* 30(2): 285–309.

Rasmussen, M. V. (2004) 'It sounds like a riddle: security studies, the War on Terror, and risk', *Millennium: Journal of International Studies,* 33(2): 381–395.

Roe, P. (2008) 'Actor, audience(s) and emergency measures: securitization and the UK's decision to invade Iraq', *Security Dialogue,* 39(6): 615–635.

Salter, M. (2008a) 'Imagining numbers: risk, quantification, and aviation security', *Security Dialogue,* 39(2–3): 243–266.

Salter, M. (2008b) 'Securitization and desecuritization: a dramaturgical analysis of the Canadian Air Transport Security Authority', *Journal of International Relations and Development,* 11(4): 321–349.

Scanlan, J. and G. Loescher (1983) 'U.S. foreign policy, 1959–80: impact on refugee flow from Cuba', *The ANNALS of the American Academy of Political and Social Science,* 467(1): 116–137.

Schuster, L. (2003) 'Common sense or racism? The treatment of asylum-seekers in Europe', *Patterns of Prejudice,* 37(3): 233–256.

Sen, A. (1999) *Development as freedom.* Oxford: Oxford University Press.

Smith, P. J. (2007) 'Climate change, mass migration and the military response', *Orbis*, 51(4): 617–633.

Stritzel, H. (2007) 'Towards a theory of securitization: Copenhagen and beyond', *European Journal of International Relations*, 13(3): 357–383.

Stritzel, H. (2011a) 'Security as translation: threats, discourse, and the politics of localisation', *Review of International Studies*, 37(5): 2491–2517.

Stritzel, H. (2011b) 'Security, the translation', *Security Dialogue*, 42(4–5): 343–355.

Tickner, J. A. (1992) *Gender in international relations. Feminist perspectives on achieving global security*. New York: Colombia University Press.

Trombetta, M. J. (2008) 'Environmental security and climate change: analysing the discourse', *Cambridge Review of International Affairs*, 21(4): 585–602.

United Nations Development Programme (UNDP) (1994) *Human development report 1994*. Oxford: Oxford University Press.

Van Munster, R. (2005) *Logics of security: the Copenhagen School, risk management and the War on Terror*. Political Science Publications, 10/2005. Odense: University of Southern Denmark.

Walker, R.B.J. (1997) 'The subject of security'. In: K. Krause and M. C. Williams (eds.), *Critical security studies. Concepts and cases*. London: UCL Press: 61–82.

Watson, S. D. (2012) '"Framing" the Copenhagen School: integrating the literature on threat construction', *Millennium: Journal of International Studies*, 40(2): 279–301.

Wæver, O. (1995) 'Securitization and desecuritization'. In: R. D. Lipschutz (ed.), *On security*. New York: Colombia University Press.

Wæver, O. (2002) 'Identity, communities and foreign policy: discourse analysis as foreign policy theory'. In: L. Hansen and O. Wæver (eds.), *European integration and national identity*. London: Routledge: 20–49.

Wæver, O. (2004) *Aberystwyth, Paris, Copenhagen. New 'schools' in security theory and their origins between core and periphery*. Paper prepared for the annual meeting of the International Studies Association, Montreal, March 17–20.

Wæver, O. (2008) 'Peace and security: two evolving concepts and their changing relationship'. In: H. G. Brauch, U. Oswald Spring, C. Mesjasz, J. Grin, P. Dunay, N. C. Behera, B. Chourou, P. Kameri-Mbote, and P. H. Liotta (eds.), *Globalization and environmental challenges. Reconceptualizing security in the 21st century*. Hexagon series on human and environmental security and peace, Volume 3. Heidelberg, Germany: Springer-Verlag: 99–111.

Wijblijvenhier (2013) *'Marokkanen' debat is institutionalisering van discriminatie* (only availbale in Dutch). Available at: www.wijblijvenhier.nl/18900/marokkandenbat-is-institutionalisering-van-discriminatie (last visit 24 September 2014).

Wilkinson, C. (2007) 'The Copenhagen School on tour in Kyrgyzstan: is securitization theory useable outside Europe?', *Security Dialogue*, 38(1): 5–25.

Wilkinson, C. (2011) 'The limits of spoken words: from meta-narratives to experiences of security'. In: T. Balzacq (ed.), *Securitization theory. How security problems emerge and dissolve*. London: Routledge: 94–115.

Williams, M. C. (2003) 'Words, images, enemies: securitization and international politics', *International Studies Quarterly*, 47(4): 511–531.

Williams, M. J. (2008) '(In)Security studies, reflexive modernization and the risk society', *Cooperation and Conflict*, 43(1): 57–79.

Wyn Jones, R. (1999) *Security, strategy, and critical theory*. London: Lynne Rienner Publishers.

3   A Pragmatic Framework for Analysis

The four schools on securitisation each adopt a relatively narrow view on securitisation. Each individual school is therefore challenged when needing to account for complex processes of securitisation in which different conceptualisations of security are present. For instance, in a securitisation process a certain group may promote its human security by challenging dominant institutions, which is in line with Critical Security Studies' definition of security. Others can interpret this as a confrontational attempt leading to instability and state conflict, in correspondence with the Copenhagen School's conceptualisation of security. Insights from both schools are thus needed to account for this securitisation process.

To analyse such diverse understandings and interpretations in a securitisation process, this chapter develops a new pragmatic framework for analysis. This framework integrates all four schools to allow for their interplay and is made well applicable to explaining complex processes of securitisation traceable in empirical studies. It thus adopts a pragmatic outlook. The aim is not to verify the validity or explanatory value of one single school, but is instead to provide an in-depth and well-informed account of empirical processes for which it pragmatically makes use of different theoretical insights.

To account for complexity in securitisation processes, context and the audience are central to the framework for analysis. It draws on recent developments in securitisation literature that understand securitisation as a 'Situated Interactive Activity' (Balzacq 2005: 179). Such literature presents securitisation as a contextual embedded and interactive process (between a securitiser and its audience) that can take on various meanings. For instance, due to dynamic interactions between a securitiser and an audience, the meaning of security may change or other security measures may develop than those originally envisaged by the securitiser.

The main assumption of the framework is that the context of a securitisation process and interactive processes between a securitiser and its audience(s) inform what theoretical insights of the schools on securitisation are relevant. In other words, this framework for analysis allows for all the theoretical insights of all four schools to be applied and to interact in the study of empirical processes of securitisation. Their relevance will, however, vary per securitisation process; each informed by a particular context and interaction processes between a securitiser and its audience.

Such a flexible application of the four schools on securitisation does not imply that there are no general securitisation trends to be traced. In certain empirical studies the theoretical insights of one school on securitisation may appear dominant. I consider it, however, unlikely that one school will be able to explain a full securitisation process when seeking to explore this process in depth. The theoretical insights of one school may suffice if the analysis would take on a more abstract form. For instance, when the analysis focusses only on the start and end point of a securitisation process, leaving aside the whole in-between process in which different actors can become engaged who may disagree on or hold different views on certain issues. An in-depth understanding of a securitisation process therefore implies engaging with diverse understandings held by the actors involved (these understandings could, however, become shared or dominant in the course of the securitisation process). It should take into account the potential array of directions in which a securitisation process can develop which can lead to different outcomes. For such an analysis, it is constructive to make use of different theoretical insights on securitisation, and not to be limited to the insights of one school.

This is not the first attempt that draws on different schools on securitisation. Some studies use insights of both the Copenhagen School and the Paris School (see e.g., Abrahamsen 2005; Huysmans 2006, especially ch. 1, 4, and 5; Aradau and Van Munster 2007; Huysmans and Buonfino 2008; Neal 2009;), or try to make the Copenhagen School and Critical Security Studies more complementary to one another (Floyd 2007; 2011). Some combine the conceptualisation of security as defined by the Copenhagen School with the logic of risk management (Methmann and Rothe 2012), or examine both speech acts and everyday techniques of security (see e.g., Van Munster 2005; Elbe 2008; Mythen and Walklate 2008). Despite this work being done, there is no study that integrates all four schools into one framework for analysis. The pragmatic framework for analysis, as outlined in this chapter, is developed in such a manner that it can practically and interactively employ theoretical insights of all four schools to conduct a rich analysis of securitisation processes. In this manner, this framework for analysis is something different than a theory offering new ways to understand and explain securitisation. It is meant to guide the empirical analysis by providing a structure that allows the analyst to flexibly draw on existing theoretical insights that are relevant to the material under study.

Before outlining this framework for analysis in detail, the following section introduces the role of context and the audience in the study of securitisation.

The Securitiser, the Audience, and the Context

To account for complexity in empirical studies on securitisation, an increasing number of scholars, frequently referred to as the '"second generation" of more contextual securitization scholars' (Stritzel 2011a: 2492), argue that the audience and context need to become central in the analysis of securiti-sation (see e.g., Balzacq 2005, 2011; Huysmans 2006; Stritzel 2007; 2011a, 2011b; McDonald 2008; Salter 2008; Wilkinson 2011). Through an analysis of context, it is possible to understand why a securitisation process can take on different meanings in diverse settings and circumstances, or why in a certain contextual environment a particular concept of security dominates. A central role for the audience(s) can offer insight into the interactive and dynamic pro-cess of securitisation and therefore into processes of dominance, diversity, and change. Therefore, by adding these two factors (the context and the interac-tion with the audience) to the analysis, one can grasp the more complex and dynamic processes through which securitisation unfolds.

Context here refers to a set of more structural factors 'that pervade the context in which participants are nested . . .' (Balzacq 2005: 186), such as interests and values, political agendas, the setting of the securitisation pro-cess, existing policies, existing knowledge (Balzacq 2005), 'institutional and political histories' (Huysmans 2006: 5), power relations (Stritzel 2007), policy discourses, and 'the predominant social views, trends, ideological and political attitudes . . .' (Balzacq 2005: 186). Such contextual factors shape the manner in which a securitisation process unfolds. For instance, the 'institutional and political histories' (Huysmans 2006: 5) of an organisation may influence the manner in which this organisation perceives security (see discussion Huys-mans 2006: 4–5). Or, the setting of a securitisation process can allow for dia-logue or for specific practices to emerge. For instance, a securitising move can have a different meaning depending on whether it takes place in a United Nations (UN) summit in which each country has a vote, or whether it unfolds in a G8 meeting where only a number of countries are represented. The contex-tual environment of a securitisation process can also relate to material factors. As argued by Balzacq (2005), there may be actual hazards imposed on us, such as a natural disaster, which can affect actors' perceptions (which can be both the securitiser and the audience). It is important to keep in mind, however, that while material structures can shape perceptions, the essence of a hazard can-not be determined solely on the basis of its impact. Some cultures would not perceive a typhoon simply as a natural hazard, but as an act of god in addition to being a disaster.

Such a more situated analysis of securitisation is helpful to understand why and how a securitising move emerges. As argued by Hammerstad (2012: 5): 'certain securitizations are promoted by bureaucracies if they confirm institu-tional values, advance institutional goals or confirm existing power relations'. An analysis of contextual factors therefore helps to understand why an issue becomes subjected to a securitisation process, why a securitising move draws on a particular concept of security, and promotes certain security measures. It is important to note, however, that not all second-generation securitisation scholars assume that the concept of security may vary, even when acknowl-edging that context influences the course of a securitisation process. Balzacq (2005, 2011) adopts a relatively fixed concept of security, by predominantly relying on the discourse of threat. In contrast, this framework for analysis starts from the assumption that actors involved in a securitisation process may draw on different concepts of security, informed by the context in which these actors are embedded.

These second-generation securitisation scholars provide a central role to the audience in understanding a securitisation process. An audience is not a mere receiver of a securitising move. Securitisation should be understood as a relational and interactive process in which both the securitiser and the audience play an active role (Balzacq 2005: 187, 2011; Roe 2008; Salter 2008; Stritzel 2011b). The response of an audience to a securitising move should be contextualised as well. Context provides the audience(s) with a 'frame of reference' (Balzacq 2005: 192) that shapes the audience's perception of the securitising move. As argued by Balzacq (2005: 182): 'the context "selects" or activates certain properties of the concept, while others are concealed' (Balzacq 2005: 182). It therefore depends on the audience's contextual environment what element of a securitising move will be heard. As a consequence, the audience is central in understanding the manner in which a securitisation process unfolds. A study conducted by Hammerstad (2012) on the securitisation of Zimbabwean immigrants by the South African urban poor, for instance, shows how a securitisation process may take on a different form when it reaches its audience. By means of violent protests and riots, the South African urban poor tried to securitise the mass influx of Zimbabweans. The South African foreign policy and security elite did respond to this securitising move. However, it perceived the hostile response of the South African urban poor as a potential threat, instead of the Zimbabwean immigration itself. This perception of the South African foreign policy and security elite is informed by a discourse of 'African solidarity' which did not resonate with the argument of the urban poor that Zimbabwean immigrants pose a threat to national security. This study by Hammerstad exemplifies how securitisers and audiences may hold different perceptions of similar processes, and how these perceptions are shaped by their context.

Moreover, the context does not only affect what is heard in a securitisation process, but also the manner in which the audience will respond to a securitising move. The response is of course strongly related to the audience's interpretation of the securitising move. For instance, if an audience does not perceive the issue under securitisation to pose a national security threat, this audience is unlikely to support military action. But in addition, an audience's response can be influenced by other contextual factors, such as the setting in which the audience is based. If the securitiser and its audience are both active in a UN debate, the possibilities for interaction are higher, as compared to a situation where an NGO tries to respond to a securitising move taking place in a bureaucratic setting where it does not have full access. Each setting differs in 'who may speak, what may be said, and what is heard' (Salter 2008: 323). Moreover, in the contextual literature on the audience's response, attention has been given to the role of power (see e.g., Hansen 2000; Stritzel 2007; Roe 2008; Vuori 2008).

The audience's power relation vis-à-vis a securitiser may affect its capacity to respond to a securitising move (Stritzel 2007: 363, 365; see also Vuori on the role of power, 2008: 70–71, 77). As argued by Vuori (2008: 70): 'Security is a "structured field of practices" where some people and collective actors are more privileged to speak and construct security issues than others . . .' For instance, the audience may be a subordinated group to the securitiser, such as migrants subjected to regimes of border controls. These groups may not have the power to counter a securitising move, but will experience its consequences. This question of subordinate power has furthermore been discussed in relation to non-democratic regimes, where the general public, but also ministries and NGOs, have fewer opportunities to respond to a securitising move (see e.g., discussion Stritzel 2007: 363).

A related aspect is that the response of an audience can be influenced by perceptions of authority and expertise. In certain issue areas, some actors may hold the image of the legitimate authority, or of the expert who knows how to optimally manage a situation. For instance, in the area of immigration, daily professionals who work with border controls have established a certain amount of control over the governance of immigration (Bigo 2002). In such situations, other audiences may be overruled or may hold less perceived legitimate power to influence the securitisation process. As argued by Roe (2008: 618), 'The military sector of security often carries with it a certain degree of legitimacy in terms of the government's—or, more precisely, the military's—ability to act without the consent of the general public and/or other securitising audiences'.

To sum up, the primary message of recent securitisation literature is that the analysis should take the context and securitiser–audience relations into account to understand positions, interpretations, and reactions in a securitisation process. By doing so, the analysis can trace the complex and diverse manners in which a securitisation process unfolds.

The Three-Stage Framework for Analysis

The pragmatic framework for analysis consists of three stages. The first stage is the securitising move by the securitiser (the starting point of a securitisation process), the second stage centres on the audience's response to this move, and the final stage is the outcome of a securitisation process. By dividing the securitisation process into these three stages, actors are given a central role. It needs to be examined specifically what happens to the initial securitising move, as initiated by the securitiser(s), when it is being received by a particular audience, and how this unfolds in a particular set of outcomes. But, as discussed above, the securitiser's and audience's understandings are not solely shaped by their specific actions and by interaction processes, but are informed by the context in which their actions are made. The contextual environment provides a structural embedding to the securitisation process and informs the manner in which the securitiser and the audience understand security.

Precisely by making interaction processes and the views and positions of actors central in this framework for analysis, the study of securitisation can seek to grasp change and dynamism. It allows for an in-depth account of different understandings of security and of security measures in a securitisation process. The next three sections will outline the three stages of the framework for analysis and will explain how different theoretical insights can be relevant to examine a securitisation process.

Stage One: The Securitising Move

To examine a securitising move, it is important to understand how it emerged and what message it conveys. This section first sets out how to analyse the emergence of a securitising move. The second part of the section outlines the study of the securitising move's message. I will demonstrate how the different theoretical insights on securitisation can be applied in a flexible manner to examine a securitising move in a contextualised and detailed manner.

The Emergence of a Securitising Move

I distil three perspectives to describe how a securitisation process emerges. This is based on the analytical tool components of a securitisation process. As discussed in chapter 2, the analytical tool components suggest by what mechanism, by what actor, and at what level of politics securitisation unfolds.

The first perspective, as most strongly developed by the Copenhagen School and built upon by Critical Security Studies and the Risk School, focusses on securitising moves in the form of speech acts (the mechanism), executed by elite actors as the securitiser, taking place at the level of high politics. I will refer to this perspective as the speech act perspective. The second perspective, as developed by the Paris School and built upon by the Risk School, is directed to everyday and routine techniques of security as a securitisation mechanism, which is executed by professionals of an organisation as the securitiser, and takes place at an administrative level of politics. I will refer to this perspective as the routine-technocratic perspective. The third perspective, as developed by Critical Security Studies, focusses on physical acts that attempt to articulate human choice, as the manner through which securitisation emerges (the mechanism). These acts predominantly appear in the form of protests (e.g., a street protest or even a silent protest, as discussed in chapter 2). Critical Security Studies assumes that these acts are executed by social movements (the securitiser) functioning largely at a grass root level of politics. I will refer to this perspective as the protest perspective.

There may be securitising moves consisting of a combination of these perspectives. For instance, a ministry may decide to present human rights as a matter of security (a speech act), because its human rights and conflict departments have started to collaborate more intensively and have come to share certain policy regulations (a routine development). In this manner, routine-technocratic processes and speech acts intersect. Or a securitising move may be a combination of a protest and a speech act; for instance, in case of a street protest using catchy slogans to frame an issue in terms of security.

Which of the three perspectives is relevant to the analysis of a securitising move is informed by the context in which the securitisation process is based. For instance, when researching a securitisation attempt in the context of a UN summit on human rights, it is likely for the analyst to trace developments according to the speech act perspective. During such a summit, politicians, Ministers, Secretaries etc., engage in high-level speeches to get a message across. But, the same study may trace longer-term routine policy processes that have gradually been taken for granted and have come to form the basis of the international discourse on human rights and security. Furthermore, in the context of a tense political climate where there is wider unrest in the civil society, insights of the protest perspective can become relevant.

The Message of a Securitising Move

The message of a securitising move draws on the content components of a securitisation process. These are about the meaning of security, the endorsed security measures and suggest whether a school understands securitisation as a negative or positive process.

I do not pre-select which concept of security is present in a securitising move. A securitising move does not have a fixed negative or positive character; instead securitisation processes can take on various forms in different settings and circumstances. While drawing on this open perception of security, it is important not to lose sight of the historical connotations associated with the concept of security. As argued by the Copenhagen School, the concept of security carries a considerable amount of historical baggage (Wæver 1995; see also discussion Conca 1994); it has been a central concept in matters of state security, defence, and war in many parts of the world. For that reason, the negative conceptualisation of security as envisaged by the Copenhagen School may have a strong embedded meaning that travels across different contexts. At the same time, authors have shown that this concept is not fixed. Trombetta (2008) demonstrates how specific connotations associated with environmental discourse impact on the definition of security, such as notions of an interconnected world, risk, prevention, and cooperation. The interest of the framework for analysis is therefore to grasp 'the social, political and historical contexts in which particular discourses of security (even those defined narrowly in terms of the designation and articulation of threat) become possible' (McDonald 2008: 573).

In adopting such an open understanding of security, the concept(s) of security endorsed by the securitiser is made independent of the manner through which a securitising move emerges. In other words, a speech act does not necessarily have to be linked to the Copenhagen School's concept of security, neither does a routine-technocratic mechanism have to be connected to the

Paris School's notion of unease, nor do protests have to be based on Critical Security Studies' concept of human security. Instead, a securitising move can be associated with a wide range of conceptualisations of security. For instance, a protest act (Critical Security Studies' securitisation mechanism) can be based on another concept of security than the notion of human security. Protests may take the form of riots targeting a specific group (see Hammerstad 2012) and can therefore promote a confrontational understanding of security along the lines of the Copenhagen School. Similarly, speech acts (the Copenhagen School's securitisation mechanism) may for instance endorse the Paris School's concept of unease. According to the Paris School, the concept of unease should be understood as a subtle one that associates itself with less spectacular notions, such as worry or disturbance. This conception of security does not, at first glance, neatly correspond with the characteristics of a visible and significant speech act. But there can be situations where a discursive context is created (through speech acts) in which issues become associated with a notion of unease. Imagine a parliamentary session on international crime in which occasional reference to processes of immigration is made to exemplify how international crime spreads (for a similar type of example, see Huysmans and Buonfino 2008). Even though no specific speech acts on migration are performed to present it as a matter of great insecurity, such a discursive context fuels a sense of unease about immigration. As soon as such statements become more extreme, they rather point to the conceptualisation of security as developed by the Copenhagen School. Therefore, the assumption here is that the concept of security used in a securitising move may vary and does not fundamentally connect to any perspective on the emergence of a securitising move.

For similar reasons, the logic of security measures promoted in the securitising move is not pre-determined. In contrast to what seems to be implied by the established schools on securitisation, the framework for analysis does not assume that a certain concept of security and logic of security measures are fundamentally connected to one another in a securitisation process. The Copenhagen School, for instance, argues that the concept of security defined in terms of survival, existential danger, and confrontation results in a logic of confrontation, competition, and defence. But Methmann and Rothe (2012; see also chapter 4) have demonstrated that climate change may be conceptualised as an existential threat, while the developed security measures follow a logic of risk management. This example shows that different insights on securitisation are required to account for the concept of security and the logic of security measures promoted.

Another situation that could arise is that security measures change in meaning in the course of a securitisation process. Initially, a certain security measure can be considered exceptional, in line with the Copenhagen School. But it can gradually become normalised and regulated, in line with the Paris School's logic. Such a process takes place in the European Union (EU)'s border control policy. The EU's professional bureaucratic agency, FRONTEX, attempts to regulate excessive border control measures executed by individual member states through harmonisation measures (Neal 2009: 347). Exceptional practices are gradually being harmonised into measures that FRONTEX considers to be acceptable. This may reduce some of the excessiveness of these measures and protect the rights of migrants to a larger degree. But at the same time, these harmonisation and regulation measures legitimise a certain amount of exclusionary security practices by presenting them as normal and acceptable day-to-day affairs. These regulations reaffirm ideas that the EU should attempt to maintain the society in its current form and should prevent deviating groups from entering, such as economic immigrants from Africa. This feeling of unease has become distributed and reaffirmed in a subtle way through regulation and harmonisation measures instead of being imposed through the execution of excessive and exceptional security measures.

I furthermore assume that securitisers can have different understandings of certain security measures. For instance, a Western NGO may promote bottom-up security measures in a developing country aiming to increase the resilience of local communities to climate change. The NGO's presentation and rationale behind these measures may fit the logic of human security as outlined by Critical Security Studies. However, the local communities themselves (the NGO's audience) may perceive these measures as unwanted interference and as a confrontational act of Western actors trying to change or even destroy their culture and practice, more in line with the Copenhagen School's logic of security measures. Therefore, the interpretation of a security measure, and the associated logic, is shaped by the context in which a securitisation process develops.

In sum, the study of the emergence and message of a securitising move should not be limited to a narrow theoretical understanding of securitisation. I outlined three perspectives that can be used to examine how a securitisation process emerges: the speech act perspective, the routine-technocratic perspective, and the protest perspective. Similarly, different insights on the content components of securitisation can be applied in the analysis of a securitising move's message. The context of the securitising move informs which of these insights are relevant in the analysis.

Stage Two: The Audience's Response

In line with the recent trend in securitisation literature, the audience obtains a central role in the framework for analysis. The aim of stage two is to examine how the audience reacts to a securitising move, including how it perceives (interprets) the securitising move.

An audience can respond to a securitising move in a series of different ways, depending on the context shaping the audience's interpretation of and reaction to this move. It is important to note that the audience analysed does not have to be, necessarily, the audience targeted by the securitiser. While the audience targeted in the securitising move indeed plays an important part (see e.g. Balzacq 2005, 2011; Salter 2008; Vuori 2008; Léonard and Kaunert 2011), there may be other audiences that become involved (Stritzel 2011b). Certain actors may respond to a securitising move without being targeted specifically, since it intersects with their field of authority, or because they hear about the securitising move through the media, or because the move will impact their daily lives. For instance, the securitisation of immigration may be directed to the general public in order to convince them of a certain policy change; yet, at the same time, the migrants themselves are affected by the securitising move. To take another example, a defence ministry may securitise an issue of climate change among the political elite; meanwhile, other ministries may respond to this move since it intersects with their field of interests and authority. Therefore, a range of audiences may become involved in a securitisation process.

Partly because of the involvement of different audiences, the direction in which a securitising move travels cannot always be controlled by the securitiser (see discussion Stritzel 2011b; see also Wagnsson 2000: 18, quoted in Wilkinson 2011). It is exactly the multifarious relationships between the securitiser and different sets of audiences, informed by different contexts, that make securitisation so complex. Furthermore, each audience is embedded in a specific context (which may, nonetheless, overlap with that of other audiences). This can affect the manner in which it interprets or reacts to a securitising move. As discussed in the beginning of this chapter, an audience's response can be influenced by factors of power (its capacity to respond to a securitising move, its position vis-à-vis the securitiser), established perceptions of authority and expertise, and the setting in which the securitiser and the audience find themselves (e.g., whether the setting allows for dialogue). Dominant political trends, policy discourse, national history, institutional interests, etc., may also impact on the audience's perception of the securitising move (e.g., whether the securitising move makes sense to the audience, or whether the audience considers the securitising move to be inappropriate).

It is more likely for the audience to accept the securitising move, if this move resonates with the audience's context; for instance, with its institutional remit. But, if the audience has a different interpretation of the securitiser's arguments, the securitisation process can take on a different meaning. For instance, the previously discussed study by Hammerstad (2012) shows that the South African political elite interpreted the securitising move by the South African urban poor differently than intended by the securitisers.

To analyse such complexity, it is important to allow for different insights on the content components of securitisation to be applied in the analysis of the audience's response to a securitising move. Take the case of river enlargement in the Netherlands. For one inhabitant, the enlargement means greater human security since it reduces the flood risk to its home. But, for other inhabitants the enlargement poses a direct threat to their current living situation since they are required to move due to the enlargement (this example is based on discussions in Roth and Warner 2007; Roth and Winnubst 2009; Warner and Van Buuren 2011). As a result, each inhabitant defines the threat differently, draws on different concepts of security and is likely to react in a different manner to a securitising move on river enlargement. Also, it is important to take into consideration that an audience may not engage with any notion of security. Instead, its identity or institutional experience is informed by a different concept. For instance, a development organisation may perceive problems and issues through a development lens. As a consequence, the organisation does not accept the securitising move.

Response Scenarios to a Securitising Move

An audience can react in diverse sets of ways to a securitising move. I outline seven response scenarios that can be traced when analysing an audience's reaction to a securitising move: simple agreement, forced compliance, voluntary non-response, non-acceptance and desecuritisation, non-acceptance and backfire, alternative securitisation (including backfire), and (argumentative) struggles. These scenarios account for a wide variety of responses, and are meant to make sense of the diverse manners in which an audience can react to a securitising move. It should be noted, however, that these scenarios serve as ideal-types and are likely to intersect in reality.

To start with the scenario of *simple agreement*. This scenario unfolds if the audience interprets the securitising move in line with the securitiser, and accepts the securitising move. Such a compatible interpretation by the audience is more likely to be traced when the audience's frame of reference is highly compatible with that of the securitiser, such as when cultural differences are small, when the actors (the securitiser and audience) operate in similar institutional environments, or when both actors share a similar political agenda. A compatible interpretation does not, however, necessarily guarantee the acceptance of a securitising move. This furthermore depends on the audience's power in relationship to the securitiser (see Stritzel 2007), its perceptions of authority and of legitimate expertise (see e.g., Bigo 2002; Vuori 2008), the audience's interests and institutional responsibilities, etc. The acceptance of a securitising move can depend on the audience's relation with the securitiser; whether they share a particular history or whether they are close allies. The chances for the audience to be receptive to the securitising move are likely to increase when the audience holds a positive view of the securitiser. Furthermore, as argued by Stritzel (2007: 370), 'the better the positional power of securitizing actors, the easier it is for them to establish their preferred individual text as a dominant narrative for a larger collective'. Moreover, it can be beneficial if the securitiser and the audience are actively engaged in a setting characterised by opportunities for interaction to build shared understandings.

A second scenario of *forced compliance* can be traced if the audience holds a subordinate position to that of the securitiser and has limited means to respond to a securitising move (see Stritzel 2007 on the importance of power, and p. 372 on the monopoly of a securitiser). The audience, possibly unwillingly, has to experience the consequences of a securitising move. This can occur in non-democratic regimes, where the public has little means to counter authorities, or when immigrants suffer from stricter border controls. This scenario can unfold independent from the question whether the audience interpreted the securitising move in its pure form or in a somewhat different manner. In both scenarios, the audience will have to bear the consequences of the securitising move, due to its limited means to respond.

A third scenario of (*voluntary*) *non-response/non-engagement* is when the securitising move is incompatible with the audience's own perceptions related to the issue under securitisation, or with its cultural values and interests. As a consequence, it does not to respond at all or in a very limited manner. The audience does not see the relevance of actively engaging in a discussion over a framing that it perceives as false, irrelevant or incorrect, especially if the stakes are not considered high. This scenario can be considered an unsuccessful securitisation process from the perspective of the securitiser, in case the audience in question is the one the securitiser aimed to target.

A fourth scenario of *non-acceptance and desecuritisation* refers to a situation in which the audience rejects the securitising move (after either having interpreted it correctly or in a different fashion), and tries to desecuritise the issue under securitisation. Desecuritisation is defined here as a situation in which an audience actively aims to get (or keep) an issue outside the security domain. This can be contrasted to the above scenario of voluntary non-response in which the audience is simply disengaged with the issue. In this scenario, the securitiser does think the stakes are high enough to actively counter the securitising move. Such a scenario can be traced in the response from aid agencies to a report by the US army arguing that development aid in Afghanistan can be used as a strategy to gain trust among the local population (see Oxfam International 2010). As a response of non-acceptance and desecuritisation, a group of aid agencies released a report called 'Quick Impact, Quick Collapse'. They argued that the militarisation of development aid risks making development work political and short-term focussed, and makes citizens 'targets of armed opposition groups' (Oxfam International 2010).

A fifth scenario is *non-acceptance and backfire*. This scenario is when the audience's rejection of the securitising move results in a situation of '*backfire*' (Stritzel 2011b: 350, emphasis in the original). Backfire means that the securitising move is not only not-accepted, but the audience's response also further worsens the objectives of the securitiser. A scenario of backfire for instance unfolded for the United Kingdom (UK)'s Labour Government during the time of the Iraq War. The British public was highly sceptical of Britain's interference in this war, and of its legitimacy in the first place. Thousands of people decided to protest against military intervention in Iraq (BBC 2003). To convince the public of such military action, Prime Minister Tony Blair warned of '"bloody consequences", if Iraq was not confronted' (Blair quoted in BBC 2003). But such statements have only added fuel to the fire (BBC 2003). It motivated hundreds thousands of people to march on the streets and deteriorated the public's trust in the Labour Government.

This scenario can relate to the above situation of desecuritisation, if the audience actively aims to recast the issue away from security. However, it does not necessarily have to be about desecuritisation. For instance, an audience may refuse to pursue collaboration with the securitiser as a consequence of a securitising move. This negatively affects the securitiser's objectives but does not necessarily represent a situation of desecuritisation. The audience is not specifically aiming to keep an issue outside the security domain. Moreover, backfire has a specific effect, which makes it different from mere desecuritisation. Its defining feature is that the audience's response further worsens the securitiser's objectives. This is not necessarily the effect of a desecuritisation attempt.

A sixth scenario is that of *alternative securitisation*. In this scenario, the audience holds a different interpretation of the securitising move to the one of the securitiser and has the capacity to take the securitisation process forward independent from the support of the securitiser (see e.g., the case on the securitisation of Zimbabweans immigrants by Hammerstad 2012). In this situation, the securitising move takes on a new course once it reaches an audience, possibly detached from the initial securitising move. This scenario can also result in a situation of backfire when the alternative securitisation process further worsens the objectives of the initial securitising move. For instance, the concept of human security has been used to legitimise military intervention or to justify border control practices (Liotta 2002; Duffield and Waddell 2006; Huysmans and Squire 2009; Oels 2012). This usage of the concept of human security contrasts with the ideals of universal human rights, common security and inclusiveness, as advocated by its original promoters.

A seventh scenario is that of *(argumentative) struggles* between the securitiser and the audience(s) over the framing and/or interpretation of the issue under securitisation, questions of governance, and related questions of authority (see Hajer 1995, on argumentative struggles). These struggles can also revolve around the desecuritisation of the issue. Struggles can take place through speech acts, institutional exchange or bureaucratic fights over institutional responsibility, but can also take on physical forms by means of protests (see e.g., Wilkinson 2007; Vuori 2011). For that very reason, the word *argumentative* is placed between brackets. Some audiences only have access to physical forms of communication, while not having the means to engage in verbal dialogue with the securitiser (see discussion in Wilkinson 2007). These struggles can take place between different audiences, who hold different perceptions and ideas of the securitising move.

It is important to note that not only the question of framing is at stake in such struggles, but also the positioning of the actors involved (Hajer 1995: 53). The framing of an issue influences which actor (the securitiser or the audience) may claim the right to authority and obtains control over the issue under securitisation. For instance, a defence ministry becomes an important player when immigration is framed as a matter of defence. Meanwhile, a development cooperation ministry is granted authority when the issue is presented as a matter of development. Such (argumentative) struggles can only emerge, however, if the participating actors hold sufficient capital to engage in dialogue or protests.[1] The participating actors also need to perceive the stakes high enough to engage in (argumentative) struggles to convince one another about the validity of their perspective or of their authority of governance. On what grounds the (argumentative) struggle can be won, depends on several contextual factors, such as the reputation of the actor's knowledge over the issue under securitisation (see Bigo 2002 on the authority of expertise), and power relations (e.g., one actor may hold greater power if it has the authority over the available budget).

These struggles do not have to result in a clear winner and loser. It could be that this process of receiving and employing arguments gradually forms a shared understanding among the involved actors (Wyn Jones 1999: 112; see also discussion in Risse 2000; Checkel 2001). As argued by Wyn Jones, 'argumentation and disputation can have—and have had—profound effects even on the practice of security . . .' (Wyn Jones 1999: 112). Wyn Jones (1999: 156–158) in particular refers to the profound effect of peace movements on traditional security politics in the 1980s through their promotion of the term 'common security'. He argues, in line with scholars such as Risse-Kappen (1994), Kaldor (1995), Checkel (1993) and many others, that this promotion of a more positive and collaborative understanding of security motivated states, such as the United States and the former Soviet Union, to continue discussing arms controls and even to develop less offensive defence strategies.

In sum, an audience may engage in several response scenarios to react to a securitising move. To make sense of these various possible reactions, seven response scenarios are developed: simple agreement, forced compliance, voluntary non-response, non-acceptance and desecuritisation, non-acceptance and backfire, alternative securitisation, and (argumentative) struggles. In order to understand the different ways in which a securitising move can be understood by its audience, it is relevant to draw on different insights on the content components of securitisation as provided by the four schools.

Stage Three: The Outcome of a Securitisation Process

This final step of the framework assesses the overall consequences of the securitisation process in terms of relative positions of power (also referred to as positional power). The key question is whether the securitisation process resulted in a 'reconfiguring [of] existing relations of power' (Stritzel 2007: 370) of the involved actors (the securitiser(s) and the audience(s)). In other words, has the securitiser or the audience gained or lost in power due to the securitisation process, have power positions remained unaffected, or have the securitiser and the audience both gained or lost in power?

This can be assessed by examining the ability of the actor(s) 'to influence collective meaning constructions' (Stritzel 2007: 372), and by analysing what actor has been more influential in determining how the issue under securitisation should be governed. The latter refers to the question of how the securitisation process has affected the securitiser's and audience's influence over the endorsed security measures and the related field of governance. For instance, if examining the securitisation of the Ebola virus, the following questions could be asked: Which securitiser has been most powerful in this securitisation process: the aid workers, border security specialists, the World Health Organisation or the UN Security Council? How influential has the audience been (e.g., those governments that have been less active in addressing the virus)? What is the main outcome: additional aid or enhanced border security measures at various airports? And who has been granted the authority to execute these measures, and who benefits or suffers from it? Or, in case of a failed or changed securitisation process in which an audience did not accept the endorsed security measures by the securitiser, it can be examined how this affects the securitiser's and audience's position in the respective governance field. Has the securitiser lost its power due to its own securitising move?

The ability to influence meaning constructions is about whether the securitiser or the audience has been more influential (or equally influential) in determining how the issue under securitisation (in this case, climate migration) is presented or perceived. For example, as I will discuss in chapter 6, partly due to India and UK interactions in the securitisation process on climate migration, the UK's Foreign and Commonwealth Office eventually adapted its securitising move. This case shows that an audience has a certain degree of power over the securitiser's conceptualisation of security.

In short, the outcome of a securitisation process centres on questions of power. The aim is to grasp the actual effects of the securitisation process in terms of power politics: who gains and who loses, or whether this is a win-win or lose-lose situation.

Applying the Pragmatic Framework for Analysis

The next three chapters will review the securitisation process on climate migration through the lens of the framework for analysis set out in this chapter. I examine whether it is indeed useful to draw on different theoretical insights on securitisation, and analyse how the securitisation process is informed by its contextual environment and by interactions between the securitiser and its audience.

The analysis is structured according to the three stages of a securitisation process: chapter 4 reviews the securitising move(s) on climate migration (stage one); chapter 5 addresses the response to this move by its audience (stage two); and chapter 6 examines the outcome of this securitisation process (stage three). The analysis aims to provide a rich and in-depth understanding of the securitisation of climate migration.

Note

1. Capital refers to the actor's level of authority, the freedom or capacity to engage in protest, the actor's level of access to the debate, etc.

References

Abrahamsen, R. (2005) 'Blair's Africa: the politics of securitization and fear', *Alternatives*, 30(1): 55–80.

Aradau, C. and R. Van Munster (2007) 'Governing terrorism through risk: taking precautions, (un)knowing the future', *European Journal of International Relations*, 13(1): 89–115.

Balzacq, T. (2005) 'The three faces of securitization: political agency, audience and context', *European Journal of International Relations*, 11(2): 171–201.

Balzacq, T. (2011) 'A theory of securitization: origins, core assumptions, and variants'. In: T. Balzacq (ed.), *Securitization theory. How security problems emerge and dissolve*. London: Routledge: 1–30.

BBC (2003) 'Million march against Iraq war', *BBC*, 16 February. Available at: http://news.bbc.co.uk/2/hi/uk_news/2765041.stm (last visit 30 September 2014).

Bigo, D. (2002) 'Security and immigration: towards a critique of the governmentality of unease', *Alternatives*, 27(1): 63–92.

Checkel, J. (1993) 'Ideas, institutions, and the Gorbachev foreign policy', *World Politics*, 45(2): 271–300.

Checkel, J. (2001) 'Why comply? Social learning and European identity change', *International Organization*, 55(3): 553–588.

Conca, K. (1994) 'In the name of sustainability: peace studies and environmental discourse', *Peace & Change*, 19(2): 91–113.

Duffield, M. and N. Waddell (2006) 'Securing humans in a dangerous world', *International Politics*, 43(1): 1–23

Elbe, S. (2008) 'Risking lives: aids, security and three concepts of risk', *Security Dialogue*, 39(2–3): 177–198.

Floyd, R. (2007) 'Towards a consequentialist evaluation of security: bringing together the Copenhagen and the Welsh Schools of security studies', *Review of International Studies*, 33(2): 327–350.

Floyd, R. (2011) 'Can securitization theory be used in normative analysis? Towards a just securitization theory', *Security Dialogue*, Special Issue on the Politics of Securitization, 42(4–5): 427–439.

Hajer, M.A. (1995) *The politics of environmental discourse. Ecological modernization and the policy process*. Oxford: Clarendon Press.

Hammerstad, A. (2012) 'Securitization from below: the relationship between immigration and foreign policy in South Africa's approach to the Zimbabwe crisis', *Conflict, Security & Development*, 12(1): 1–30.

Hansen, L. (2000) 'The little mermaid's silent security dilemma and the absence of gender in the Copenhagen School', *Millennium: Journal of International Studies*, 29(2): 285–306.

Huysmans, J. (2006) *The politics of insecurity. Fear, migration and asylum in the EU*. London: Routledge.

Huysmans, J. and A. Buonfino (2008) 'Politics of exception and unease: immigration, asylum and terrorism in parliamentary debates in the UK', *Political Studies*, 56(4): 766–788.

Huysmans, J. and V. Squire (2009) 'Migration and security'. In: M. Dunn Cavelty and V. Mauer (eds.), *Handbook of security studies*. London: Routledge.

Kaldor, M. (1995) 'Who killed the Cold War?', *Bulletin of the Atomic Scientists*, 51(4): 57–60.

Léonard, S. and C. Kaunert (2011) 'Reconceptualizing the audience in securitization theory'. In: T. Balzacq (ed.), *Securitization theory. How security problems emerge and dissolve*. London: Routledge: 57–76.

Liotta, P. H. (2002) 'Boomerang effect: the convergence of national and human security', *Security Dialogue*, 33(4): 473–488.

McDonald, M. (2008) 'Securitisation and the construction of security', *European Journal of International Relations*, 14(4): 563–587.

Methmann, C. and D. Rothe (2012) 'Politics for the day after tomorrow: the political effect of apocalyptic imageries in global climate governance', *Security Dialogue*, 43(4): 323–344.

Mythen, G. and S. Walklate (2008) 'Terrorism, risk and international security: the perils of asking 'what if'?', *Security Dialogue*, 39(2–3): 221–242.

Neal, A. W. (2009) 'Securitisation and risk at the EU border: the origins of FRONTEX', *Journal of Common Market Studies*, 47(2): 333–356.

Oels, A. (2012) *The governmentalization of security in neoliberal times: the case of climate change induced migration*. Paper presented to the international workshop 'The securitization of climate-induced migration: critical perspectives', Hamburg, 10–12 June.

Oxfam International (2010) *Aid agencies sound the alarm on the militarization of aid in Afghanistan*. Press release, 27 January 2010. Available at: www.oxfam.org/en/grow/ pressroom/pressrelease/2010–01–27/aid-agencies-sound-alarm-militarization-aid-afghanistan (last visit 23 September 2014).

Risse, T. (2000) '"Let's argue!": communicative action in world politics', *International Organization*, 54(1): 1–39.

Risse-Kappen, T. (1994) 'Ideas do not float freely: transnational coalitions, domestic structures, and the end of the Cold War', *International Organisation*, 48(2): 185–214.

Roe, P. (2008) 'Actor, audience(s) and emergency measures: securitization and the UK's decision to invade Iraq', *Security Dialogue*, 39(6): 615–635.

Roth, D. and J. Warner (2007) 'Flood risk, uncertainty and changing river protection policy in the Netherlands: the case of "calamity polders"', *Journal of Economic and Social Geography*, 98(4): 519–525.

Roth, D. and M. Winnubst (2009) 'Reconstructing the polder: negotiating property rights and "blue" functions for land', *International Journal of Agricultural Resources, Governance and Ecology*, 8(1): 37–56.

Salter, M. (2008) 'Securitization and desecuritization: a dramaturgical analysis of the Canadian Air Transport Security Authority', *Journal of International Relations and Development*, 11(4): 321–349.

Stritzel, H. (2007) 'Towards a theory of securitization: Copenhagen and beyond', *European Journal of International Relations*, 13(3): 357–383.

Stritzel, H. (2011a) 'Security as translation: threats, discourse, and the politics of localisation', *Review of International Studies*, 37(5): 2491–2517.

Stritzel, H. (2011b) 'Security, the translation', *Security Dialogue*, 42(4–5): 343–355.

Trombetta, M. J. (2008) 'Environmental security and climate change: analysing the discourse', *Cambridge Review of International Affairs*, 21(4): 585–602.

Van Munster, R. (2005) *Logics of security: the Copenhagen School, risk management and the War on Terror*. Political Science Publications, 10/2005. Odense: University of Southern Denmark.

Vuori, J. A. (2008) 'Illocutionary logic and strands of securitization: applying the theory of securitization to the study of non-democratic political orders', *European Journal of International Relations*, 14(1): 65–99.

Vuori, J. A. (2011) 'Religious bites: Falungong, securitization/desecuritization in the People's Republic of China'. In: T. Balzacq (ed.), *Securitization theory. How security problems emerge and dissolve*. London: Routledge: 186–211.

Warner, J. and A. Van Buuren (2011) 'Implementing room for the river: narratives of success and failure in Kampen, the Netherlands', *International Review of Administrative Sciences*, 77(4): 779–801.

Wæver, O. (1995) 'Securitization and desecuritization'. In: R. D. Lipschutz (ed.), *On security*. New York: Colombia University Press.

Wilkinson, C. (2007) 'The Copenhagen School on tour in Kyrgyzstan: is securitization theory useable outside Europe?', *Security Dialogue*, 38(1): 5–25.

Wilkinson, C. (2011) 'The limits of spoken words: from meta-narratives to experiences of security'. In: T. Balzacq (ed.), *Securitization theory. How security problems emerge and dissolve*. London: Routledge: 94–115.

Wyn Jones, R. (1999) *Security, strategy, and critical theory*. London: Lynne Rienner Publishers.

4 Stage One
Securitising Moves on Climate Migration

The most prominent securitising moves on climate migration took place in the United Nations (UN) Security Council debates on climate change of 2007 and 2011. In both debates, over 50 states participated (55 in 2007, and 62 in 2011). Never before had a UN Security Council debate attracted contributions of that many delegations. The debate of 2007 has even been named the key starting point of the more widespread securitisation of climate change, including related issues such as climate migration (Brauch 2009). In these debates, the spectre of climate migration was amongst the key issues that countries referred to as a means to exemplify global warming's security implications.

This chapter examines securitising moves on climate migration, and hence focusses on the securitisers, their actions, and main messages. I start with an analysis of the two UN Security Council debates. Through the lens of the pragmatic framework for analysis set out in chapter 3, the aim is to provide a macro-level insight into securitising moves performed in these debates. This will demonstrate which states act as the key securitisers, how they conceptualised climate migration, and what action they have tried to promote to address the issues at hand. An analysis of the UN Security Council debates is particularly interesting, as the Council is the key avenue where one would expect exceptional measures to be promoted to deal with identified threats (Methmann and Rothe 2012: 334). But as the analysis will show, the securitisers did not endorse exceptional measures. Instead, their focus is largely on preventive measures in the area of development, conflict prevention, and particularly in that of climate change.

As a next step, I zoom in on one of the key securitisers of climate migration: the United Kingdom (UK)'s Foreign and Commonwealth Office. The FCO was the initiator of the UN Security Council debate of 2007 and has been amongst the most active promoters of the climate–security–migration nexus. This micro-level analysis will help to understand how its securitising move emerged, the reasons driving it, and particularly it will delve into the connection with climate politics and diplomacy.

Securitising Moves at the UN Security Council Debates

The debate of 2007 was the first-ever UN Security Council debate fully focussed on the issue of global warming (including climate migration).[1] The

UK had put much effort into getting the Council to accept the issue of climate change as an agenda item. The UK particularly had to persuade the United States (US) because of its position on climate change at the time, but China and Russia were sceptical as well for reasons I will return to in the next chapter. In the end, the debate was accepted on the basis that there would be no negotiated outcome, no presidential statement or resolution.[2]

The debate four years later did produce a presidential statement. It expressed the concern 'that possible adverse effects of climate change may, in the long run, aggravate certain existing threats to international peace and security' (UNSC 2011a). But having a debate on climate change in the UN Security Council remained very sensitive. In 2013, the UK, together with Pakistan, attempted to hold another UN Security Council debate on the topic (King 2013; Krause-Jackson 2013), but this initiative was blocked by Russia and China (see chapter 5 for details on their reasons). As a result, the UN Security Council only held a closed-door informal debate on climate change, which was not recorded and not open to the media.

The macro-level analysis will focus on the UN Security Council debates of 2007 and 2011, as no primary data is available for the latest debate held in 2013. This assessment is conducted by means of a content analysis software tool called 'Discourse Network Analyzer' (Leifeld 2013). This is a technique to detect what actors act as coalitions that unite on particular statements, commonly referred to as discourse coalitions. By applying this tool to the UN Security Council debates, I can demonstrate what state actors act as the securitisers on climate change, and more specifically on climate migration, and how other state coalitions position themselves on this topic. It shows what arguments they make and what actions they propose to address the issues at hand.

Through a reading of the transcripts and reportings of the two UN Security Council debates (Detraz and Betsill 2009; Sindico 2007; UNSC 2007a, 2007b, 2011b, 2011c; Worsnip 2011; Methmann and Rothe 2012; King 2013), I knew that both debates were characterised by a stark divide between groups of states supporting and opposing the debate. My aim was to get insight into what exact state coalitions supported or opposed the debate, what their key arguments were in favour or against having a debate on climate change in the UN Security Council, their view on the link between climate change and security in general, and specifically their positioning on the securitisation of climate migration. Many more specific issues than climate migration were discussed in the debate (such as water scarcity, food insecurity, health risks), but these were not included in the analysis.

This analysis was conducted in two steps. *As a first step* for both debates, I examined the general positioning of states on climate change and security. I reviewed whether the states supported or opposed the debates, how they framed climate change, and whether they agreed with the argument that climate migration is a security issue (see below for the exact selection of examined statements). In this step of the analysis, I do not go into much detail about states' positions on climate migration (this detail is provided, however, in the second step of the analysis). Instead, the focus is more on the general understanding of climate change (whether states framed it in terms of security, and if yes how, or whether, they framed it in a different manner) and on the general positioning of states in the debate. Climate migration is part of a wider securitisation process on climate change. For that reason it is important to grasp the overall framing of climate security and how states view the respective UN Security Council debates, in order to understand what role climate migration plays in that regard. Based on this analysis, I can detect what states act as the securitisers on climate change (including climate migration) and what states belong to the opposing coalition to the securitising moves.

To select the group of securitisers in both the 2007 and 2011 debate, I analysed what states supported the following statements: This debate is welcome; Climate change fits the UN Security Council's mandate (in short, Fits UNSC mandate); Climate change is a security issue (in short, CC is a security issue); Climate change can exacerbate conflict (in short, CC can exacerbate conflict); Climate change is a matter of human security (in short, human security); Climate insecurity is a potential risk (in short, a risk); Climate migration is a security issue (in short, CM is a security issue). These statements were selected on the basis of a reading of the transcripts and other reportings of the UN Security Council debates (Detraz and Betsill 2009; Sindico 2007; UNSC 2007a, 2007b; 2011b, 2011c; Worsnip 2011; Methmann and Rothe 2012; King 2013), and are meant to give an overview of the key lines of argumentation. In addition, not preselected statements were examined, to trace outliers in the debate. This led to the inclusion of statements about 'Energy security', which visualises how the US was connected to the debate of 2007.

The statement 'Climate change is a security issue' has been broadly defined. It includes sentences by states in the debate referring to implications for human security (unless this was framed as a risk), but also sentences in which climate change was framed as a security threat or as an emerging threat, and sentences where states simply spoke of security implications. In addition, I included some more specific statements in the analysis on the climate–security nexus to obtain insight into how the actors understood security in the climate security discourse. Cases in which states explicitly used the term *human security* when discussing climate change, have been categorised under the statement of 'Climate change is a matter of human security'. The statement of 'Climate change is a potential risk' was strictly defined. I only connected states to that statement if they explicitly discussed climate insecurity as a potential risk. For example, Australia and Cape Verde were both concerned about the link between climate change and security, but purposefully represented it as a risk (as opposed to a clear matter of security), that could potentially materialise in future. But this 'risk' statement does not include those states arguing explicitly that climate change has security implications, or is a threat, while occasionally using the word *risk* (for instance, by using the term *security risks*). Such phrases have been placed under the broad statement of 'Climate change is a security issue'. The statement 'Climate change can exacerbate conflict' includes sentences in which states argue that climate change *will* exacerbate conflicts/or will *cause* conflicts, and sentences stating that climate change *risks* to exacerbate conflicts. Finally, the statement 'Climate migration is a security issue' has been broadly defined. It includes phrases ranging from climate migration being a grave security threat to climate migration being a matter of human security. As I will discuss in more detail below, in a second step in the analysis, I examine more detailed statements on climate migration.

To select the opposing coalition in the 2007 and 2011 debate, I analysed what states supported the following statements: Use other UN forums to discuss climate change; Climate change belongs to the UN Framework Convention on Climate Change (UNFCCC); Climate change does not fit the UN Security Council's mandate (in 2011 this was called 'UNSC should not address climate change' as more statements were framed along those lines); Climate change is a matter of sustainable development; There is a lack of evidence connecting climate change and security; Climate change poses a threat to small island states (this statement is only highlighted for those states arguing against the general conceptualisation of climate change in terms of security, to show the contradiction in their argument). Similar to the statements of the securitisers, these statements were selected on the basis of a reading of the transcripts and other reportings of the UN Security Council debates (Detraz and Betsill 2009; Sindico 2007; UNSC 2007a, 2007b, 2011b, 2011c; Worsnip 2011; Methmann and Rothe 2012; King 2013). This analysis did not include any specific statements on climate migration, since these countries rejected a security discourse on climate migration and thus largely did not engage with the issue (see chapter 5 for details). In few instances, climate migration was mentioned. That was in the context of the broader statement 'There is a lack of evidence connecting climate change and security', and have thus been categorised under that statement.

As a second step, I performed a more in-depth analysis of the core group of securitisers and of the core counter coalition in both debates. I regard only those states that share at least four statements to be the core group of securitisers and the core opposing coalition (with the exception for the core opposing coalition in the 2007 debate, where I select those states that support at least three of the same statements). For the core group of securitisers, I examined more detailed statements on climate migration, on the meaning of security, and what security measures were promoted in the debate. For the core opposing coalition, I reviewed what types of actions or policy measures they promoted in the debate.

The next subsections will show the results of this analysis, with a focus on the securitisers (details on the positioning of the opposing coalition are discussed in chapter 5). I will start with a review of the debate of 2007, followed by the one of 2011.

The 2007 UN Security Council Debate

Figure 4.1[3] provides an overview of the respective state positions and relations (including all 55 states) in the UN Security Council debate of 2007.[4] This

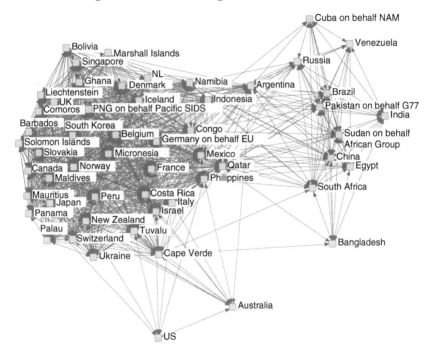

Figure 4.1   An Overview of State Positions in the 2007 UNSC Debate

Note: Any two states are connected when they share at least one of the selected statements.

overview is derived from the selected statements outlined above, seeking to provide insight into the general positioning of states in the debate. This analysis shows that it has been a divided debate, with two main groups and a few outliers. The main group consists of the securitisers in favour of the respective UN Security Council debate, performing securitising moves on climate change and specifically on climate migration. These are mostly European states and small island states. The states on the other side of the spectrum represent the opposing group, to which I return to in the next chapter. In this latter group, the emerging developing countries play a key role.

Figure 4.2 shows more specifically how the group of securitisers (and its outliers) is aligned through the set of examined statements. A total of 34 states welcomed the respective UN Security Council debate, and 16 states argued that climate change issues do fit the Council's mandate aimed to protect international peace and security. The latter statement thus appeared more controversial amongst the securitisers. The widening mandate of the Council, including non-traditional security issues (such as climate change), is a highly sensitive topic amongst many developing countries and emerging economies, as the Council's decision making is controlled by its five permanent members holding veto power (the US, UK, Russia, China, and France) (Biermann and Boas 2008). Many of the securitisers therefore remained silent on this particular question,

Figure 4.2 States Supporting Securitising Statements in the 2007 UNSC Debate

Note: A line between a statement and a state means that the state agreed with that statement.

while welcoming the debate and framing climate change in terms of security. A total of 34 states connected climate change to security, and 15 states linked climate change to situations of conflict. In contrast, only 4 states explicitly argued climate change was a matter of human security, and even fewer spoke of climate insecurity as a potential risk (as opposed to being a clear matter of security). The topic of climate migration also frequently came up. A number of 23 states referred to climate migration when making their case that climate change threatens international peace and security or when expressing concerns for small island states populations (see Figures 4.3 and 4.5 for details).

It is interesting to see how the US positioned itself as an outlier (see Figures 4.1 and 4.2). The US did not make any explicit statements supporting the debate, but it also did not openly object to it either. This would have placed the US in the camp of the emerging developing countries and Russia instead of with its European allies. It thus tried to keep its statements below the radar. As shown in Figure 4.2, the only matter it did speak of was energy security, while it did not make any explicit connections between climate change and security. At the time of the debate, Bush was still president of the US. Under his presidency, the US had withdrawn from the Kyoto Protocol and refused to take on any binding mitigation targets under the UNFCCC. For the same reason, the US was not supportive of the respective UN Security Council debate, as it could put additional pressure on the US to act.[5]

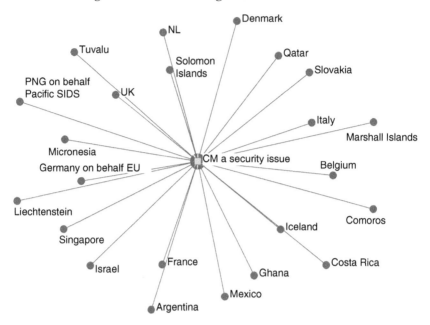

Figure 4.3 States Aligned with the Statement that Climate Migration is a Security Issue

Figure 4.4 shows those securitisers (positioned on the left side of the spectrum) that are very closely aligned to one another and together form a more cohesive network.[6] These states are the leading securitisers on the issues of climate change and climate migration. This core coalition of securitisers largely consists of European states, small island states and a few Latin American countries.[7] The UK is one of the key securitisers, but so are actors such as Germany speaking on behalf of the EU, and Papua New Guinea speaking on behalf of the Pacific Small Island Developing States (Pacific SIDS). Mexico also belongs to the group of securitisers. But Figure 4.4 shows that it is positioned somewhat more closely to the opposing coalition, compared to the other key securitisers. This is because Mexico does not agree with the statement that climate change fits the UN Security Council's mandate. Instead, it has supported the opposing group in arguing that climate change issues need to be discussed in other UN forums.

Figures 4.2 and 4.3 have shown that climate migration was presented in terms of security. But it did not demonstrate through what concept of security climate migration has been discussed: did the securitisers express concerns about the basic needs and livelihoods of the climate migrants (in line with Critical Security Studies' concept of security), or did they portray climate migration as a subtle risk, or as a serious threat? Figure 4.5 provides a detailed analysis of the statements on climate migration and security made by the core coalition as selected in Figure 4.4. It shows that climate migration has been presented in rather alarmist terms. Most of the statements about climate migration reflect a Copenhagen School language of fear and exceptionality, based on a negative

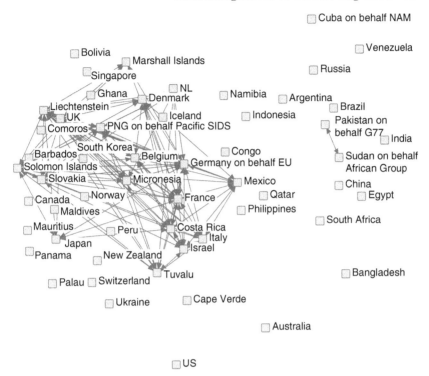

Figure 4.4 The Core Group of Securitisers in the 2007 UNSC Debate

Note: Any two states are connected when they share least four statements.

conceptualisation of security. States use terms such as unprecedented and uncontrollable migration, climate refugees, mass displacement, mass exodus, and portray climate migration as a driver of conflict. In that light, Margaret Beckett, UK representative acting as President to the Council, argued: 'An unstable climate will exacerbate some of the core drivers of conflict, such as migratory pressures and competition of resources' (UNSC 2007a: 2). Along similar lines, Mr. De La Sablière, representing France, referred to 'massive population movements' as one of the 'four impacts [which] are convincing evidence of the threat to peace posed by climate change. . . . It is clear that natural disasters and rising water could increase the number of refugees and displaced persons and could result in uncontrollable migratory flows' (UNSC 2007a: 11). Mr. Beck, representing the Solomon Islands, also warned of climate migration to raise awareness of the security implications of climate change: 'Today we are accommodating the internal movement of people. Soon it will spill over into the international scene . . .' (UNSC 2007b: 13). This shows how the spectre of climate migration was actively played on to make argument that climate change causes insecurity.

The same applies to the manner in which this core coalition conceptualised the overarching issue of climate change as a matter of security. Most states

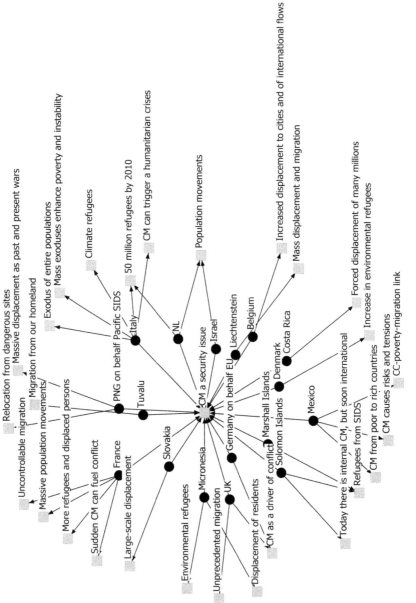

Relocation from dangerous sites
Massive displacement as past and present wars
Migration from our homeland
Exodus of entire populations
Mass exoduses enhance poverty and instability

Climate refugees

50 million refugees by 2010
CM can trigger a humanitarian crises

Population movements

Increased displacement to cities and of international flows

Mass displacement and migration

Forced displacement of many millions

Increase in environmental refugees

CC-poverty-migration link

CM causes risks and tensions

CM from poor to rich countries

Refugees from SIDS

Today there is internal CM, but soon international

Mexico

Costa Rica

Denmark

Marshall Islands

Solomon Islands

Germany on behalf EU

CM as a driver of conflict

Displacement of residents

UK

Unprecedented migration

Micronesia

Environmental refugees

Slovakia

Large-scale displacement

France

Sudden CM can fuel conflict

More refugees and displaced persons

Massive population movements

Uncontrollable migration

Tuvalu

PNG on behalf Pacific SIDS

CM a security issue

Italy

NL

Israel

Liechtenstein

Belgium

Figure 4.5 Statements on Climate Migration Made by the Core Group of Securitisers in the 2007 UNSC Debate

in this coalition draw on quite alarmist Copenhagen School-style statements. They spoke of national and international security threats, and compared climate change to situations of war, crime, or terrorism (UNSC 2007a, 2007b). For example, the UK argued that the disruption of climate change will be on the 'scale of the two world wars' (UNSC 2007a: 2), Tuvalu spoke of a 'warming war', and Denmark referred to Darfur as an example of climate-related conflict (UNSC 2007b). Detraz and Betsill (2009) argue that such statements were often made in the context of broader concerns of human security (also when the term 'human security' was not explicitly mentioned). States indeed frequently highlighted the vulnerability of developing countries to situations of climate insecurity, and expressed concerns for economic development and human wellbeing in terms of food and water security (Detraz and Betsill 2009: 311). I would argue, however, that the overall tone of the debate remained rather alarmist. Broader concerns about economic development, migration, food, and water security obtain a threatening image when being connected to notions of war and conflict. Moreover, the debate portrays the vulnerable (the developing world) as 'the dangerous enemies' (Methmann and Rothe 2012: 336). The Global South is portrayed as the region where climate-related conflict, climate migration, and related chaos is most likely to occur, which may cause tensions and distress in neighbouring states and in other parts of the world. In line with the Copenhagen School's concept of security, such a presentation of climate security creates a sense of otherness and a confrontational image of a stable Global North versus the fragile Global South. As argued by Methmann and Rothe (2012: 336), the debate produces a discourse in which the vulnerable are presented as 'a threat for national security in the Western world or even for international security'.

Interestingly, this core coalition of securitisers making these alarmist security statements on climate change and climate migration did not seek to propose any more traditional or exceptional security measures to counter the identified threats (Methmann and Rothe 2012). No reference was made to military solutions, border measures to stop climate migrants, nor was it proposed that the UN Security Council should be given a mandate to force countries to reduce their greenhouse gas emissions (GHG) emissions. The latter would represent a rather exceptional measure (Trombetta 2008: 599). It would allow a group of five countries as permanent members of the Council, including the major emitters of China and the US, to decide on the fate and the policy of the rest of the world. Meanwhile, climate policy has thus far been governed by a consensus-based institution: the UNFCCC.

Instead of proposing any extreme security measures along the lines of the Copenhagen School's logic, the core coalition of securitisers largely endorsed what they saw as more soft preventive measures to avoid scenarios of uncontrollable climate migration. A number of proposals focussed on conflict prevention. The securitisers remained somewhat implicit as to what conflict prevention exactly entails (see Figure 4.6: it shows all explicit statements on conflict prevention by the core group of securitisers). By and large, they

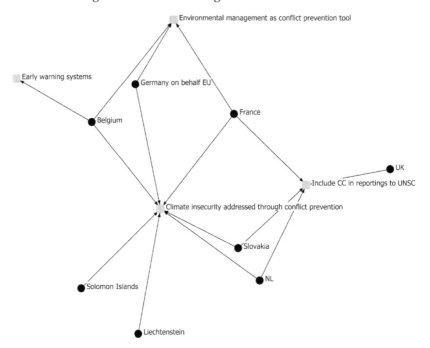

Figure 4.6 All Conflict Prevention Statements in the 2007 UNSC Debate Made by the Core Group of Securitisers

argued that climate change has to be taken into account as one of the underlying causes of conflict in the UN's conflict analysis and reportings. Moreover, as will become clearer in the analysis of the debate of 2011, some states in the core coalition of securitisers proposed to use development tools to address climate-induced societal problems, such as migration, to prevent conflict from emerging (Sindico 2007). As argued by Sindico (2007: 31), the promotion of sustainable development becomes a central part of conflict prevention strategies.

However, most proposals in the 2007 UN Security Council debate focussed on measures in the field of climate policy (see Figure 4.7: it shows the climate actions proposed by at least two states of the core group of securitisers).[8] The core coalition of securitisers argued for more efforts on adaptation and disaster management, and promoted action in the field of mitigation. The respective states pleaded for more use of renewable energy, argued for clean energy technology and a low carbon economy, and highlighted the need to reach a new UNFCCC deal. From that understanding, drawing on the argument by Methmann and Rothe (2012), alarmist Copenhagen style security statements are combined with the endorsement of more mundane and technocratic measures of prevention and risk management in the context of the UNFCCC. As I will explain in more detail in the subsequent section on the

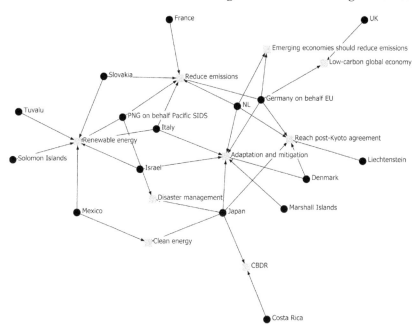

Figure 4.7 Key Climate Actions Proposed in the 2007 UNSC Debate by at Least Two States of the Core Group of Securitisers

FCO's securitising move, such measures can best be described through the logics of security measures as provided by the Paris School and the Risk School. In line with the Risk School's logic, the securitisers seek to promote preventive and cooperative (but top-down) measures (such as a new UNFCCC deal) to address climate change (Trombetta 2008). Moreover, following the Paris School's insights, they endorse a low-carbon economy and technocratic measures in the realm of renewable energy to mitigate the risk of climate change, while seeking to secure the basic structures of the current energy and market-based society (Swyngedouw 2010: 222). It is important to note, however, that even though the securitisers do not perceive and present such measures in exceptional terms, its audience can have a different interpretation. As discussed in chapter 3, security measures can have different meanings for different actors, as informed by their contextual environment. As I will explain in chapter 5, specifically proposals for *binding* mitigation action can by emerging developing countries be understood in more exceptional and drastic terms.

There were also a few states, mainly small island states, who proposed actions in line with Critical Security Studies' logic of human security. The Solomon Islands proposed a people-centred approach, and Papua New Guinea stressed the role of traditional knowledge in climate policy and that local communities should be empowered. But such proposals with a more bottom-up and empowerment focus were not provided by a large number of states, and thus represent the minority in this debate.

The 2011 UN Security Council Debate

The debate of 2011 shows a somewhat similar picture to the debate of 2007 (see Figure 4.8).[9] In this debate, the group of securitisers is even more clearly visible.[10] As a consequence, the group of states positioned more in the middle of the two extreme ends in the debate is more clearly visualised (Cuba, Bolivia Tanzania, Singapore, Colombia, South Korea, Barbados on behalf of CARICOM, and Pakistan).

Again, the core coalition of securitisers (see the states on the left side of the spectrum in Figure 4.9) consists of largely European states and small island states.[11] This time also some African countries are part of this core coalition. The argument has been made that the UN Security Council debate reflect the traditional North–South divide in which the developing countries and Western countries are positioned on opposite ends (see e.g., Worsnip 2011). But this analysis shows that the picture is more complex than that. The securitisers are not just European countries, but find support from the Small Island States

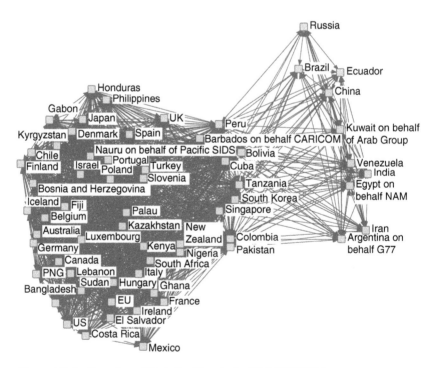

Figure 4.8 An Overview of State Positions in the 2011 UNSC Debate

Note: Any two states are connected when they share at least one of the selected statements.

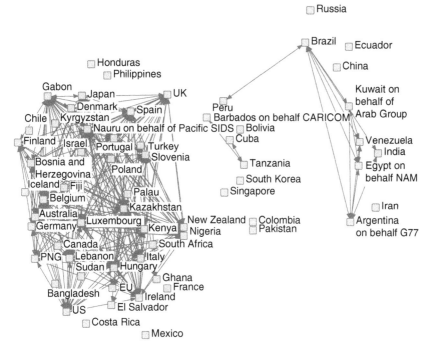

Figure 4.9 The Core Group of Securitisers and the Core Opposing Coalition in the 2011 UNSC Debate

Note: Any two states are connected when they share at least four statements.

and from a number of African countries. In the debate of 2011, also Bangladesh, and some Latin American countries, and are closely associated with the securitiser's coalition, even though they do not belong to the core coalition of securitisers. Even Pakistan, who was amongst the key opponents of the 2007 debate, became the initiator of the informal UN Security Council debate of 2013 (together with the UK; King 2013). It is also interesting to note that while the representative of the Group of G77 plus China (in short, G77) in both debates positioned itself in the opposing coalition, a number of the countries it represents were positioned closer to the side of the securitisers (see e.g., the positions of Ghana, Kenya, Gabon, and in 2011 Bangladesh also positioned itself on the side of the securitisers). As I will discuss in more detail in the forthcoming chapters, this reflects an increasing fraction of the G77 coalition in the climate change negotiations. Many developing countries commenced partnerships with Western countries as a means to pressure emerging economies to do more to limit their GHG emissions.

Another finding is that the US is part of the 2011 core coalition of securitisers. With the Obama administration, the US has tried to take a more collaborative stand in international politics and especially vis-à-vis its Western European allies. US Democrats have since Obama's election actively used alarmist security arguments to promote mitigation action in US Congress (Hayes and Knox-Hayes 2014). In 2009, John Kerry, as the chair of the Senate Foreign Relations Committee, argued: 'Many today do not see global climate change as a national security threat, but it is profoundly so. . . . In Copenhagen this December, we have a chance to forge a treaty that will profoundly affect the conditions of life on our planet itself' (Kerry quoted in Hayes and Knox-Hayes 2014: 88). But climate change mitigation continues to be a sensitive topic in the US congress (McCright et al. 2014), which makes it difficult for the US to actively raise its profile on these matters on an international level. This is well reflected in the 2011 UN Security Council debate where it did not make any statements about climate action in terms of mitigation and adaptation (see Figure 4.11 for details). Instead, as the remaining part of the analysis will show, the US focussed its statements in the UN Security Council debate primarily on questions of conflict prevention. It remained silent on the role for climate policy and politics in lessening the security implications of climate change.

The issue of climate migration is, similar to the situation of 2007, discussed in rather alarmist terms (see Figure 4.10). Following the Copenhagen School's repertoire, climate migration is portrayed as a factor driving conflicts or tensions, and concerns for large-scale population movements have often been expressed. As argued by New Zealand (2011b: 6); 'Put simply, whole populations could be on the move, and by any measure that is a security threat'. The same applies to the overarching issue of climate change. States speak of implications for national security, conflict, and compare it to the threat posed by terrorism. A change is that a larger number of states explicitly use the term *human security* to discuss the implications of climate change (a shift from 4 to 8). But most states do not take that much further, thereby not connecting climate change to a more inclusive notion of security as developed by Critical Security Studies. For instance, Japan and the EU only mention the word *human security* but other than that mainly speak about more exceptional threats and implications for conflict. Kenya is one of the few states that really goes into more depth regarding the basic human needs affected by climate change.

Also in this debate did the securitisers not propose any military, defensive or reactionary measures to address the identified threats. Instead, the focus remained on endorsing preventive action and practices of risk management on climate change. In the 2011 debate, widely shared statements focussed on collaboration, international assistance and building resilience in the realm of climate governance (Figure 4.11 shows those actions proposed by at least four states of the core securitising group). This shows that the Risk School's logic of positive prevention and risk management was particular prominent in statements by the core securitisers in the debate of 2011, with the focus on cooperative action and international support. States highlight the need to salvage a new climate deal in the UNFCCC to tackle the issues at hand, and the need to provide adaptation resources for developing countries. Climate action also continued to be the main focus of the most recent debate of 2013. According to

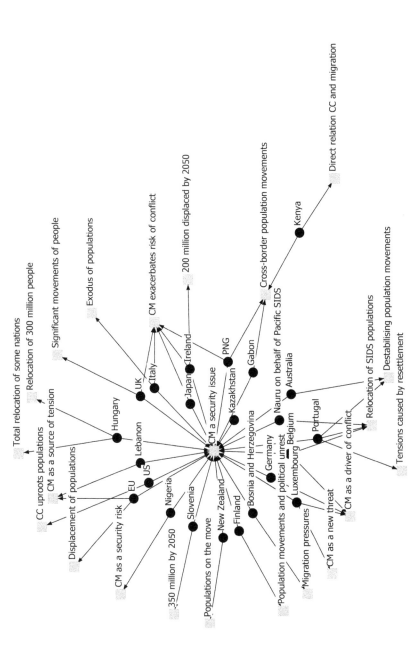

Figure 4.10 Statements on Climate Migration Made by the Core Group of Securitisers in the 2011 UNSC Debate

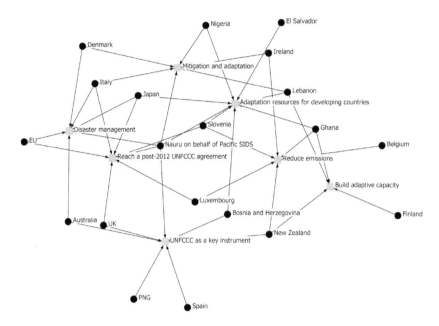

Figure 4.11   Key Climate Actions Proposed in the 2011 UNSC Debate by at Least Four
States of the Core Group of Securitisers

Slovenia's Ministry of Foreign Affairs (2013) 'speakers called for immediate
action by world leaders, based on scientists' recommendations. The economy
has to switch to low-carbon sources, laying particular emphasis on renewables,
while the global community needs to cooperate closely'.

The 2011 debate did become somewhat clearer as to what conflict prevention entails in the field of climate security and migration. As visualised in Figure 4.12, development cooperation is being reframed in such a manner that it
becomes a policy of conflict prevention. Development cooperation is then not
(solely) focussed on achieving sustainable development, but primarily aimed
to prevent escalations, unrest and violent conflict and situations of uncontrollable migration.

In sum, European states together with small island states represent the key
securitisers in both UN Security Council debates on climate change (including
climate migration). They were supported by a number of developing countries,
particularly from Latin America and Africa. This core coalition of securitisers
has used rather alarmist statements on climate migration to make their case.
But they did not propose extreme measures to address the identified security
threats. Instead, alarmist statements by the securitisers are connected with the
endorsement of measures of risk management and prevention.[12] The majority
of the types of measures proposed reside in the field of climate governance,
with a focus on adaptation and mitigation actions.

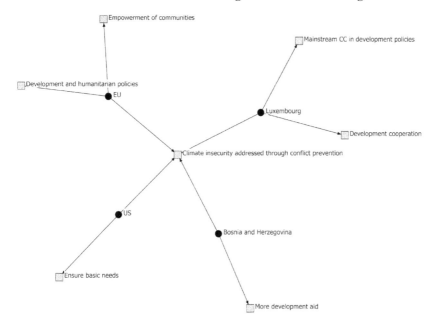

Figure 4.12 States in the Core Group of Securitisers in the 2011 UNSC Debate that Connect Conflict Prevention and Developing Cooperation

A question remains why states used language of fear and threat to endorse risk management and preventive measures in the field of climate change, instead of exceptional action as the Copenhagen School would suggest. As argued by Buzan et al. (1998: 5), in a securitising move, new issues are 'staged as existential threats to a referent object by a securitizing actor who thereby generates endorsement of emergency measures'. Methmann and Rothe (2012) argue that climate change (including of climate migration) is dramatised to such a degree that political actors seem incapable to tackle it. As a consequence, technocratic measures are seen as the only reliable solution. The security discourse 'is so exaggerated that it prompts the opposite: routine and micro-practices of risk management' (Methmann and Rothe 2012: 337).

In this chapter, I provide an alternative (but complementary) explanation. In the micro-level analysis conducted in the next section, I zoom in on the reasons for the UK's FCO to present climate migration in rather alarmist terms to promote climate action. The main argument is that the securitising move on climate migration emerged and developed as a *conscious* and *strategic* attempt. The aim was to convince the international community and particularly the emerging developing countries to take more ambitious and binding action on the mitigation of GHG emissions and to accept a global deal on climate change. The analysis particularly centres on the period of 2000–2010 when the narrative was developed and became institutionalised. Recent changes to this narrative, and related to that its functioning under the Coalition Government that commenced in 2010, will be discussed in chapter 6.

The UK's FCO's Securitising Move: A Strategy in Climate Diplomacy

The FCO has been amongst the leading actors in portraying climate migration as a matter of security, both within the UK and internationally, as part of a wider narrative on climate change and security (Trombetta 2008; Brauch 2009; Harris 2012). The FCO was the UK ministry that thought of the idea to hold a debate on the topic of climate change (including climate migration) in the UN Security Council in 2007 and pushed for it to happen, both domestically and internationally.[13] In the early 2000s, the FCO was tasked to convince the international community that climate change was an important and urgent matter to be addressed in the UNFCCC. As I will demonstrate, it is in that context that innovative strategies, such as the respective securitising move on climate migration, emerged to endorse low-carbon development and a global climate agreement amongst the international community that would succeed the Kyoto Protocol.

This development set in during the early 2000s. It was a time when the topic of climate change was granted a high profile in the Labour Government (Sinha 2010). Prime Minister Tony Blair announced that climate change would become one of the top priorities for the UK's foreign policy agenda. Similar to states such as Germany and also the EU (Hatch 2007; Scheurs and Tiberghien 2007), Blair envisioned for its government a leadership role in stimulating the international community to achieve greater action and agreement on climate change. In 2004, he officially announced that global warming would become a top priority at the UK's presidency of the G8 and the EU in 2005 (Blair 2004, 2005; *The Guardian* 2004; BBC 2005). But according to Margaret Beckett, Secretary for the Department for the Environment, Food and Rural Affairs from 2001 until May 2006 and then Foreign Secretary until June 2007, Blair already expressed his interest to make climate change a key foreign policy issue during the 2002 UN World Summit on Sustainable Development.[14] During the presidency rounds of the G8 and EU, Blair indeed put much emphasis on the issue of climate change. For instance, the chair's summary of the G8 summit, provided by Blair (2005), states:

All of us agreed that climate change is happening now, that human activity is contributing to it, and that it could affect every part of the globe. . . . We will advance the global effort to tackle climate change at the UN Climate Change Conference in Montreal later this year. Those of us who have ratified the Kyoto Protocol remain committed to it, and will continue to work to make it a success.

As a consequence of these developments, the FCO was tasked to integrate climate change in its foreign policy work. The FCO's environmental diplomacy fully transformed into the specific niche of *climate change* diplomacy. The FCO's Environmental Policy Department (established in 2000) changed name twice, first into the Climate Change and Energy Group in 2004, then into the Climate Change and Energy Department in 2010 (FCO 2005: 8).

The FCO's climate change diplomacy aims to mobilise the international community to reduce GHG emissions, with an emphasis on achieving a low carbon global economy (FCO 2004: 84; 2005: 12–13, 129–134; 2007: 69–73; 2008: 70–73; 2009a: 39–44; 2010; 2011: 3, 9, 31; 2012: 9, 10, 39; 2013: 11; 2014: 38; Ashton 2011). The FCO tries to achieve this objective by promoting two policy trajectories. The first is a binding international agreement, including the major emitters, under the UNFCCC, and the second is to stimulate voluntary action towards a low-carbon economy (Ashton 2011: 7). According to John Ashton, Head of the Environmental Policy Department from 2000–2002[15] and the FCO's Special Representative for Climate Change from June 2006 until June 2012,[16] most energy should be spent on achieving the first option: 'It is simply not credible to argue that bottom up alone offers what we need. Only a binding regime can create a force field strong enough to align those countless choices' (Ashton 2011: 7). This corresponds with the line taken by the UK Government arguing for a global binding agreement on climate change (Blair 2004, 2005; Brown 2009; Davey, UK Energy and Climate Change Secretary 2012; Davey in HM Government 2014: ministerial foreword).[17]

It is interesting to note that the promotion of adaptation measures has played a relatively minor role in the FCO's climate change diplomacy. In contrast to mitigation action aiming to prevent dangerous levels of climate change by reducing GHG emissions, adaptation starts from the assumption that some or even extreme climate change may occur. Adaptation is about making societies resilient to climate change impacts (e.g., think of the construction of dikes to protect coastal areas from more extreme storm surges). Few of the FCO's departmental reports produced since the creation of the FCO's Climate Change and Energy Group in 2004 mention adaptation to climate change (in the following reports there is little to no engagement with the issue: FCO 2004, 2005, 2006, 2007, 2008, 2009a, 2011, 2014).

This changed somewhat in the run up to and following the UNFCCC conference in Copenhagen of December 2009, when climate change adaptation obtained a somewhat more important role. The Copenhagen Conference was considered an important political event as it aimed to finalise a new deal on climate change that would also include a comprehensive programme on adaptation (Liverman and Billet 2010). The failure of the Copenhagen Conference and the lack of ambitious mitigation pledges further strengthened the argument that action on adaptation is essential; an argument particularly made by the Least Developed Countries and the Alliance of Small Island States. Thus, for the FCO to remain credible in its efforts to promote mitigation action, it needed to engage with adaptation more seriously to account for the needs of the most vulnerable countries to climate change. The FCO for instance created a UK Climate Security Envoy for Vulnerable Countries in October 2008

(FCO 2009a: 40); a position fulfilled by Robin Gwynne.[18] In a visit to Bangladesh, Gwynne argued that '[the] UK is committed to helping Bangladesh build cyclone shelters, develop early warning systems and carry out more research' (quoted in FCO 2009b).

Despite these efforts to do more with adaptation, by and large, the FCO's adaptation policy remains vaguely defined and is subordinate to the goal of climate change mitigation.[19] Even the departmental reports of 2012 and 2013, which provide a specific heading on climate change adaptation, do not go into detail on adaptation strategies. Instead, the FCO immediately connects the discussion to policies on mitigation: 'Adapting to climate change, and incorporating low carbon, green growth into broader growth policies are central to the FCO prosperity agenda which informs policy-making throughout the organisation' (FCO 2012: 40). And as stated in 2013: 'the FCO is working alongside DECC, and through our Posts, to create political conditions to achieve an ambitious global deal to cut emissions, consistent with limiting global temperature increases to two degrees Celsius and helping countries adapt to inevitable impacts of climate change' (FCO 2013: 40). The latest departmental report of 2014 even no longer mentions climate change adaptation (FCO 2014; it does once refer to loss and damage, p. 18). Meanwhile, it seems regular practice in the FCO to outline strategies on climate change mitigation. Departmental reports provide a whole list of examples, such as emission trading schemes (see e.g., FCO 2007 2009a), 'a near zero emissions coal-power generation project' to be implemented in China (FCO 2007: 72), the creation of 'Low Carbon Development Zones' in countries such as China (FCO 2009a: 41), or a future project on joint UK/India 'collaboration on industrial energy efficiency' (FCO 2011: 9). Thus, mitigation serves as the primary policy objective promoted by the FCO.

In the early 2000s, FCO officials searched for narratives that could help to promote action towards the mitigation of climate change. The securitising move on climate migration came up as part of a narrative on climate change and security that amplified the negative consequences of inaction on climate change. John Ashton had a central role in the development of this narrative.[20] His perspective was that the FCO cannot change governments' priorities and interests at the UNFCCC Conference of the Parties. Instead, the FCO needs to influence the domestic political conditions as these shape governments' political agendas. As argued by Ashton:

> When a negotiator goes off to a UNFCCC negotiation, what really matters is their mandate and their mandate comes from domestic politics. You cannot change those alignments and mandates by the negotiation itself. You have to get into the domestic politics.[21]

Diplomats were asked to highlight that low-carbon development could provide economic gains and business opportunities, and to warn of negative economic implications and of security threats associated with inaction, such as climate migration.[22] Such arguments should lift climate change to a higher position on states' domestic political agendas. As argued by Ashton: 'It seemed to us . . . that if you wanted to push up ambition and urgency in responding to climate change then it would be a good idea to make the climate security discourse more prominent in the broad debate'.[23] This narrative also resonated with wider strategic thinking of the 2000s in the Labour Government (PM Strategy Unit 2005: 135; see also Blair 2004; Cabinet Office 2009). For instance, a 2005 report by the Prime Minister's Strategy Unit stated that:

> The UK government should use its presidency of the G8 to reinvigorate the climate change agenda and emphasise the links to future risks of instability and crisis as an additional justification for immediate action on climate change.
>
> (PM Strategy Unit 2005: 135)

Thus, the securitising move on climate migration formed part of a larger security narrative on climate change. It functions as a strategic diplomatic narrative to mobilise action towards a low carbon global economy.

The idea of this narrative did not emerge out of thin air. The image of climate migration being a major security threat stems from debates on *environmental* degradation, conflict and migration that were particularly prominent in the 1980s and 1990s in academia and in some policy circles (on this discourse, see Trombetta 2008; Vogler 2009; Hartmann 2010). In the 2000s, these debates made a very prominent re-entry, but this time with a focus on *climate* migration and security (see e.g., CNA 2007; DCDC 2007; Schwartz and Randall 2003; Smith and Vivekanada 2007). For instance, in 2007, the UK defence think tank, the Development Concepts and Doctrine Centre (DCDC), warned of large-scale climate migration from Africa to the EU (DCDC 2007: 29). Prominent figures, such as Lord Stern (quoted in McKie 2013), have also warned that unabated climate change may cause great insecurity, including mass climate migration and armed conflict:

> Hundreds of millions of people will be forced to leave their homelands because their crops and animals will have died. The trouble will come when they try to migrate into new lands, however. That will bring them into armed conflict with people already living there. Nor will it be an occasional occurrence. It could become a permanent feature of life on Earth.

Moreover, there are number of UK-based think tanks and NGOs that have raised concerns about insecurity caused by climate change, such as climate migration. For example, in 2007 the London-based NGO International Alert warns that 'large-scale migration carries high risk of conflict because of the fearful reactions it often receives and the inflammatory politics that often greet it' (Smith and Vivekananda 2007: 3). This NGO has been in contact with the FCO and other UK ministries on the theme of climate change and security.[24] E3G is another strategic think tank which has actively promoted ideas on climate change and security within the UK Government and abroad. This think tank was co-established in 2004 by John Ashton, Nick Mabey (a former official in the FCO's Environment Policy Department, the FCOs lead for the Johannesburg Earth Summit in 2002, and advisor to the PM's Strategy Unit) and Tom Burke (former FCO advisor to Ashton in his role as Special Representative on Climate Change) (E3G 2014). Considering their background, this think tank clearly has strong lines with the FCO's strategic thinking on climate change. This discursive and wider strategic environment provided favourable conditions through which the FCO could develop, strengthen and employ its securitising move based on notions of conflict and images of mass migration.

The FCO's securitising move on climate migration became particularly visible in 2006 when Margaret Beckett became Foreign Secretary. Prime Minister Tony Blair had asked her to make climate change a top priority in the UK's foreign policy.[25] It was a time that the Copenhagen UNFCCC Conference was approaching; a vital moment to achieve a new global deal on emission reduction. Climate change became an official strategic priority for the FCO under the banner of 'delivering climate security' (FCO 2007: 70) and Beckett actively made a case to prevent a situation of climate insecurity on an international level. The aim was to change the political conditions necessary for a new deal. Beckett raised the issue of climate security in Berlin, India, Mexico, the US, and in the UN Security Council (see FCO 2007: 71; see for instance Beckett 2006a, 2006b, 2007; UNSC 2007a). The debate at the UN Security Council was particularly considered a high-profile move, as demonstrated by the high amount of attention by the press (see e.g., Clark 2007; Leopold 2007; Pilkington 2007; The New York Times 2007), and by follow-up debates in the UN General Assembly in 2009 and in the UN Security Council in 2011 (UNGA 2009; UNSC 2011b, 2011c). The debate was aimed to grasp the attention of heads of states and to create additional momentum to make action on climate change a key priority.[26] It functioned as part of a wider diplomatic strategy by the FCO towards the Conference of the Parties in Copenhagen.[27] The rationale was to reframe climate change in terms of security in order to convince states to accept a binding deal on climate change in the UNFCCC, in the name of national and international security.[28] As commented by an FCO official:

It is like the old water wars debate. Arguing that climate change is going to cause security problems helps you gain more international attention. This in turn can generate pressure on States to make the difficult compromises needed to agree on a successful post-Kyoto framework.[29]

In the words of Margaret Beckett:

[W]hen people talk about security problems they do so in terms qualitatively different from any other type of problem. Security is seen as an imperative not an option. . . . So understanding and flagging up the security aspects of climate change has a role in galvanising those governments who have yet to act.

(Beckett 2007; see also Brauch 2009: 90)

In her speeches, Beckett frequently referred to the issue of climate migration to depict a scenario of dangerous climate change in the hope to convince states that urgent mitigation action is necessary (Beckett 2006b, 2007; UNSC 2007a). She argued that the consequences of climate change, such as migration, 'reach to the very heart of the security agenda. Consequences of flooding, disease and famine—and, from that, migration on an unprecedented scale' (Beckett, UNSC 2007a: 18). David Miliband, Beckett's successor as Foreign Secretary from June 2007 until May 2010, continued to perform public speeches on security, climate change and migration (Miliband and Steinmeier 2008; Miliband 2009; see Ministerial Foreword to FCO 2010). Along these lines, Miliband, as Foreign Secretary, stated: '. . . if we do not act to cut emissions responsible for climate change, we do know what the result could be: rising sea levels that threaten millions, causing mass migration . . .' (FCO 2010; Ministerial foreword; see also Miliband 2009). In similar vein, Beckett has warned:

By tackling climate change we can lessen the push factors driving immigration. If we don't tackle it, we have to brace ourselves for population shifts on a scale we have never seen before.

(Beckett 2006a)

The Foreign Secretaries actively used these warning messages following a Copenhagen School repertoire in the hope to mobilise greater action on climate change. In an alarmist manner, practices of risk management and prevention have thus been promoted.

In 2009, the FCO even created a Climate Security Team. Its primary task was to use a security narrative on climate change in its diplomatic relations to change the political conditions necessary for a global deal on climate change. As argued by the Head of the FCO's Climate Security Team:

In my team, we look at a strategy to raise awareness of the security risks of climate change to other countries, with the hope that we can influence political conditions around negotiations on a UNFCCC deal on reducing global emissions.[30]

Speech acts on climate migration were perceived as an effective vehicle to achieve the key objectives of climate change diplomacy:

I think the migration strand is quite useful, because when you are trying to persuade other governments that this [climate change] is an important issue, migration is a very visible thing, it is a political thing, a thing that the electorate cares about. So, depending on the country, it can be a good avenue to engage politicians.[31]

The FCO's Climate Security Team, for example, discussed the implications of climate migration in diplomatic encounters in countries for which general cross-border migration already presents a concern, such as the US, Spain, and India.[32] Just recently, in September 2012, the name of this team changed into the Global Strategic Impacts Team to engage with a wider range of narratives than just those on security, such as economic arguments (see chapter 6 for more details).[33]

As part of its task, the Global Strategic Impacts Team, including the previously named Climate Security Team, aims to raise the interest of security establishments in climate change. Part of the aim is to show that the military has a societal responsibility to become more energy efficient and therefore required to contribute to the mitigation of climate change. In this manner, a security narrative on climate change (including its arguments on climate migration) is meant to 'green' the military.[34]

But this is not all the FCO has tried to achieve through its communication with security establishments. It is primarily meant to support the FCO's objective to promote greater action and agreement on climate change. The rationale is that when climate change is considered part of national security and defence planning, it may help to persuade politicians and the wider policy community on climate change to agree to binding mitigation targets under the UNFCCC.[35] As argued by Ashton: 'The security constituency is always a powerful one and if the security constituency becomes agitated about something then by and large it increases the chances that something is being done about it'.[36] In that context, the FCO, in collaboration with the UK Department of Energy and Climate Change and the Ministry of Defence (MOD), created a UK Climate and Energy Security Envoy. The position was held by Rear Admiral Neil Morisetti, and ran from 2009 until the end of 2012 (in January 2013, he became the successor of John Ashton, as the FCO's Special Representative for Climate Change). The primary assignment of the UK's Climate Change and Energy Security Envoy was to engage 'the defence and security community [within the UK and those of other states] on climate security to help create the political conditions necessary for a global deal on climate change' (FCO 2010: 21; see also FCO 2011). Thus, his duty was to add to the FCO's securitising move on climate migration aiming to promote climate action. The fact that Rear Admiral Neil Morisetti, a recently retired Royal Navy officer, succeeded Ashton as the FCO's Interim Special Representative for Climate Change further exemplifies the FCO's strategy to involve security communities as a way to promote climate action.

It is important to note that the FCO's call for climate change mitigation did not emerge from a fear that climate migrants will migrate en masse to the UK and to other Northern regions or that climate change would cause great conflict. The objective to promote climate change mitigation is not a product of such security arguments, but exists independently, and is promoted by a range of policy strategies; the security narrative being only one. The securitising move on climate migration emerged from a strategic interest on climate change, and not from any substantial fear of climate migrants. It emerged from the FCO's diplomatic work on climate change, and developed as a rhetorical political strategy, to see climate change as a security issue in order to achieve greater political action on climate change and low carbon development.[37] Some interviewees in the FCO also openly said that they were not convinced by arguments on climate or environmental conflicts provided by academics such as Homer-Dixon, but that they used them to make a clear narrative and a strong case to address climate change in the UN Security Council. This does not preclude, however, that some of the officials using this narrative have come to support and believe in the argument that climate change causes migration which poses a security risk.

This strategic character driving the FCO's securitising move is not necessarily unique and radical. Other actors have also drawn on security narratives to promote climate action; sometimes in interaction with the FCO. The FCO's securitising move on climate migration has, to some degree, been supported by the Department of Energy and Climate Change (DECC), the UK's lead department on UNFCCC negotiations (Davey in HM Government 2014: ministerial foreword).[38] While DECC considers the FCO to be the lead actor on climate change and security,[39] DECC has occasionally drawn on the climate change, migration, and security argument as one of its communicating strategies in climate change negotiations.[40] Furthermore, as mentioned, the UK's MOD and DECC supported the FCO's securitising move by co-financing the UK's Climate and Energy Security Envoy. In addition, as shown in the previous section, Germany, the EU, but also small island states have used speech acts on climate change, migration, and security to promote climate action (see e.g., Stripple 2002; German Advisory Council on Global Change 2007; Miliband and Steinmeier 2008; European Commission 2011). Germany is one of the FCO's key partners. The FCO and the German Environment Ministry have already been discussing the topic since 2001 (Brauch 2009: 88). And in the footsteps of the UK, Germany initiated the second UN Security Council debate on the security implications of climate change, held in 2011.

The FCO sees such states as 'message multipliers' of its security narrative on climate change and climate migration.[41] By strengthening this coalition, the FCO tries to put more pressure on those states that it wants to convince to sign up to binding mitigation targets under the UNFCCC, such as the US and the emerging developing countries. As discussed in the previous section, the US does perform securitising moves itself, but it is to a lesser degree connected to the promotion of climate action. The US establishment is divided when it comes to ideas about climate security. Security establishments in the US, such as the Pentagon, have addressed the topic of climate change and national security (including the topic of climate migration) (see Townsend and Harris 2004; see also the US-based report by CNA 2007). But according to the FCO, the term climate security does not resonate in the US congress. It is better to talk about the need to secure the US energy efficiency, or even energy security, if aiming to promote climate action in US congress.[42]

Emerging Developing Countries as a Core Audience

The FCO regards emerging developing countries, such as India, Brazil, and China, as part of its core target group of 'major energy users' (FCO 2007: 71), even though these countries are not historically responsible for climate change. As argued by an Official with the FCO's Climate Change and Energy Department:

> We are not going to achieve the two degree target unless we include some of the major emitters in the developing world, primarily China, but countries such as India and Indonesia also belong to that group. We think it is unsustainable if they have the same emission targets as the poorest in the world. Therefore, there should be a binding framework, with binding targets, which includes these countries. But such targets will of course still be differentiated depending on the economic state of a country.[43]

These countries therefore belong to the core audience of the FCO's securitising move.

It was particularly since the mid-2000s that the FCO, and the UK at large, started to centre on this group of countries in climate change diplomacy. The emission shares of China and India tripled (for India, it almost tripled) between the 1990s and 2009 (IEA 2011: 23, 24). For the first time since 2008, the total share of emissions from Non-Annex I countries (developing countries) exceeded those of Annex I countries (industrialised countries) (IEA 2011: 7; see also Oels 2013: 6). Emissions by China, followed by India, account for most of this increase. In terms of total emission shares per country, China even became the world's top emitter of carbon dioxide. The UK Government thus argues that industrialised countries are no longer singularly responsible for the mitigation of climate change. The group of emerging developing countries should also contribute. For instance, according to *The Guardian*, Prime Minister Blair stated in 2006 that 'if all Britain's carbon emissions were stopped in one fell swoop, they would be replaced within two years by the increase in Chinese emissions' (Sturcke 2006 in *The Guardian*, paraphrasing Blair).

The UK is not alone in efforts to push emerging developing countries to commit themselves to binding and more ambitious mitigation efforts. In UNFCCC debates, the EU has put in much effort to convince the key emerging developing countries, such as China and India, to sign up to binding mitigation targets (Bäckstrand and Elgström 2013). This is essential to get the US to support a new UNFCCC deal. The US has always argued that it will not participate in any climate change agreement that lacks mitigation commitments for the emerging developing countries (Bäckstrand and Elgström 2013). Moreover, even the Least Developed Countries (LDC) and the Alliance of Small Island States (AOSIS) have argued that these emerging developing states need to start mitigating under a binding international agreement.[44] During the 2011 UNFCCC conference in Durban, the LDCs and AOSIS maintained that while

the rich industrialised countries are required to do more due to their historical responsibility, the emerging developing countries need to accept binding
mitigation targets in future years to maintain temperature rise below two
degrees (Black 2011). For that very reason, the current climate negotiations
are focussed on achieving one global deal in which all state parties contribute
to the mitigation of climate change (for more details, see chapters 5 and 6). It is
in this wider political context, that the FCO's position regarding fast-growing
emitting developing countries was able to develop.

It is important to note that the FCO's securitising move has a particular
emphasis on promoting *binding* mitigation targets by emerging developing
countries. As I will discuss in more detail in forthcoming chapters, it is this
aspect that has made the securitising moves particularly sensitive amongst its
audience (the emerging developing countries). As will be exemplified in chapter 5, leading developing countries have perceived it, or at least portrayed it,
as unjust when being pushed to commit to *binding* mitigation targets under the
UNFCCC (Dubash 2012). That does not mean, however, that emerging developing countries have taken no voluntary (non-binding) action to mitigate climate change. China has taken action to become more energy efficient and to
sustain economic growth through renewable energy technologies on a voluntary
(non-binding) level. China has worked with low-carbon technology while not
being committed to international binding mitigation targets. For instance, in
2011, China's investments in wind power installations account for 43 percent
of the global market (Harvey 2012). It is also investing in renewable energy to
reduce air pollution levels. Not always is such action driven by the interest to
save climate change, however. As argued by Figueres, the UNFCCC Executive Secretary: 'They actually want to breathe air that they don't have to look
at. . . . They're not doing this because they want to save the planet. They're
doing it because it's in their national interest' (Figueres quoted in Yoon 2014).

The Paris School and the Risk School's Logics of Security Measures

What logic of security measures best describes the action on climate change
mitigation promoted by the FCO? What mitigation measures does the FCO
hope, and assume, that other states will take, when accepting binding targets
under the UNFCCC? The closest fit is the logic of technocratic management,
proactivity and control described by the Paris School, combined with the logic
of positive prevention and risk management, as outlined by the Risk School.
It is important to note that this analysis is based on the manner in which the
FCO itself presents mitigation policy; even though some critical reflections
are also included. As argued in chapter 3, security measures, including climate
change mitigation, may have different meanings to different groups, and for
that reason can be described through different logics. It is relevant to understand what logic(s) fits the FCO's own representation and understanding of climate change mitigation as provided in its departmental reports and speech acts.
This can, as a next step, then be contrasted to alternative views on mitigation;

as will be done in chapter 5 when examining India's reaction to the FCO's securitising move.

First of all, in line with the Paris School's logic, technocratic measures play an important role in the FCO's approach to, and understanding of, mitigation. It builds on the assumption that the usage and adoption of energy efficient technology simultaneously helps governments to tackle climate change (FCO 2004, 2005, 2006, 2007, 2008, 2009a, 2011, 2012; see also Beckett 2006a, 2007; Hague 2010; Ashton 2011). The FCO equates climate change mitigation with the creation of a 'low-carbon, high growth, global economy' (FCO 2008, 2009a), based on notions of carbon markets, emission trading, and technologies of clean energy and energy efficiency (FCO 2004, 2005, 2006, 2007, 2008, 2009a, 2011, 2012; see also Beckett 2006a, 2007; Hague 2010; Ashton 2011). In the words of Methmann and Rothe (2012: 331–332), 'the whole problem of climate is boiled down to a question of the right "low carbon technology"'. By means of low carbon technological development, states should prevent dangerous level of climate change, while being able to secure energy supplies and current levels of energy demand. For example, the 2006–2007 FCO departmental report argues in favour of:

> developing technologies and innovation and strengthening the commitment of other governments to increase the development and demonstration of technologies that will accelerate the shift to a global low-carbon economy. Carbon capture and storage is a key technology as it is the only way to take carbon emissions out of power generated by fossil fuel.
>
> (FCO 2007: 71)

Second, in line with the Paris School's logic of security measures, technocratic measures function to regulate, manage, and control deviating factors (in this case, the surplus of GHG emissions) as a means to preserve the normal societal order; one that is based on current patterns of consumption. The FCO stresses the need for green technology to secure *affordable* energy for UK citizens (see in particular FCO 2004; 2007). As argued in the FCO's departmental report for 2006–2007:

> During 2006, the FCO integrated its energy and climate security work more fully, recognising that the UK's national security and economic prosperity depend on reliable, affordable supplies of energy and a stable climate. Our overall energy goal is to deliver reliable supplies of energy to UK consumers at affordable cost, while reducing carbon emissions. We can meet these combined challenges only if the UK is an active and influential member of the international community. And we will only be able to persuade others of the merits of working together to tackle climate change if we can demonstrate and persuade our international partners that climate policies and energy security can exist together.
>
> (FCO 2007: 64)

Therefore, the interest is not to structurally change the energy demand of consumers; instead, the existing consumption patterns can be preserved through the management of climate change by means of technological innovation. This policy discourse on low carbon technology and energy is deeply embedded within the UK Government at large. An analysis by Lovell, Bulkeley, and Owens (2009) shows that the areas of climate change and energy have increasingly converged in UK policy development since the early 2000s through a focus on energy efficiency. Climate change was no longer presented as a matter of environmental politics, but of energy security and energy technology. The discourse is also active in other regions, such as in the EU (Trombetta 2008: 598). In 2007, the EU produced an 'Energy and Climate Package' (Trombetta 2008: 598), thereby integrating climate and energy policy. Over the years, the FCO has aimed to influence the EU's position on climate change. As stated in the 2006–2007 departmental report: 'The FCO's network of overseas Posts lobbied EU governments in the run up to Lahti, underlining the important opportunity the summit offered for the EU to tackle climate and energy security together for the first time' (FCO 2007: 50). The aim was to 'fast track delivering a stable climate and secure affordable low-carbon energy for EU citizens' (FCO 2007: 19).

Related to that, in the FCO's understanding of mitigation, low carbon development works as a vehicle to maintain a world order based on the notion of economic growth. Beckett (2006a) stressed that 'the choice between economic growth and a stable climate is a false one. We have to have both. And we can have both'. Along these lines, the FCO created a Prosperity Fund 'which promotes sustainable, global economic growth through support for an open global economy, avoiding dangerous climate change and enhancing energy security' (FCO 2012: 10). This can be described as a neoliberal mitigation policy: to keep the basic structures of the market-based society intact through technological innovation (see also Swyngedouw 2010: 222). The FCO's perspective of mitigation takes on the form of what Biermann (2012: 6) refers to as a 'risk-averse approach, conserving the world as it is . . .'

This policy can from a Paris School perspective be criticised for having exclusionary and thus negative effects; since a market-based world society historically benefited the Global North over the Global South. From this perspective, climate change mitigation works through technocratic, economic, regular, and managerial practices as a result of which 'we have to change radically, but within the contours of the existing state of the situation . . ., so that nothing really has to change' (Swyngedouw 2010: 219). Consequently, the neo-liberal economic system is secured and the divisions between its losers and winners are maintained. In more radical terms, the FCO's policy objective to convince leading developing states to commit to binding mitigation targets, can even be seen as serving the interests of the Global North who already established a good standard of living and level of economic growth (see chapter 5 for such an understanding).

While acknowledging that such a mitigation policy may have exclusionary effects, it is debatable whether it is fair to provide it with such a critical assessment. In many ways, the FCO's take on mitigation can be described by means of the more positive logic of positive prevention and risk management. First of all, the FCO is occupied with securing the economic security for UK citizens (see e.g., FCO 2007: 64), and not with consciously excluding others from economic gain. From many understandings of justice, there is no harm in ensuring the wellbeing of your own society (see e.g., Kymlicka 1995). Second, the FCO perceives, or at least portrays, low carbon development as a policy that could benefit citizens from poorer countries as well. In that manner, it values a collaborative approach. As argued in its 2003–2004 departmental report, adopting technologies of low carbon development 'will help to tackle climate change, to improve the **security of energy supplies** and bring **clean, affordable energy** to remote communities in developing countries'. (FCO 2004: 85, emphasis in the original). In the words of Beckett (2006a):

> We all have an interest in continuing economic growth. We all want to see the developing world lift itself out of poverty. But at the moment that growth and development is being driven by the burning of the fossil fuels which cause climate change. In other words, the very process which is making people's lives better across the world today is destroying their future.

The FCO also collaborates with emerging developing countries on climate change mitigation. The FCO for instance helped finance a collaborative project between the EU and China that generates low-carbon development in China (see e.g., FCO 2007: 72); a project based on knowledge sharing to the benefit of both parties (European Commission 2010). Therefore, the approach to mitigation as presented by the FCO is instead characterised by the logic of positive prevention and positive risk management. Its efforts are focussed on collaborative (yet top-down) efforts aiming to prevent future harm.

Of course, this can be interpreted as a sign that the FCO seeks to get other states to 'buy in' to its arguments about collaboration in order to maintain the UK's economic growth. Even though the FCO is clearly driven by economic interests, it seems a bit radical to condemn any effort of the FCO to promote a low-carbon economy. Low-carbon technologies do help to mitigate climate change, and in the current market-based world order it seems among the most effective strategies to move forward; not just from the perspective of industrialised countries, but also of major developing states that aim to maintain energy security and economic growth.

Thus, the FCO's understanding of climate change mitigation reflects elements of the Paris School's and the Risk School's logics of security measures. It corresponds with the Paris School's logic because of the technocratic character of the endorsed policy measures that maintain characteristics of the present market and consumer-based society. From a Paris School's perspective, it can be argued that the FCO's approach to mitigation is focussed on controlling the market-based order through technocratic and economic adjustments that may benefit particular groups over others. However, the manner in which the FCO itself presents mitigation action is rather focussed on collaboration and positive prevention of future harm, in line with the Risk School's positively oriented, yet problem-solving logic. It is fair to say the FCO does not consciously intend to maintain world inequality through the mitigation of climate change, even though this may very well be an (unintended) consequence.

In sum, the analysis has demonstrated that the FCO's securitising move emerged as a strategy developed in its climate change diplomacy. The aim has been to promote greater action towards the mitigation of GHG emissions, particularly by endorsing a new deal under the UNFCCC. The emerging developing countries form its core audience. Due to their increasing emission shares, the FCO has been trying to persuade them to sign up to strict and binding commitments under the UNFCCC.

Concluding Discussion

This chapter examined securitising moves on climate migration, with a particular focus on the actions by the UK's FCO. A large number of states have performed securitising moves on climate migration, from both the Global North and the Global South. But the European countries and the small island states have been the leading securitisers. Interestingly, their securitising moves were not based on a concept of security and logic of security measures as provided by one school on securitisation. The securitising moves draw on negative images of climate migration, while promoting more technocratic, but positively orientated, measures in terms of prevention, risk management and international collaboration. This representation of climate migration particularly resembles the Copenhagen School's concept of security. Meanwhile, the mitigation practices promoted reflect the logics of security measures as outlined by the Paris School and the Risk School. This shows how insights from different schools on securitisation are needed to understand the meaning and focus of a securitising move; in this case the Copenhagen, Paris, and the Risk School.

This discrepancy between the concept of security used and the logic of security measures promoted, raises the question why such alarmist language has been used to promote the risk management of climate change, instead of promoting exceptional action as would be assumed by the Copenhagen School. The micro-analysis of the FCO exemplifies how a securitising move can be strategically constructed or played on by political actors to 'sell' particular policy action, such as a global deal under the UNFCCC. The analysis showed how the alarmist narrative emerged and developed as one of the diplomatic strategies that FCO officials consciously and deliberately used to promote mitigation action. This insight on the role of strategy helps to explain why alarmist security language and policies of risk management can go together.

Another interesting finding is that speech acts were key to understand the emergence and promotion of securitising moves on climate migration (referred to as the speech act perspective, in chapter 3). The UN Security Council debates were full of high-profile securitising statements expressed by prominent state actors. Speech acts were also a central feature of the FCO's diplomatic strategy. This strategy revolves around communication, lobbying, and is based on a very specific security narrative developed to promote climate action. It is through language that the FCO hopes to promote binding mitigation action, and it is also the language used by the FCO to which its audience primarily reacts (see chapter 5).

In addition to that, the analysis gave insight into the role of routine and technocratic processes to understand the emergence of the FCO's securitising move, along the lines of the Paris School (the routine-technocratic perspective, as defined in chapter 3). Day-to-day diplomats in the FCO's Climate Change and Energy Department were vital actors in developing, crafting, and performing this speech act strategy on climate change, migration, and security. As discussed, it was already in the early 2000s that these ideas emerged in the FCO; long before the high-profile UN Security Council debate of 2007. Moreover, according to Margaret Beckett, it was John Ashton's good reputation within the FCO that convinced the FCO diplomats to use the narrative on climate security in their diplomatic work.[45] This shows how less visible internal dynamics within an organisation are important to get a securitising move off the ground in the first place.

A key question remains how an audience will respond to these securitising moves on climate migration. Will it be successful? As I will demonstrate in the next chapter, the Government of India easily interprets the FCO's securitising move on climate migration as pure rhetoric. The securitising move provides an image of the UK (and other states using similar arguments) as if attempting to deflect attention away from its own responsibilities on climate change and to put the blame on India by creating scare stories on climate migration.

To further delve into this, the next chapter will analyse how the emerging developing countries, as the core audience, have reacted to securitising moves on climate migration. The micro-analysis of the audience perspective will trace how the Government of India responds to the FCO's securitising move.

Notes

1. As discussed in the introduction chapter, in 1992 the UN Security Council also made a brief statement referring to ecological threats to peace and security. But the 2007 debate is the first that specifically focussed on the issue of climate change.
2. Interview, UK Government Official, 6 October 2011, London.
3. These figures are developed through the software of NetDraw (Borgatti 2002).
4. I used some abbreviations to make the figures more readable. CC stands for climate change. CM stands for climate migration. PNG stands for Papua New Guinea, NL for the Netherlands. US for the United States. UK for the United Kingdom. SIDS for Small Island Developing States. NAM for Non-Aligned Movement. G77 for the Group of 77 plus China. UNSC for the UN Security Council. UNFCCC for the United Nations Framework Convention on Climate Change. CBDR for common but differentiated responsibilities.
5. Interview, UK Government Official, 6 October 2011, London.
6. A cohesive network among the parties of the opposing group shows when selecting all states sharing at least three statements.

7. Specifically, the core group of securitisers in 2007 consists of: Belgium, Costa Rica, Denmark, France, Germany on behalf of the EU, Israel, Italy, Japan, Liechtenstein, Marshall Islands, Mexico, Micronesia, The Netherlands (NL), Papua New Guinea (PNG) on behalf of the Pacific SIDS, Slovakia, Solomon Islands, Tuvalu, and the UK. Those states not connected by an arrow (such as Canada or the Maldives) do not belong to this selected core group of securitisers.

8. CBDR in Figure 4.7 stands for common but differentiated responsibilities.

9. To obtain an overview of state relations, the debate was analysed through the set of preselected statements for the general analysis of state positions, as outlined in the beginning of this section.

10. I used some abbreviations to make the figures more readable. CC stands for climate change. CM stands for climate migration. PNG stands for Papua New Guinea, NL for the Netherlands. US for the United States. UK for the United Kingdom. SIDS for Small Island Developing States. NAM for Non-Aligned Movement. CARICOM for the Caribbean Community including the Caribbean Common Market. G77 for the Group of 77 plus China. UNSC for the UN Security Council. UNFCCC for the United Nations Framework Convention on Climate Change.

11. Specifically, the core group of securitisers in 2011 consists of: Australia, Belgium, Bosnia and Herzegovina, Denmark, EU, El Salvador, Finland, Gabon, Germany, Ghana, Hungary, Ireland, Italy, Japan, Kazakhstan, Kenya, Luxembourg, Nauru on behalf of the Pacific SIDS, New Zealand, Nigeria, Papua New Guinea, Portugal, Slovenia, Spain, the UK, and the US.

12. As mentioned, the proposed measures were at least not intended to be exceptional, from the perspective of the securitisers. Some of its audiences, however, can interpret certain measures as being exceptional (see chapter 5).

13. Interview, UK Government Official, 6 October 2011, London. Interview, Margaret Beckett, 23 November 2011, London.

14. Interview, Margaret Beckett, 23 November 2011, London.

15. From 2002–2006, Ashton was seconded to a think tank, E3G. This think tank has also actively promoted ideas on climate change and security. During this time, he continued to be influential in forming the FCO's position on climate security. This is exemplified by his return in the FCO in 2006 when he was granted the prestigious position of Special Representative for Climate Change, having ambassadorial status.

16. In January 2013 this position was temporarily fulfilled by Rear Admiral Neil Morisetti, who first served as the UK's Climate and Energy Security Envoy from 2009 until the end of 2012 (GOV.UK 2013b). In September 2013, Sir David King, a former Government's Chief Scientific Advisor, became the new FCO's Special Representative on Climate Change (GOV.UK 2013a).

17. It should be noted, however, that the Coalition Government (which commenced in 2010) puts somewhat less priority on the goal to achieve a global deal on climate change compared to the Labour Government. See chapter 6 for more details.

18. The position is no longer in place.

19. The FCO did produce 'An adaptation plan for the FCO' (FCO 2010); a departmental plan each governmental department was required to make (Defra 2010). This plan particularly discusses measures to assess the types of risks climate change may produce, in terms of extreme weather events, water stress, migration, and violent conflict. It to a lesser degree outlines actual adaptation policies or funds that can be implemented or promoted by means of diplomatic endeavors. It furthermore describes the task to promote the shift towards a low carbon political economy as its core work (FCO 2010: 2, 14).

20. Interview, Official of the British High Commission in Delhi, 19 August 2011, Delhi, India; Interview, UK Government Official, 6 October 2011, London; Telephone interview, FCO Official, 17 November 2011; Telephone interview, John Ashton, the FCO's Special Representative for Climate Change (from June 2006–June 2012)

and head of the former Environmental Policy Department, 31 January 2012 and 24 May 2012. Nick Mabey is another official who has been identified by interviewees as an important player in the creation of these narratives. Mabey was employed in FCO's Environment Policy Department in the early 2000s and was the FCOs lead for the Johannesburg Earth Summit in 2002. He currently runs E3G, a think tank which he set up together with Ashton, and continues to work on topics of climate security.

21. Telephone interview, John Ashton, Special Representative for Climate Change (from June 2006–June 2012), 31 January 2012.
22. Interview, Official of the British High Commission in Delhi, 19 August 2011, Delhi, India.
23. Telephone interview, John Ashton, Special Representative for Climate Change (from June 2006–June 2012), 31 January 2012.
24. Based on interviews held in 2011, with the FCO, International Alert, and involved researchers.
25. Interview, Margaret Beckett, 23 November 2011, London. See also FCO 2007: 19, 7.
26. Interview, Margaret Beckett, 23 November 2011, London.
27. Interview, UK Government Official, 6 October 2011, London.
28. Interview, UK Government Official, 6 October 2011, London.
29. Telephone interview, FCO Official, 24 March 2011.
30. Interview, Head of the FCO's Climate Security Team, Climate Change and Energy Department, 8 March 2011, London.
31. Interview, Head of the FCO's Climate Security Team, Climate Change and Energy Department, 8 March 2011, London.
32. Interview, Deputy Head of the FCO's Climate Security Team, Climate Change and Energy Department, 31 October 2011 and a telephone interview on 24 May 2012 and 1 June 2012.
33. This is based on email communication in February 2013 with the Climate Security Team (at that time, called: Global Strategic Impacts Team).
34. Interview, Head of the FCO's Global Strategic Impacts Team (formerly called: Climate Security Team), Climate Change and Energy Department, 8 March 2011, London. Final email communication was in February 2013.
35. Interview, Official of the British High Commission in Delhi, 19 August 2011, Delhi, India.
36. Telephone interview, John Ashton, Special Representative for Climate Change (from June 2006–June 2012), 31 January 2012.
37. Interview, UK Government Official, 6 October 2011, London.
38. While DECC is the lead department in the UNFCCC negotiations, the FCO adds to such negotiations by aiming to create the political conditions necessary for a global deal on climate change by means of other avenues, for instance by means of diplomatic bilateral discussions.
39. Telephone interview, DECC official, 31 January 2012.
40. Telephone interview, DECC official, 31 January 2012.
41. Based on interviews held in the FCO conducted in 2011 and 2012. See also Ashton 2011, on the need to use narratives to strengthen coalitions in the UNFCCC (see p. 10, 12).
42. Speech and question round, Deputy Head of the FCO's Global Strategic Impacts Team, Climate Change and Energy Department, 19 October 2012, University of Sussex.
43. Interview, FCO Official, the FCO's Climate Change and Energy Department, 23 January 2012. See also an interview statement by the UK's Minister of State on Energy and Climate change in King 2012.
44. This contrasts to periods in the 1990s and early 2000s in which developing countries acted as a negotiating block in UNFCCC negotiations 'aiming to resist pressure from the developed countries' (Gupta 1999: 200), including from the UK.
45. Interview, Margaret Beckett, 23 November 2011, London.

References

Ashton, J. (2011) *Only diplomacy: hard-headed soft power for a time of risk, scarcity and insecurity*. Speech at Chatham House, London, 21 February. Available at: www.chathamhouse.org/publications/papers/view/109591 (last visit 19 September 2014).

Bäckstrand, K. and O. Elgström (2013) 'The EU's role in climate change negotiations: from leader to "leadiator"', *Journal of European Public Policy*, 20(10): 1369–1386.

BBC (2005) 'Q&A: UK presidency of the EU', *BBC*, 22 September. Available at: http://news.bbc.co.uk/1/hi/world/europe/4124350.stm (last visit 19 September 2014).

Beckett, M. (2006a) *Beckett: Berlin speech on climate change and security*. Speech at British Embassy, Berlin, 24 October. Available at: http://ukingermany.fco.gov.uk/en/newsroom/?view=Speech&id=4616005 (last visit 22 March 2013). This speech is no longer available online.

Beckett, M. (2006b) Speech on climate security at the event 'Climate security: risks and opportunities for the global economy'. Council on Foreign Relations, New York, 21 September. Available at: www.cfr.org/energy-security/climate-security-risks-opportunities-global-economy-video/p11539 (last visit 19 September 2014).

Beckett, M. (2007) *Margaret Beckett on climate change. The case for climate security*. Speech at Royal United Services Institute, London, 10 May. Available at: www.rusi.org/events/past/ref:E464343E93D15A/info:public/infoID:E4643430E3E85A/ (last visit 19 September 2014).

Biermann, F. (2012) 'Planetary boundaries and earth system governance: exploring the links', *Ecological Economics*, 81(September): 4–9.

Biermann, F. and I. Boas (2008) 'Protecting climate refugees: the case for a global protocol', *Environment*, 50(6): 8–16.

Black, R. (2011) 'Climate talks end with late deal', *BBC*, 11 December. Available at: www.bbc.co.uk/news/science-environment-16124670 (last visit 15 October 2014).

Blair, T. (2004) 'Full text: Blair's climate change speech', *The Guardian*, 15 September. Available at: www.guardian.co.uk/politics/2004/sep/15/greenpolitics.uk (last visit 19 September 2014).

Blair, T. (2005) *Chair's summary*. G7/G8 summit meetings, Gleneagles, 8 July. Available at: www.g8.utoronto.ca/summit/2005gleneagles/summary.html (last visit 19 September 2014).

Borgatti, S. P. (2002) *NetDraw software for network visualization*. Lexington, KY: Analytic Technologies.

Brauch, H.-G. (2009) 'Securitizing global environmental change'. In: H.-G. Brauch, U. Oswald Spring, C. Mesjasz, J. Grin, P. Dunay, N. C. Behera, B. Chourou, P. Kameri-Mbote, and P. H. Liotta (eds.), *Globalization and environmental challenges. Reconceptualizing security in the 21st century*. Hexagon Series on Human and Environmental Security and Peace, Volume 3. Heidelberg, Germany: Springer-Verlag: 65–102.

Brown, G. (2009) *Brown: for the planet, there is no plan B*. Speech at Major Economies Forum, 19 October. Available at: www.youtube.com/watch?v=NYnVf33l4mE (last visit 19 September 2014).

Buzan, B., O. Wæver, and J. de Wilde (1998) *Security: a new framework for analysis*. Boulder, CO: Lynne Rienner.

Cabinet Office (2009) *Security for the next generation: national security strategy update*. London: Crown Copyright/Cabinet Office.

Clark, A. (2007) 'Climate change threatens security, UK tells UN', *The Guardian*, 18 April. Available at: www.guardian.co.uk/environment/2007/apr/18/greenpolitics.climatechange (last visit 19 September 2014).

CNA, Military Advisory Board (2007) *National security and the threat of climate change*. Arlington, VA: The CNA Corporation.

Davey, E., UK Energy and Climate Change Secretary (2012) *COP18: statement from UK Energy and Climate Change Secretary*. Available at: www.gov.uk/government/speeches/cop18-statement-from-uk-energy-and-climate-change-secretary (last visit 19 September 2014).

Department for Environment, Food and Rural Affairs (DEFRA) (2010) *Archive: adaptation across government*. Available at: http://archive.defra.gov.uk/environment/climate/programme/across-government.htm (last visit 19 September 2014).

Detraz, N. and M. Betsill (2009) 'Climate change and environmental security: for whom the discourse shifts', *International Studies Perspectives*, 10: 303–320.

Development, Concepts and Doctrine Centre (DCDC) (2007) *The DCDC Global Strategic Trends Programme 2007–2036*. London: Crown Copyright/MOD 2007 (3rd edition).

Dubash, N. (2012) 'Looking beyond Durban: where to go from here?', *Economic & Political Weekly*, 47(3): 13–17.

E3G (2014) *E3G staff. Directors & founders*. Available at: www.e3g.org/people (last visit 30 September 2014).

European Commission (2010) *Climate action. China-EU near zero emission coal project*. Available at: http://ec.europa.eu/clima/dossiers/nzec/index_en.htm (last visit 15 October 2014).

European Commission (2011) *Common statement by the European Union, least developed countries and the alliance of small island states*. Available at: http://ec.europa.eu/commission_2010–2014/hedegaard/headlines/news/2011–12–09_01_en.htm (last visit 19 September 2014).

Foreign and Commonwealth Office (FCO) (2004) *Departmental report. 1 April 2003–31 March 2004*. London: FCO/Crown Copyright.

Foreign and Commonwealth Office (FCO) (2005) *Departmental report. 1 April 2004–31 March 2005*. London: FCO/Crown Copyright.

Foreign and Commonwealth Office (FCO) (2006) *Departmental report. 1 April 2005–31 March 2006*. London: FCO/Crown Copyright.

Foreign and Commonwealth Office (FCO) (2007) *Departmental report. 1 April 2006–31 March 2007*. London: FCO/Crown Copyright.

Foreign and Commonwealth Office (FCO) (2008) *Departmental report and resource accounts. 1 April 2007–31 March 2008*. Volume 1. London: FCO/Crown Copyright.

Foreign and Commonwealth Office (FCO) (2009a) *Departmental report 1 April 2008–31 March 2009*. London: FCO/Crown Copyright.

Foreign and Commonwealth Office (FCO) (2009b) *Robin Gwynn: tenacity and a sense of responsibility to power climate change objectives*. Available at the UK Web Archive: http://webarchive.nationalarchives.gov.uk/20130217073211/http://ukinbangladesh.fco.gov.uk/en/about-us/working-with-bangladesh/climate-change/global-discussion/uk-climate-security-envoy (last visit 19 September 2014).

Foreign and Commonwealth Office (FCO) (2010) *Preparing for global climate change—an adaptation plan for the FCO*. London: FCO, Global and Economic Issues Directorate.

Foreign and Commonwealth Office (FCO) (2011) *Annual report and accounts 2010–2011 (For the year ended 31 March 2011)*. London: FCO/Crown Copyright.

Foreign and Commonwealth Office (FCO) (2012) *Annual report and accounts 2011–2012 (For the year ended 31 March 2012)*. London: FCO/Crown Copyright.

Foreign and Commonwealth Office (FCO) (2013) *Annual report and accounts 2012–2013 (For the year ended 31 March 2013)*. London: FCO/Crown Copyright.

Foreign and Commonwealth Office (FCO) (2014) *Annual Report and Accounts 2013– 2014 (For the year ended 31 March 2014).* London: FCO/Crown Copyright.

German Advisory Council on Global Change (2007) *World in transition: climate change as a security risk.* Berlin: German Advisory Council on Global Change.

GOV.UK (2013a) *Foreign Secretary's new Special Representative for Climate Change.* Available at: www.gov.uk/government/news/foreign-secretarys-new-special-repre sentative-for-climate-change (last visit 30 September 2014).

GOV.UK (2013b) *Rear Admiral Neil Morisetti. Introduction of Rear Admiral Neil Morisetti as Special Representative for Climate Change.* Available at: www.gov.uk/ government/people/neil-morisetti (last visit 19 September 2014).

Gupta, J. (1999) 'North-South aspects of the climate change issue: towards a construc tive negotiating package for developing countries', *Review of European Community & International Environmental Law*, 8(2): 198–208.

Hague, W. (2010) *The diplomacy of climate change.* Speech to the Council of For eign Relations, New York, 27 September. Available at: www.gov.uk/government/ speeches/an-effective-response-to-climate-change-underpins-our-security-and- prosperity (last visit 15 October 2014).

Harvey, F. (2012) 'Clean technology: what is the future of green energy?', *The Guardian*, 2 October. Available at: www.guardian.co.uk/sustainable-business/clean-technology- green-energy-future (last visit 19 September 2014).

Harris, K. (2012) *Climate change in UK security policy: implications for development assistance?* Overseas Development Institute (ODI) Working Paper 342. London: ODI.

Hartmann, B. (2010) 'Policy arena. Rethinking climate refugees and climate conflict: rhetoric, reality and the process of policy discourse', *Journal of International Devel opment*, 22(2): 233–246.

Hatch, M. T. (2007) *The Europeanization of German climate change policy.* Paper pre pared for the European Union Studies Association Tenth Biennial International Con ference, Montreal, Canada, May 17–19.

Hayes, J. and J. Knox-Hayes (2014) 'Security in climate change discourse: analyzing the divergence between US and EU approaches to policy', *Global Environmental Politics*, 14(2), 82–101.

HM Government (2014) *Paris 2015. Securing our prosperity through a global climate change agreement.* London: Crown Copyright.

International Energy Agency (IEA) (2011) CO_2 *emissions from fuel combustion. High lights.* IEA statistics. OECD/IEA: Paris.

King, E. (2012) 'China and Russia block UN Security Council climate change action', *Responding to Climate Change (RTCC)*, 19 February. Available at: www.rtcc. org/2013/02/18/china-and-russia-block-un-security-council-climate-change-action/ (last visit 30 September 2014).

Krause-Jackson, F. (2013) 'Climate change's links to conflict draws UN attention', *Bloom berg*, 15 February. Available at: www.bloomberg.com/news/2013–02–15/climate- change-s-links-to-conflict-draws-un-attention.html (last visit 30 September 2014).

Kymlicka, W. (1995) *Multicultural citizenship.* Oxford: Oxford University Press.

Leifeld, P. (2013) *Discourse network analyzer.* Available at: https://github.com/leifeld/ dna/releases (last visit 27 September 2014).

Leopold, E. (2007) 'UK puts climate change in U.N. Council', *Reuters*, 17 April. Avail able at: www.reuters.com/article/2007/04/18/environment-globalwarming-un-britain- dc-idUSN1736824820070418 (last visit 21 September 2014).

Liverman, D. and S. Billet (2010) 'Copenhagen and the governance of adaptation', *Environment: Science and Policy for Sustainable Development*, 52(3): 28–36.

Lovell, H., H. Bulkeley, and S. Owens (2009) 'Converging agendas? Energy and climate change policies in the UK', *Environment and Planning C: Government and Policy*, 27(1): 90–109.

McCright, A. M., C. Xiao, and R. E. Dunlap (2014) 'Political polarization on support for government spending on environmental protection in the USA, 1974–2012', *Social Science Research*, 48: 251–260.

McKie, R. (2013) 'Climate change "will make hundreds of millions homeless"', *The Guardian*, 12 May. Available at: www.theguardian.com/environment/2013/may/12/climate-change-expert-stern-displacement (last visit 30 September 2014).

Methmann, C. and D. Rothe (2012) 'Politics for the day after tomorrow: the political effect of apocalyptic imageries in global climate governance', *Security Dialogue*, 43(4): 323–344.

Miliband, D. (2009) *David Miliband warns of global threats from climate change.* Speech shown by ITN News. Available at: www.youtube.com/watch?v=dct_ePtqP5k (last visit 22 September 2014).

Miliband, D. and F.-W. Steinmeier (2008) *Europe has to rise to the security challenges of climate change.* Joint Contribution by Foreign Secretary David Miliband and German Foreign Minister Frank-Walter Steinmeier, 13 March. Available at: http://ecc-platform.org/index.php?option=com_k2&view=item&id=1485:europe-has-to-rise-to-the-security-challenges-of-climate-change&Itemid=750 (last visit 22 September 2014).

Ministry of Foreign Affairs, Republic of Slovenia (2013) *The UN Security Council examines the security implications of climate change.* Available at: www.mzz.gov.si/nc/en/newsroom/news/article//31725/ (last visit 30 September 2014).

Oels, A. (2013) 'Rendering climate change governable by risk: from probability to contingency', *Geoforum*, 56(1): 17–29.

Pilkington, E. (2007) 'UK to raise climate talks as security council issue', *The Guardian*, 16 April. Available at: www.guardian.co.uk/world/2007/apr/16/greenpolitics.climatechange (last visit 23 September 2014).

Prime Minister (PM)'s Strategy Unit (2005) *Investing in prevention. An international strategy to manage risks of instability and improve crisis response.* London: Crown Copyright/PM's Strategy Unit.

Scheurs, M. and Y. Tiberghien (2007) 'Multi-level reinforcement: explaining European Union leadership in climate change mitigation', *Global Environmental Politics*, 7(4): 19–46.

Schwartz, P. and D. Randall (2003) *An abrupt climate change scenario and its implications for United States national security.* Available at: www.fas.org/irp/agency/dod/schwartz.pdf (last visit 9 February 2015).

Sindico, F. (2007) 'Climate change: a security (council) issue?', *The Carbon and Climate Law Review*, 1(1): 29–44.

Sinha, U. K. (2010) 'Climate change and foreign policy: the UK case', *Strategic Analysis*, 34(3): 397–408.

Smith, D. and J. Vivekananda (2007) *A climate of conflict: the links between climate change, peace and war.* London: International Alert.

Stripple, J. (2002) 'Climate change as a security issue'. In: E. A. Page and M. Redclift (eds.), *Human security and the environment. International comparisons.* Cheltenham: Edward Elgar: 105–127.

Sturcke, J. (2006) 'We must pay now to avoid climate disaster, says Blair', *The Guardian*, 30 October. Available at: www.guardian.co.uk/business/2006/oct/30/greenpolitics.economicpolicy (last visit 23 September 2014).

Swyngedouw, E. (2010) 'Apocalypse forever? Post-political populism and the spectre of climate change', *Theory, Culture & Society*, 27(2–3): 213–232.

The Guardian (2004) 'Blair demands international action to aid Africa', *The Guardian*, 7 October. Available at: www.guardian.co.uk/world/2004/oct/07/politics.foreignpolicy (last visit 19 September 2014).

The New York Times (2007) 'UN attacks climate change as a threat to peace', *The New York Times*, 17 April. Available at: www.nytimes.com/2007/04/17/world/europe/17iht-climate.5.5324498.html?_r=2 (last visit 23 September 2014).

Townsend, M. and P. Harris (2004) 'Now the Pentagon tells Bush: climate change will destroy us', *The Guardian/The Observer*, 22 February. Available at: www.guardian.co.uk/environment/2004/feb/22/usnews.theobserver (last visit 23 September 2014).

Trombetta, M. J. (2008) 'Environmental security and climate change: analysing the discourse', *Cambridge Review of International Affairs*, 21(4): 585–602.

United Nations General Assembly (UNGA) (2009) *Climate change and its possible security implications*. 85th plenary meeting, 3 June.

United Nations Security Council (UNSC) (2007a) *Letter dated 5 April 2007 from the permanent representative of the United Kingdom of Great Britain and Northern Ireland to the United Nations addressed to the president of the Security Council*. Meeting records, S/PV.5663, 5663rd meeting (Part I), 17 April, New York.

United Nations Security Council (UNSC) (2007b) *Letter dated 5 April 2007 from the permanent representative of the United Kingdom of Great Britain and Northern Ireland to the United Nations addressed to the president of the Security Council*. Meeting Records. S/PV.5663, 5663rd meeting (Part II), 17 April, New York.

United Nations Security Council (UNSC) (2011a) *Statement by the president of the Security Council*. The 6587th Meeting, 20 July, New York.

United Nations Security Council (UNSC) (2011b) *Maintenance of international peace and security. Impact of climate change*. Letter dated 1 July 2011 from the permanent representative of Germany to the United Nations addressed to the Secretary-General. Meeting records, S/2011/408, 6587th meeting (Part I), 20 July, New York.

United Nations Security Council (UNSC) (2011c) *Maintenance of international peace and security. Impact of climate change*. Letter dated 1 July 2011 from the permanent representative of Germany to the United Nations addressed to the Secretary-General. Meeting records, S/2011/408, 6587th meeting (Part II), 20 July, New York.

Vogler, J. (2009) 'The European Union and the 'securitisation' of the environment'. In: E.A. Page and M. Redclift (eds.), *Human security and the environment. International comparisons*. Cheltenham: Edward Elgar Publishing Limited: 179–198.

Worsnip, P. (2011) 'West, Russia divided over U.N. council climate role', *Reuters*, 20 July. Available at: www.reuters.com/article/2011/07/20/us-climate-un-idUSTRE76J7QY20110720 (last visit 30 September 2014).

Yoon, S. (2014) 'Biggest emitter China best on climate, Figueres says', *Bloomberg*, 14 January. Available at: www.bloomberg.com/news/2014–01–13/top-global-emitter-china-best-on-climate-change-figueres-says.html (last visit 30 September 2014).

5 Stage Two

The Response from Emerging Developing Countries

The emerging developing countries are amongst the key audiences of securitising moves on climate migration. The securitising moves have been performed to convince these countries of the need to adopt binding mitigation targets under the United Nations Framework Convention on Climate Change (UNFCCC), in the name of international peace and security. In this chapter, I examine how the emerging developing countries have responded to such securitising moves. I start by providing a macro-level analysis of the positioning of the emerging developing countries in the 2007 and 2011 UN Security Council debates held on the topic of climate change (including climate migration). As discussed in chapter 4, these debates are amongst the key settings where securitising moves on climate migration have been performed to make the case that climate change urgently needs to be addressed to prevent insecurity.[1]

This will provide a background to the micro-level analysis, where I focus on the case of India. Specifically, I examine how the Government of India has responded to the securitising move on climate migration by the United Kingdom (UK)'s Foreign and Commonwealth Office (FCO), as analysed in chapter 4. India is often regarded as major emitter, as its total emission shares almost tripled between the 1990s and 2012 (PBL 2013: 50). In 2012, its total emissions were about four times higher than the UK's total emissions (PBL 2013: 50). India is thus one of the key countries that the FCO aims to convince to adopt stricter mitigation targets (FCO 2007: 71);[2] primarily by means of binding commitments under the UNFCCC (Ashton 2011: 7).

Through the perspective of the pragmatic framework for analysis on securitisation as developed in chapter 3, I will review India–UK interactions and India's response to the FCO's securitising move aiming to promote binding mitigation action. Moreover, I will delve into the argument that securitising moves on climate migration provide India with another reason to justify strict border control measures to stop so-called Bangladeshi climate refugees (see e.g., German Advisory Council on Global Change 2007: 123; Friedman 2009a; White 2011: 71–72). To assess such concerns, I will examine whether the FCO's securitising move has had such an unintended effect.

Emerging Developing Countries in the UN Security Council Debates

The major emerging developing countries (in particular, India, China, and Brazil) have opposed securitising moves on climate change (including climate migration) in both UN Security Council debates. They find support from other emerging economies, such as Russia, and from oil-producing countries, such as Egypt and Iran. Figures 5.1 and 5.2 visualise how these countries are situated on the opposite side of the spectrum when compared to the securitisers (see chapter 4 for a detailed discussion on the selection of statements that underlies these figures).[3]

Figures 5.3 and 5.4 show more specifically how the opposing coalition in the 2007 and 2011 debate is aligned through the set of examined statements.[4] One of the main concerns of the opposing coalition is the increasing encroachment of the UN Security Council on non-traditional security areas, such as climate change and climate migration. With the exception of China and Russia, the emerging developing countries and emerging economies do not have special voting powers in the UN Security Council, and thus prefer climate change to be discussed in forums where they do have decision-making power

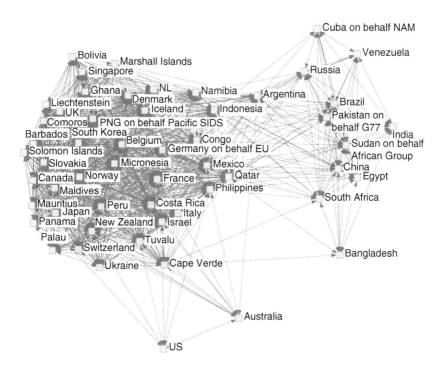

Figure 5.1 An Overview of State Positions in the 2007 UNSC Debate

Note: Any two states are connected when they share at least one of the selected statements.

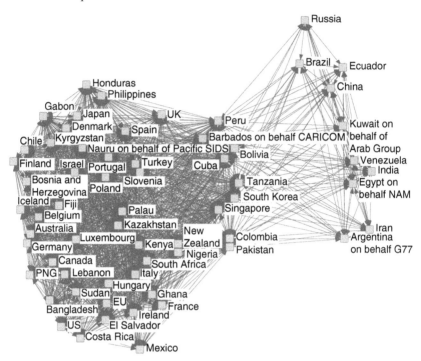

Figure 5.2 An Overview of State Positions in the 2011 UNSC Debate

Note: Any two states are connected when they share at least one of the selected statements.

(see Figures 5.3 and 5.4 for such statements). But even China and Russia who are permanent members to the Council, thus holding veto-power, have argued against this debate (see e.g., King 2013a; Krause-Jackson 2013). China and Russia, similar to other emerging economies, value their sovereignty and related principles of non-intervention (Humphrey and Messner 2006: Keeler 2011). Therefore, these states try to prevent the UN Security Council of expanding its mandate over an even a wider range of issues that it considers to be of national authority, including climate change.

In addition to expressing these concerns, most states in the opposing coalition stress that climate change should primarily be seen as a matter of sustainable development (see Figures 5.3 and 5.4), instead of being an issue of security. They prefer the UN Commission on Sustainable Development, General Assembly, and in particular the UNFCCC, to address climate change. In these forums, the emerging economies and developing countries are well represented. When framing climate change in terms of sustainable development, it has a better institutional fit with these UN forums.

But this framing also says something about their perspective of climate security and climate migration. The opposing coalition is uncomfortable with a security framing of climate change, and is not keen on discussing topics such

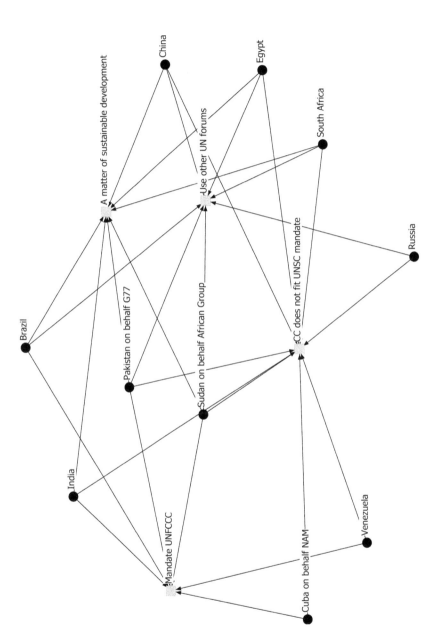

Figure 5.3 Statements Connecting at Least Three States of the Opposing Coalition in the 2007 UNSC Debate

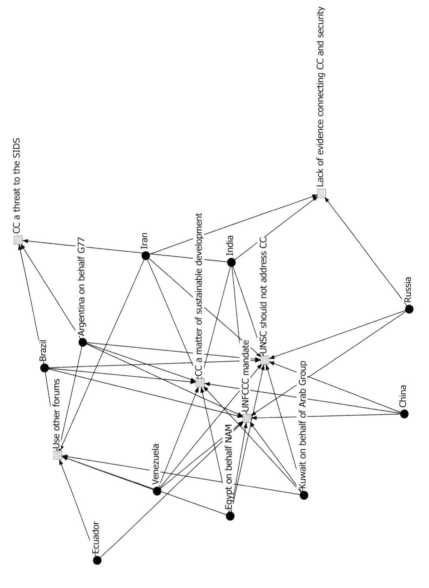

Figure 5.4 Statements Connecting at Least Three States of the Opposing Coalition in the 2011 UNSC Debate

as climate conflicts and climate migration. Instead, it prefers to discuss climate change through a development lens, with a focus on poverty reduction and economic growth. Related to that, the opposing coalition is sceptical of direct linkages between climate change, migration, and security. In the debate of 2011 Russia, Iran, and India argued that there is insufficient evidence connecting climate change and security (see Figure 5.4), and thus rejected alarmist claims about climate conflict, mass climate migration, and the like (Brazil was also sceptical of linking climate change and security, but did acknowledge there may be indirect connections). In the debate of 2007 Russia, India, and Brazil had expressed similar concerns (these, however, do not show in Figure 5.3 as their statements were too distinct to be grouped in one category).[5] In this context, Brazil argued that '. . . utmost caution must be exercised in establishing links between conflicts and the utilization of natural resources or the evolution of climate on our planet' (UNSC 2007a: 20). Along similar lines, Russia stated that: 'I would like to make an appeal to avoid panicking and overdramatizing the situation, which does not help us reach long-term comprehensive agreements in this area' (UNSC 2007b: 17). With regards to climate migration, India argued that 'possible consequences in terms of border disputes, migration, energy supplies, societal stress, and the like can hardly be discussed in any meaningful manner' due to the ignorance of strong uncertainty in the analysis of climate change (UNSC 2007a: 22).

Interestingly, in the debate of 2011, a number of countries sceptical of a security framing of climate change (including climate migration), did agree that the survival of the Small Island Developing States (SIDS) is threatened by climate change, and thus accepting this link between climate change and security (see Figure 5.4).[6] It was difficult for many countries to morally disagree with this argument, in contrast to discussions about climate wars (see also Kurtz 2012). Not to appear inconsiderate, critical states such as China, Russia, Brazil, and India highlighted the situation of the SIDS (though China and Russia did not frame this in terms of security, and are therefore not connected to this statement in Figure 5.4). Brazil, for instance, commented that 'The rather indirect relationship between security and climate change in no way diminishes the urgency of supporting countries and populations that are most vulnerable to climate change, in particular small island developing States, many of which face truly existential challenges' (UNSC 2011: 8).

The 2011 UN Security Council debate followed in the footsteps of a meeting on climate change and security (including climate migration) held at the UN General Assembly in 2009, which can explain why security statements on the SIDS have become more prominent. The SIDS were very central in the debate in the UN General Assembly. The UN General Assembly had discussed (and later accepted) a draft resolution on climate change and security, proposed by the SIDS. As a result, much of the debate was about the moral duty of the international community to support the SIDSs in their quest to protect their survival (see also Kurtz 2012). As argued by Australia:

[T]here was a lot of discussion among us on what the resolution was really about—whether it was really about climate change, security or development. I think that, in the end, we realized it was about all those things, but mostly it was really about respect—respect for some of the smallest and least powerful States [small island states] represented in this General Assembly . . . I would like to congratulate those countries that initially were not enthusiastic about aspects of the resolution but that decided on principle not to block it. To those, I say thank you.

(UNGA 2009: 10)

In this setting, even the most critical countries of the climate change–security nexus did not want to object to the argument that the SIDS are threatened by climate change, out of principle and most likely some moral pressure. Such sentiments appear to have influenced the tone of the 2011 debate held in the UN Security Council.

Another key finding is that many statements by the emerging developing countries in the opposing coalition reflect their positions taken in the UNFCCC negotiations. Figure 5.5[7], based on the 2007 UNSC debate, shows how they highlighted the responsibility of industrialised countries in both the mitigation and adaptation to climate change. They furthermore promoted the principles of historical responsibility and common but differentiated responsibilities (in short, CBDR in Figure 5.5). This suggests that the emerging developing

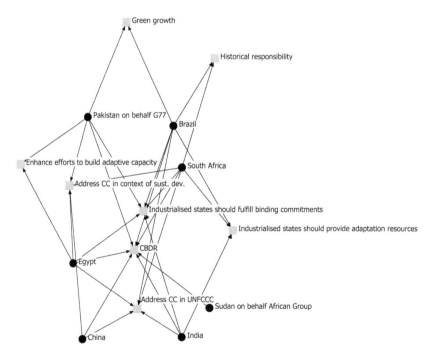

Figure 5.5 Actions and Measures Proposed by at Least Two States of the Core Opposing Coalition in the 2007 UNSC Debate

countries were well aware of the strategic intent driving securitising moves on climate change and climate migration in the UN Security Council debates, aiming to convince these states to take more mitigation action under the UNFCCC. It explains much of their opposition to the UN Security Council debates, and to specific securitising moves on climate change and climate migration. The emerging developing countries wanted to make sure that the UN Security Council debates would not shift the primary mitigation responsibility away from industrialised states (King 2013a; see the analysis of India in this chapter for a more detailed discussion).

Another trend that matched the UNFCCC negotiations is the position of South Africa. South Africa has shifted its position in the UN Security Council debates from being an opponent of securitising moves to being more closely associated with the securitisers, including many European states (see Figures 5.1 and 5.2). In the UNFCCC negotiations, South Africa has also positioned itself somewhat closer to the European states in recent years (see chapter 6 for details). During the climate change negotiations in Cancun of 2010, South Africa was largely in favour of the idea that emerging developing countries should adopt binding emission cuts, while India and China strongly opposed this (Qi 2011). Moreover, South Africa hosted the 2011 climate change negotiations in Durban, and thus had an interest to make these negotiations run smoothly. This has likely influenced its position in the UN Security Council debate of 2011, which took place just a few months prior to the Durban negotiations.

In sum, the emerging developing countries are part of the opposing coalition to securitising moves on climate migration. These states have argued against a security framing of climate change, including the issue of climate migration. Instead, they unite around the argument that climate change is a matter of sustainable development, and should be discussed other decision-making forums, of which in particular the consensus-based UNFCCC. Moreover, a number of states in the opposing coalition were not convinced that scenarios of climate migration and of climate conflict are valid, as these lack sufficient scientific evidence.

The macro-level analysis suggests that the emerging developing countries were well aware of the strategic interests driving securitising moves on climate migration, and partly for those reasons actively tried to counter them. The micro-level analysis in the next section will shed more light on that finding. I will demonstrate that much of India's scepticism to securitising moves on climate migration can be explained when analysing the securitisation process in the context of climate change politics and negotiations.

India's Response to Securitising Moves on Climate Migration

In this section, I will zoom in on India's response to securitising moves on climate migration. A particular focus will be on its response to the FCO's securitising move, a move that aims to persuade India to accept binding mitigation targets under the UNFCCC. The analysis primarily concentrates on the *central* Indian government, also known as the Government of India. India is a federation that consists of 29 states. Each state has an elected government and is authorised to make its own legislation in areas such as state-level land policies, state-level climate change policies, law and order, etc. The Government of India (the central government) is tasked to provide unity between such policies and has the means to overrule state law when these are inconsistent with national law (Government of India 2011: Part XI). In the realm of climate change, the Government of India also has such a coordinating and rule-setting role. It developed a National Action Plan on Climate Change. This provides the framework in which the state governments should build their State Action Plans on Climate Change. In addition to that, the Government of India has sole responsibility over a number of areas of national importance, such as defence issues and foreign relations. This means that the Government of India is responsible for foreign relations on climate change, which includes negotiations under the UNFCCC. The Government of India is therefore the main Indian governmental actor that the FCO and other securitisers have to persuade for India to accept binding mitigation targets.

I will analyse India's response to the FCO's securitising move in three policy fields: the field of international climate change negotiations, the field of India's national (domestic) policy on climate change, and the field of India's immigration policy. The focus is thus on the response by the climate change and security (including migration) community in the Government of India. The aim is to examine whether the FCO has been able to influence India's policy making on climate change, and to review whether its arguments have become intertwined with India's policy towards Bangladeshi immigrants. To analyse this, I will make use of the respective scenarios of audience responses as outlined in chapter 3.

Non-Acceptance and Backfire: India and International Climate Change Negotiations

The FCO's Global Strategic Impacts Team and the Delhi-based British High Commission have both used securitising moves on climate migration in discussions with Indian partners. These discussions particularly took place with India's security community. FCO officials for instance had conversations with retired military generals, with security-based think tanks, and with governmental officials in the Ministry of Defence.[8] As discussed in chapter 4, the key interest behind such conversations was to create favourable domestic conditions necessary to reach a global deal on climate change mitigation. The hope was that the Indian security community would convince those in India responsible for climate change policy that action on emission reduction is of utmost urgency to preserve peace and security. In addition to communications with India's security community, the FCO and other securitisers have tried to reach the elite of the Government of India through the debates on climate change held in the UN

Security Council. These debates aimed to make climate change an issue of high politics and therefore to convince countries such as India to adopt binding mitigation targets under the UNFCCC (for more details, see chapter 4).

In this section, I examine to what extent this approach has been successful to convince the Government of India to take more action in the UNFCCC. In charge of India's climate change policy is the Ministry of Environment and Forests (shortly referred to as the Environment Ministry), and in international climate change negotiations support is provided by the Ministry of External Affairs and by the Indian Prime Minister's Special Envoy on Climate Change (a position that ran until March 2010). The analysis will show there is no evidence that the security community or the UN Security Council debates have been able to persuade India's climate change community to take more action in the UNFCCC. Instead, the response to the FCO's securitising move has largely been negative. The FCO's securitising move and the respective UN Security Council debates backfired and compounded a tense negotiation environment on climate change.

Setting Out the Context

Prior to discussing India's response of non-acceptance and backfire in more depth, it is important to understand the context that accounts for the Government of India's negative reaction to securitising moves on climate migration. This reaction is in many respects informed by India's own defensive positioning in international negotiations in the UNFCCC on the mitigation of climate change. In such negotiations, India has actively counteracted claims that it represents a major emitter, which it believes to be an unjust line of argumentation (see e.g., *The Hindu* 2011). The Government of India argues that it is unfair to push India to commit to binding and ambitious mitigation targets under the UNFCCC (Rajamani 2009; *The Hindu* 2011; Dubash 2012a). If counted per capita (per citizen of a country), India has a low level of emission shares (PM's Council on Climate Change 2008; Dubash 2012a: 15). The Government of India maintains that the per capita norm is the fairest principle to guide the UNFCCC negotiations (PM's Council on Climate Change 2008: 2; Rajamani 2009: 343). When counting emission shares per capita, industrialised countries remain responsible for the largest emission shares (IEA 2011: 12; PBL 2013: 17), due to their high emissions and relatively low populations levels compared to (emerging) developing countries. For instance, in 2009, the United States (US) accounted for about 5 percent of the world population, while being responsible for 18 percent of the world emissions. Meanwhile, China and India together generated 29 percent of the world emissions, while accounting for 37 percent of the word population (IEA 2011: 11). However, China's emission shares per capita have risen considerably since then. As a result, in 2011, these were equal to the level of emissions per citizen of the European Union (EU) (PBL 2012: 15). In 2014, these have even surpassed Europe's per capita emissions (McGrath 2014). India, however, still remains far below the average per capita share of industrialised countries (PBL 2012: 13, see also p. 15; PBL 2013). In 2012, its CO_2 emissions per capita from cement production and fossil fuel use was below 2 tonne CO_2 per capita, while this was just below 10 tonne for a nation with a relatively small population size such as the Netherlands (PBL 2013:17). Related to that, India emphasises that the industrialised countries should carry the primary mitigation burden due to their historical responsibility for the problem of climate change to have emerged (Rajamani 2009; Dubash 2012a). Moreover, India maintains that if its economic growth stalls due to binding mitigation measures, it cannot grow out of poverty and hundreds of millions will suffer (Rajamani 2009; Dubash 2012a). For instance, during the 2011 Durban UNFCCC conference, the Indian Environment Minister Jayanthi Natarajan argued: 'Why should I sign away the rights of 1.2 billion people? Is that equity?' (Natarajan, cited in Third World Network 2011).

Of course, there are many counterarguments to such a position. India's per capita emissions are expected to rise substantially in coming years due to rapidly increasing energy demands (Rajamani 2009: 342). As a consequence, a moral argument has been made that India needs to adopt a more responsible approach to mitigation, since India is aware of climate science and therefore of what unmanaged greenhouse gas (GHG) emissions may cause (see discussion Rajamani 2009: 360; Dubash 2012a: 15). Despite such arguments, India is cautious of adopting binding mitigation targets under the UNFCCC, which it perceives to be an unjust proposal by industrialised countries. In the words of Chandrashekhar Dasgupta (2008), member to the Indian Prime Minister's Council on Climate Change, 'developed countries are . . . seeking to undermine the ethical basis of current international agreements on climate change. Their object is to impose a new agreement that will enable them to reduce their own commitments, while imposing additional burdens on developing countries'.

According to Michaelowa and Michaelowa (2012; see also Vihma 2011), India's position in the UNFCCC negotiations became more flexible and ambitious in the late 2000s when Jairam Ramesh took office as Environment Minister (Vihma 2011; Michaelowa and Michaelowa 2012). Part of his agenda was to change India's reputation as a deal-breaker in climate change negotiations. He wanted to adopt a more constructive negotiation position (Vihma 2011: 75). For instance, at the 2010 Cancun UNFCCC conference, he argued that 'all countries must take on binding commitments in an appropriate legal form' (cited in Pande 2011). This statement does not necessarily entail that India should adopt binding mitigation targets in the manner industrialised countries see fit. It is a broad statement that allows for a differentiation of commitments based on historical responsibility and levels of per capita emissions (Michealowa and Michaelowa 2012: 579). Despite this, domestic reactions were fierce, criticising the Minister's move (*The Economic Times* 2010; see also discussion Pande 2011; on more of such criticisms of Ramesh see discussion Vihma 2011: 83–84). The Minister was accused by the opposition and by NGOs for acting unilaterally, and for 'buckling under pressure from developed nations' (Activist Narain quoted in *The Economic Times* 2010).

Once Jayanthi Natarajan took over as Environment Minister in 2011, the Government of India largely returned to a defensive negotiation strategy on climate change (Vidal and Harvey 2011a; Dastidar 2012; Michaelowa and Michaelowa 2012: 586–587; Sethi 2012).[9] As argued by Jayanthi Natarajan, in response to the EU's demand for a new treaty legally binding to all parties under the convention: 'I wonder if this is an agenda to shift the blame on to countries who are not responsible [for climate change]. I am told that India will be blamed. Please do not hold us hostage' (Natarajan during the Durban UNFCCC conference, cited in Vidal and Harvey 2011b). Prakash Javadekar, who became Environment Minister in May 2014, seems to continue a more defensive negotiation style. During the Climate Summit of September 2014, he argued 'The moral principle of historic cannot be washed away' (quoted in Lenin 2014).

India did agree at the 2011 Durban UNFCCC conference, after a fierce negotiation on the exact text (Vidal and Harvey 2011c), to negotiate 'a protocol, another legal instrument or an agreed outcome with legal force' (UNFCCC 2012, Decision 1/CP.17). This protocol or legal instrument should include all Parties to the convention and should come into force in 2020. The State parties are still working towards this goal, aimed to be adopted during the Conference of the Parties in 2015 to be held in Paris. However, this agreement leaves many important issues undefined. It leaves the question open to interpretation whether India should accept any *binding* mitigation targets by 2020 (Gosh and Dasgupta 2011; Dubash 2012a). At least, in Indian society this agreement is not interpreted in this manner. As argued by Dubash (2012a: 13–14):

> There is little clarity on the content of what will be legally binding and who (which countries) will take on such obligations. . . . Commentators from industrialised countries tend to interpret the text as calling for all countries to take on emission reductions—a construction of symmetric responsibility—while developing countries see the principle of differentiated responsibility as alive and well.[10]

Therefore, the idea for India to accept binding and ambitious mitigation targets under the UNFCCC remains a sensitive topic (see also Wagner 2013). Prodipo Ghosh (2012: 168), Member of the Indian Prime Minister's Council on Climate Change, argues:

> First, India's (and all developing countries') concerns about economic growth and poverty eradication are legitimate, and must be fully respected in any global climate regime. . . . Second, that the cause of climate change, and one which is continuing, is the unsustainable emissions of developed countries. They will have to take leadership to drastically reduce their emissions.

India's strategy, thus far, has been to contribute to the mitigation of climate change on a more voluntary basis, and argues that industrialised countries should continue to take the lead in the mitigation of climate change. As argued by Environment Minister Prakash Javadekar (quoted in *The Economic Times* 2014): 'We are doing our action but it is not at somebody's dictation, it is on our own volition. . . . All will take responsibility, all will act but responsibility of developed countries is different and that must be recognised'. Therefore, to sum up this part, the dominant perception within the Government of India is that India should not agree to ambitious mitigation targets that are binding under the UNFCCC, which is seen as an unjust proposal by industrialised countries.

In addition to this, India has been known to be generally reluctant to engage in pragmatic negotiations and alliances with Western states (Narlikar 2006, 2011), particularly on the level of multilateral negotiations.[11] On many issues, ranging from low politics to high politics, the Government of India adopted a 'defensive, nay-saying-strategy' to Western countries, while presenting itself as the voice and representative of the developing world (Narlikar 2006: 60). As an example of such a defensive attitude, in the run up to the Rio + 20 summit of 2012, the Indian Environment Ministry argued: '[the] EU sees the Rio + 20 as a way of blunting the competitive edge of the developing economies and improve its competitiveness in a climate where the EU is facing a serious economic and financial crisis' (cited in Chaudhuri 2012). It is for that reason that:

> [o]ff the record, EU officials point out that India continues to be their most difficult strategic partner. In the eyes of many European officials, India has acquired a reputation of being an inflexible negotiator and a potential spoiler, unwilling to yield and adapt its positions where compromise seems still possible.
>
> (von Muenchow-Pohl 2012: 32;
> see also Wagner 2013)

According to Narlikar (2006: 72), such a negotiation strategy primarily stemmed from 'Nehruvian ideas of self-sufficiency and anti-imperialism' and is a stance the Indian society often expected from its government. As argued by an Indian official, 'It is easier for our minister to come back home empty-handed as a wounded hero, rather than to come back with something after having had to make a compromise' (quoted in Narlikar 2006: 72). This positioning of the Government of India has added to a complicated political climate that did not help to smooth international climate change negotiations.

Such a sceptical attitude relates to India's postcolonial history. After the British colonial rule, the Indian elite felt that the independent state of India deserved a more prominent place in global politics (Cohen 2000; Smith 2012: 373). Partly for that reason, India took on the role of a Third World leader and representative in international negotiations (see discussion Smith 2012: 373). This idea of India being a state of international significance has only strengthened in recent decades due to its rising economic power. In that political context, India is highly sensitive of Western states, and particularly of its former colonial ruler, intending to lecture India on its policy making (or when such states come across as doing so). Not only is such a lecturing style of the West at odds with India's post-colonial values of self-determination and self-sufficiency (on such values see Humphrey and Messner 2006; Narlikar 2006; Vihma 2010: 6; Wagner 2013), it also does not resonate with India's image of an emerging world power.

In that context, as I will discuss below in more detail, the Government of India has often highlighted the role of the West in securitising moves on climate migration attempting to promote mitigation action. This is interesting, since a range of developing countries, in particular the small island states, have simultaneously been involved in the construction of such security narratives to raise awareness of climate change (Stripple 2002). The Government of India nonetheless criticised the role of the West and perceived least developed countries using these security narratives as victims or puppets of the negotiation strategies of industrialised countries.[12] The remainder of the section will review in detail how the Government of India has reacted to the FCO's securitising move aiming to convince India to adopt binding mitigation targets under the UNFCCC.

India's Response of Non-Acceptance and Backfire

The Government of India has been very much aware of the policy objective guiding the FCO's securitising move on climate migration: namely, the aim to promote binding mitigation targets on climate change among states such as India. But as to be expected, the Government of India does not readily accept the binding mitigation measures promoted in the FCO's securitising move.

India does not regard the promoted binding mitigation targets as an essential, managerial, collaborative, and positive step to prevent the world from future harm; at least, not when India itself has to take these measures. Therefore, in contrast to the FCO and most other securitisers, India does not perceive the promoted climate action as a form of positive prevention and technocratic risk management, along the lines of the Risk School and the Paris School (see chapter 4 for details).

Instead, India holds a different interpretation of the argument that it should adopt binding mitigation targets under the UNFCCC. In my analysis it became clear that such action is largely perceived (or at least, portrayed) as a confrontational and competitive act by the West demanding India to do something that contradicts its principles of justice, self-determination, and potentially even harming its economic growth and its ability to combat poverty. In most extreme terms, it is perceived as 'a geopolitical stratagem by industrialized countries to contain new and emergent economic powers, particularly China, but also India . . .' (Dubash 2012b: 202). Such an understanding of binding mitigation action can best be described through the logic of security measures of competition, confrontation and exceptionality, as outlined by the Copenhagen School.

This perception of injustice and confrontation is well reflected in the following statement by Samir Saran, Vice-President of the Delhi-based Observer Research Foundation:

> Every Indian who lives in a village who may have a phone and a TV, but other than that little disposable income, still does have dreams. They dream of buying a car one day and other consumer goods. The world spends millions of dollars to tell the rest of the world to consume more through marketing and advertisement, they give people hundreds of possibilities to indulge in activities which contribute to consumption and pollution. And then on the other hand we also hear narratives [in the context of climate change negotiations] that say 'no this is not a good way to live life'. This is a discourse of differentiated lifestyles. One that seeks to limit the aspirations of the developing and emerging world. One that tells the emerging countries that they do not need to live this Western style life, that they can remain deprived, it is not a bad way to live, be happy. That happiness is not about money, not about cars. You can be happy and poor.[13]

Claims by industrialised countries that India should commit to binding mitigation targets have been received with much sensitivity,[14] and at times even anger. In line with the Copenhagen School's logic of security measures, such targets are regarded as extreme measures demanded from India by richer countries. To illustrate, in an interview, a former member of the Indian Planning Commission passionately argued in relation to the mitigation question: 'Why do you [Western countries] point out every single act of omission by India and not all of these acts of commissions and omissions of the Western countries. For heaven sake, have a perspective!'[15] Similarly, Sunita Narain, a respected environmental activist and head of the Centre for Science and Environment, argued that the promise of binding mitigation targets would represent a 'betrayal' to the Indian population and as a 'disastrous' move (*The Economic Times* 2010). Because of this, the FCO's securitising move has been regarded as demanding something extraordinary, unjust, competitive, and even confrontational. Of course, we should not forget that it is in India's self-interest to present mitigation action in such terms. Without such binding targets, India can determine its own climate policy and does not face constraints when wanting to make adjustments.

India's objection to the FCO's securitising move went, however, beyond the argument that it does not agree with the types of measures promoted. A primary objection is that the FCO's securitising move represents an unfair UNFCCC-related negotiation tactic, a rhetorical language of fear and threat to promote binding mitigation measures. This language shapes an understanding of the FCO as *demanding* something, as trying to *enforce* something, while playing on rhetorics, and thereby trying to deflect attention away from the UK's own responsibilities on climate change. It is seen as side-stepping the norms of collaboration, equity, debate, and consensus that (or at least should) underlie UNFCCC negotiations.

This perception can also be traced among the Indian security community. As argued by Gupta and Dutta (2009: 36) in a report for the security-based think tank, the Institute for Defence Studies and Analyses (IDSA), in Delhi: 'The West's agenda appears to be to use the security dimension of climate change to force the developing world to fall in line on climate change negotiations and pressurise them on governance-related issues'. Similarly, Indian Group Captain Major Kumar (2011: 96), comments that developing countries such as India are 'loath to seeing it [climate change] as a security problem—[as it] may force them to cap emissions, hamper growth'. These quotes reflect that the FCO's strategy to use a security narrative on climate migration to promote binding mitigation measures is regarded with suspicion in the Indian security community; at least, by its members who openly expressed their perspectives and concerns. The author of the first statement, Arvind Gupta, was Additional Secretary in the Ministry of External Affairs (retired in 2013), and on deputation as the Director-General of IDSA until August 2014, and was Secretary of the National Security Council Secretariat from 1999–2007. It thus seems unlikely that the Indian Security community would have influenced India's climate change decision-making in the manner the FCO saw fit.

In addition to that, there is little evidence that the security community has the actual means to influence India's international positioning on climate change, even when it would see climate change and climate migration as a major security threat. There are, for instance, no clear signs of interactions between the Indian defence and climate change community. In that context, R.R. Rashmi, the Joint Secretary on Climate Change in the Environment Ministry and part of India negotiation's team in the UNFCCC commented: 'The national security secretariat does security, that has nothing to do with climate change. There is no institutional linkage'.[16] When I attempted to arrange for an interview with the Ministry of Defence (MOD), an officer replied: 'Miss, this is the Ministry of Defence, we deal with matters of war. For climate change you should call MOEF [Ministry of Environment and Forests]'.[17] Indian officials hold a relatively traditional perception of security; an issue area limited to the MOD's mandate and related to matters of war and the military. Linkages between security and climate change and climate migration are considered misplaced, as climate change is perceived as an issue of the authority and expertise of the Environment Ministry. As argued by R.R. Rashmi, 'climate change is not a security issue, it is a scientific issue, it is adaptation. We are uncomfortable with this kind of language. We should employ measures in the realm of adaptation and prevention and not use any military or security means'.[18] Some FCO officials have acknowledged the lack of influence of the Indian security community on the Indian climate change community. An official with the British High Commission argued there are no well-developed lines of collaboration and communication between the Indian climate change community and the security community.[19]

Interestingly, however, the Indian climate change community did share the Indian security community's sceptical view of the FCO's securitising move.

As I will demonstrate below in more detail, it has interpreted statements about climate conflict, border disputes, and cross-border climate migration as scare tactics of Western countries[20] attempting to push India to commit itself to binding mitigation measures under the UNFCCC.[21] Such a sceptical attitude towards arguments on the climate change–migration–security nexus is thus widely held in the Government of India and among India's societal elite, and is not limited to perceptions of one policy community.

As a reflection of this widely shared perspective, the Government of India was highly critical of the respective UN Security Council debates of 2007 and 2011 on the security implications of climate change (including climate migration), as was discussed in the beginning of this chapter. According to Vijai Sharma, the Secretary of the Ministry of Environment and Forests from 30 June 2008 until 31 December 2010 and until this time part of India's delegation to the UNFCCC, the UK and German governments have attempted to make the climate change mitigation question extremely political by discussing it in the UN Security Council,[22] particularly since the security arguments were considered unfounded. The debate was seen as a political attempt to put additional pressure on India to commit to binding mitigation targets in the name of international peace and security. Such a sceptical reaction can be traced in the following remark by the Indian delegation during the 2007 UN Security Council debate: 'nothing in the greenhouse gas profile of developing countries even remotely reflects a threat to international peace and security, yet their taking on greenhouse gas mitigation targets will adversely impact their development . . .' (UNSC 2007a: 22). India maintained that none of the security arguments had been supported by sufficient evidence, reflecting its understanding of such statements as a matter of pure rhetoric. As argued by the Indian delegation:

> These catastrophic scenarios therefore cannot be treated as threshold events that are known in the real meaning of the word. Hence, their possible consequences in terms of border disputes, migration, energy supplies, societal stress and the like can hardly be discussed in any meaningful manner.
>
> (UNSC 2007a: 22, for a similar comment
> see UNSC 2011: 18)[23]

The Indian delegation stressed that action on climate change could only be decided on in the UNFCCC; a multilateral consensus-based forum where India could not be forced to sign up to binding mitigation targets. As the Indian delegation in the 2007 UNSC debate, 'the only context in which to discuss what can be done about the physical effects of climate change is, again, the Framework Convention [on Climate Change]' (UNSC 2007a: 22–23; see also UNSC 2011, for similar quotes by the Indian delegation).

Security framings on climate migration referring to India as the state at risk of incoming climate migrants from Bangladesh and related tensions added to India's understanding of the FCO's securitising move as a scare tactic (for such statements, see PM's Strategy Unit 2005: 54; Beckett 2006).[24] The perception is that security narratives on climate migration 'deliberately concentrate on India to demonstrate that it is in India's self-interest to sign up to binding mitigation to avoid security problems' (Boas 2014: 154). As argued by Shyam Saran, the Indian Prime Minister's Special Envoy on Climate Change from 2007 until March 2010, and during this period India's chief climate change negotiator:

> The whole world is talking about the Bangladesh–India climate conflict and cross-border climate migration, rather than focussing on its own responsibilities. Why do they focus these statements on our backyard? We need a global response on climate change rather than talking about what India as a nation should do.[25]

Related to that, Shyam Saran argued that 'the security argument put forward by the West is an attempt to deflect attention away from what they need to do themselves'.[26] As similarly commented by Samir Saran, Vice-President of the Delhi-based Observer Research Foundation: 'The climate migration, climate security discourse is a Western narrative to push for certain policy changes. . . . They want India and China to commit to binding emission cuts, so that they do not have to reduce their emissions very much'.[27] The very fact that the FCO promoted its securitising move in the UN Security Council only added to such suspicion. As argued by Vijai Sharma: 'They [the industrialised countries] seem to want to further delay the UNFCCC process, to prevent a real solution by raising new discussions'.[28] By these discussions, Sharma referred to the UN Security Council debates on security implications of climate change (including climate migration) initiated by the UK and German governments.

In addition, the climate change community of the Government of India has expressed concerns that security arguments on climate migration, including the respective UN Security Council debates, are used to break the united front of developing countries in UNFCCC negotiations, and thereby to weaken India's negotiation power in the UNFCCC. The perception is that industrialised countries, such as the UK, are forging alliances with the Least Developed Countries (LDC) and the Alliance of Small Island States (AOSIS) by means of shared concerns about the security implications of climate change, such as migration.[29] 'The fear is that the industrialized countries strategically position vulnerable nations, such as small island states or Bangladesh, as a group of states that can demand greater mitigation action from emerging developing states in the name of their security and survival' (Boas 2014: 153). As argued by Shyam Saran: 'The West tries to break this united front of developing countries. They say: look, Bangladesh, at what may happen to you, you could have major migration and a problem with India. Therefore you should join us to make India and China commit to mitigation'.[30]

This concern expressed by the Government of India is to a certain degree a legitimate one. The formation of alliances between certain groups of industrialised countries and the LDCs and AOSIS has indeed been one of the strategies in the UNFCCC negotiations (Carrington 2010; *The Guardian* 2010).

For instance, the UK aims 'to generate a voice [among vulnerable countries to climate change] that will highlight the impact of climate issues, including to exert more leverage within the UN negotiations' (FCO 2009: 40). According to Wikileaks, Connie Hedegaard, the European Commissioner for Climate Action, argued that the AOSIS '"could be our best allies" given their need for financing' (Carrington 2010; see also *The Guardian* 2010). Particularly in the 2011 UNFCCC conference in Durban, there was a notable convergence between the position of the LDCs and AOSIS and that of the EU (which includes the UK's position). They shared the argument that emerging developing countries, such as India, need to adopt binding mitigation targets in future years to prevent dangerous levels of climate change (Black 2011). During the 2012 Doha UNFCCC conference, the UK's Minister of State for Energy and Climate Change reiterated the importance of maintaining a good alliance with LDCs and AOSIS: '[It] was extremely powerful in terms of a coalition for high ambition, and I think we need to make sure that holds' (cited in King 2012a). However, some fraction within the EU, AOSIS and LDC alliance has been reported, particularly due to disagreement over the number of years in which the Kyoto Protocol needed to be extended (King 2012a; 2012b; Murray 2012).[31]

The LDCs, AOSIS, and the EU also provided a common statement to the Durban UNFCCC conference, in which they relied on a language of threat and survival:

> [W]e need not to remind anyone of the scale of climatic threats facing the most vulnerable countries in the world as a result of climate change. . . . The chance to reach our objective is getting smaller as time passes and we need to start this process today. For many countries, this is a matter of survival and this process should be able to deliver an answer to meet their worries.
>
> (European Commission 2011)

The respective UN Security Council debates analysed in chapters 4 and 5 also show that the SIDS, the EU, and some other developing countries unite in the leading coalition of securitisers. This suggests that the use of security frames may indeed result in an increasing split in the negotiation block of the Global South (see German Advisory Council on Global Change 2007: 171–173; Roberts 2011, on this divide). The following quote by the Foreign Minister of Grenada in the Durban UNFCCC conference exemplifies such tensions in the Southern negotiating block. He stated in relation to the question whether leading developing countries should sign up to binding mitigation targets: 'While they develop, we die; and why should we accept this?' (quoted in Black 2011; see also Dubash 2012a: 16). Such concerns were also expressed by a negotiator from East Africa (who stayed anonymous), who argued that the LDCs and the emerging economies have diverging interests in the negotiations towards a new post-Kyoto regime: 'Initially they were walking together but climate change has impacted people differently than anticipated and that could shape the conventional groupings. Even if it doesn't happen formally, it will shape things' (quoted in King 2013b).

In short, the Government of India has been highly suspicious of the FCO's securitising move on climate migration. The FCO's securitising move did not succeed in convincing India to adopt binding mitigation targets, nor is it conducive to more cooperative relationships between India and industrialised countries in the UNFCCC. Instead, it adds to a 'climate of mistrust' that frequently characterises climate change negotiations (Dubash 2010), and fuels a competitive negotiation environment marked by divisions between India and industrialised countries. This analysis exemplifies a response scenario of non-acceptance and backfire. Not only is the FCO's securitising move rejected in the context of climate change negotiations, but the securitising move also further weakens the chance that India will commit to ambitious mitigation targets that are binding under the UNFCCC.

Paradoxically, this response scenario represents an unsuccessful securitisation process (the Government of India does not accept a security rationale nor the promoted measures), yet at the same time supports many of the Copenhagen School's key assumptions. The FCO's securitising move does have political implications (in the form of backfire) that cannot simply be erased by an audience's rejection. In line with the Copenhagen School's conceptualisation of security and logic of security measures, the FCO's securitising move fuelled situations of confrontation, mistrust, and competition (e.g., by increasing tense relationships between India and industrialised countries in climate change negotiations). Therefore, even in a situation of unsuccessful securitisation, the Copenhagen School's insights remain relevant to grasp the political implications of a securitising move.

Climate Migration and Security in India's National Policy on Climate Change?

The previous section demonstrated that the Government of India is sceptical of the FCO's securitising move on climate migration in the context of international climate change negotiations. The question remains whether the FCO's securitising move has been able raise awareness of climate migration and security on the level of India's national (domestic) policy on climate change. In such a scenario, the FCO would be able to influence India's policy making on climate change by means of a more bottom-up process in which India would justify domestic measures on mitigation and adaptation in the name of national or even human security.

India's National Policy on Climate Change: A Situation of Non-Engagement

The primary document produced by the Government of India (the central government) outlining its national policy on climate change is the 2008 National

Action Plan on Climate Change (NAPCC) (PM's Council on Climate Change 2008). This plan is divided into eight missions: the National Solar Mission; the National Mission for Enhanced Energy Efficiency; the National Mission on Sustainable Habitat; the National Water Mission; the National Mission for Sustaining the Himalayan Ecosystem; the National Mission for a "Green India"; the National Mission for Sustainable Agriculture; and the National Mission on Strategic Knowledge for Climate Change (PM's Council on Climate Change 2008). The overall focus of this national plan is largely on technological and infrastructural development, on energy efficiency and on environmental impacts. It concentrates on technological policy developments to address adaptation and mitigation, such as water storage, energy technology and irrigation systems, without drawing clear connections to political, developmental, socioeconomic, or security consequences. The National Action Plan on Climate Change (NAPCC) does state that it aims to protect 'the poor and vulnerable sections of society through an inclusive and sustainable development strategy, sensitive to climate change' (PM's Council on Climate Change 2008: 4). However, such issues are not actively addressed. As argued by Byravan and Rajan (2012: 9), who undertook an evaluation of the NAPCC, 'development targets of the eight missions are not prioritised with clear sustainable development-focussed approaches and outcomes.' They argue that the lack of attention to development concerns, socioeconomic impacts, and to the situation of the poor, is one of the national action plan's main weaknesses (Byravan and Rajan 2012). As a result, notions of climate migration or displacement do not fit the description of the National Action Plan on Climate Change that is largely engaged with technical solutions, energy issues, and environmental impacts. Climate migration is mentioned only briefly in the description of the mission on Strategic Knowledge within the NAPCC, even though the full report on this particular mission does not once refer to the matter (Ministry of Science and Technology 2010a).

In the years following the release of the National Action Plan on Climate Change, the Government of India released full reports that outlined the respective eight climate change missions of this plan in more detail. As compared to the overarching national action plan of 2008, these full reports provide a more diverse picture regarding their engagement with human development concerns.[32] Similar to the 2008 national action plan, human and social development concerns are weakly integrated in a number of these mission reports. This is the case, for instance, with the National Solar Mission and the National Water Mission (Ministry of New and Renewable Energy 2010; Ministry of Water Resources 2011).[33] But some mission reports more actively discuss such matters (e.g., with the impacts upon traditional coping mechanisms of the poor, cultural values, food security, landlessness, skills, employment, basic services, etc.).[34] These are in particular the National Mission on Sustainable Habitat, the National Mission for Sustainable Agriculture, and to some degree the National Mission for Sustaining the Himalayan Ecosystem (Ministry of Agriculture 2010; Ministry of Urban Development 2010; Ministry of Science & Technology 2010b).

The National Mission on Sustainable Habitat and the National Mission for Sustainable Agriculture are the only two missions that refer to potential climate-related migration and displacement (Ministry of Agriculture 2010: 5, 10, 18, 19; Ministry of Urban Development 2010: 7, 8, 11). In these occasional references to climate-related migration and displacement, there is no mention of international or cross-border migration, mass movements, tensions, or violent conflict.[35] Instead, they primarily highlight the implications for climate change upon rural–urban migration (Ministry of Agriculture 2010: 10; Ministry of Urban Development 2010: 7, 8). Unlike the FCO's securitising move, the Copenhagen School's concept of security is not used in these mission reports. Nor are other conceptualisations of security clearly reflected in their representation of climate migration. Take, for instance, the following quote:

> Climate change threatens the homes, livelihoods and health of the urban poor. When disasters strike, their homes may be damaged or destroyed and they may be unable to travel to work, causing them to lose money for food and other basic needs. Droughts, floods and storms in rural areas have increased migration to cities. Poor people often live in informal settlements on land which is susceptible to climate change—flood plains, coastal lowlands or unstable hill sides. Drains and culverts are frequently blocked with rubbish. Slum dwellers often lack secure tenure, proper shelter, water, sanitation, electricity and other services. Most have no insurance. Climate change may add to their problems.
>
> (Ministry of Urban Development 2010: 7)

Even though these missions discuss the basic needs of local populations that are threatened by climate change, they do not reflect a notion of human security as defined by Critical Security Studies. Statements such as the quote above discuss the poor as if they are helpless victims that have no self-capacity to improve their human security. These missions also do not actively try to tackle oppressive structures from which humans should emancipate themselves. This does not resonate with the Critical Security Studies' definition of security; even though the focus on the vulnerability and basic needs of the poor does fit the definition of human security as provided by the UN Development Programme (1994).[36] Therefore, such statements most clearly reflect a humanitarian language of protection and development, and do not convincingly represent notions of security as defined by one of the schools on securitisation.

Despite the occasional references to climate migration, the level of engagement with climate migration in India's national policy on climate change is almost negligible. This lack of engagement with the issue of climate migration is also traceable in the reportings on climate change by the Environment Ministry (short for the Ministry of Environment and Forest (MOEF)). A major study assessing the impact of climate change in India, published by the Environment Ministry (MOEF 2010b),[37] concentrates on the physical implications of climate change and on broad trends, such as the implications for crop yields.

It does not actively address more specific human development implications of climate change; even though it occasionally touches upon such issues (e.g., it mentions the implications for farm incomes (MOEF 2010b: 82)). On a few occasions in the section on human health, the study refers to the effect of climate change upon the loss of houses and land, displacement and migration, and related life and health risks (MOEF 2010b: 102–103). It does, however, not research such social implications in any great detail. The report also does not make any connection between climate migration and conflict or cross-border movement. Instead, it expects such displacement to add to rural–urban migration processes (MOEF 2010b: 102). The principal scientific advisor on climate change of the Environment Ministry commented that the ministry concentrates on the physical implications of climate change and on the implications for entire sectors, such as the water or agriculture sectors.[38] He argues that scenarios on the social and developmental implications of climate change are fraught with uncertainty and subsequently not examined. In outlining the ministries' approach to examining climate change impacts, the scientific advisor argued:

> We develop climate change scenarios for 2020/2030, for instance, how will it impact the rivers, water availability, etc. We are not saying which community gets affected, where it will get affected. No. We look at the trends, how it affects an entire sector and then we try to integrate the analysis. So we are not asking social questions.[39]

For that reason, scenarios on (internal and cross-border) climate migration are not actively included in the reportings by the Environment Ministry. It is feared that such an endeavour would make the scientific analyses political as scenarios on climate migration would include statements on the origin and destination of migrants.[40] The principal scientific advisor on climate change argued that these reportings are meant to provide an overview of extreme and slow-onset weather events caused by climate change; independent of the question how these events should be dealt with politically, for instance, when affecting neighbouring countries. The rationale is that the Environment Ministry is not expected to provide a political interpretation or response to such cross-border events, which again is the responsibility of another ministry, such as the Ministry of External Affairs.

Explaining the Non-Engagement

This lack of engagement with the topic of climate migration can partially be explained by India's rigid and clearly demarcated governmental structure and related perceptions of authority. Each ministry is provided a narrow portfolio, having a specific defined area of authority, and there is little cross-ministerial coordination and collaboration (see discussion Narlikar 2006: 61–62). For a range of issue areas, the Government of India has created a separate ministry. For instance, in the realm of development there is a ministry on: Rural Affairs; Tribal Affairs; Women and Child Development; Housing and Urban Poverty Alleviation; Urban Affairs, etc. This creates a highly fragmented governmental structure that is difficult to coordinate. This governmental structure also translates into India's national policy on climate change. A range of ministries is involved in this policy area, particularly those in the realm of the environment, energy, agriculture, and science. While these ministries are guided by the overarching Prime Minister's Council on Climate Change and coordinated by the Environment Ministry (MOEF 2014), there is insufficient collaboration. For instance, each ministry has been granted a narrow task (e.g., the Ministry of Water Resources is responsible for water issues (Ministry of Water Resources 2011)), while the Ministry of Agriculture is responsible for matters of agricultural affairs related to climate change (Ministry of Agriculture 2010). Little synergy is created between their endeavours. In this context, the Environment Ministry, the nodal ministry on climate change, provides little attention to aspects of social development and security. It perceives itself as strictly engaged with matters of the environment,[41] being its field of authority and expertise (MOEF 2013). A lack of cross-ministerial coordination combined with strict perceptions of authority, result in narrow policy measures and sectoral approaches; while socioeconomic or so-called security issues, such as climate migration, are often cross-sectoral. This governmental structure does not help to smooth the situation for the FCO. When India itself has not developed a climate change policy that fits socioeconomic issues such as climate migration, a rigid governmental structure does not help to create more dynamism and change in India's perceptions of climate change.

Another factor is that climate change and internal displacement are largely discussed as separate matters in Indian discourse (McAdam and Saul 2010). In India, internal displacement is largely considered to be development-induced (e.g., caused by industrial projects; or related to overpopulation[42]) (McAdam and Saul 2010; *The Times of India* 2011).[43] Attention is also given to displacement caused by natural disasters (Boas 2012), in contrast, there is relatively little societal awareness of climate change factors in migratory processes (McAdam and Saul 2010). As such, the discursive environment has not been favourable for India's national policy on climate change to become actively engaged with matters of internal climate-related migration and displacement.

In short, India's national policy on climate change does not actively address the issue of climate migration and security. The Government of India's policy on climate change is particularly focussed on environmental impacts, energy efficiency, and technological development. There are a few instances where internal climate migration is discussed. But such statements do not clearly represent a language of security. For those reasons, this response to the FCO's securitising move can best be categorised under the scenario of non-engagement, as defined in the framework for analysis.

Militarisation and Border Security Practices?

Securitising moves on climate migration may have wider implications. The FCO does not have full control over which actors will respond to its securitising move, nor how such actors will interpret the move. Concerns have been raised that security narratives on cross-border climate migration and conflict, such as the one promoted by the FCO, may provide India (e.g., India's Ministry of Home Affairs) with another justification to strengthen its border regime to halt immigration flows from Bangladesh (German Advisory Council on Global Change 2007: 123; Friedman 2009a; White 2011: 71–72). As argued by Friedman (2009a), in an article in *The New York Times*, 'Climate change didn't bring this fence, but it is providing a fresh reason for its existence and ongoing expansion'. As similarly commented by an official with the British High Commission in New Delhi:

> [T]here is a risk with climate security, when not sophisticatedly discussed, for it to develop into a security policy with activities like the fence and border management issue to halt climate change migration, instead of adding to the promotion of adaptation and collaborative measures.[44]

This is considered a serious risk because securitising moves frequently refer to Bangladeshi climate migrants moving into India (in the case of the FCO, see e.g., Beckett 2006; Miliband 2009).[45] India's immigration community may have heard about these ideas and use them in support of harsh immigration practices.

Such a process would represent a response scenario of alternative securitisation, in which the securitising move would be used to pursue other measures than those originally promoted by the FCO; that of border controls and immigration policy instead of climate change mitigation policies. Fears about militarisation and strict border security practices, expressed by authors such as Hartmann (2010) and Trombetta (2014), would become a harsh reality. This section will assess to what extent such a scenario has unfolded in India, with a focus on the understandings and policy making of the central Indian Government. This will shed light on the often-made assumption that securitising moves on climate migration will lead to stricter border security practices on the Indian–Bangladeshi border (see e.g., Friedman 2009a; German Advisory Council on Global Change 2007: 123; White 2011: 71–72).

The Historical Context of Bangladesh–India Immigration

Cross-border immigration from Bangladesh (between 1947 and 1971 East Pakistan) towards India became an issue following India's partition in 1947. This region has always been characterised by a high degree of mobility, also prior to the partition (Van Schendel 2005: 210; Upadhyaya 2006: 19; McAdam and Saul 2010). It consists of a dynamic delta where rivers often change course. As a result, inhabitants were constantly moving in search of new land. But, the partition suddenly made such movements processes of international migration (Van Schendel 2005: 211; see also discussion Upadhyaya 2006: 19).

The Indian discourse towards immigrants from Bangladesh (at the time East Pakistan) was initially rather mild and welcoming (Van Schendel 2005: 192–194; Oberoi 2006: 72; Das 2011: 42).[46] The perception was that partition-refugees from the newly created Pakistan (divided into East and West Pakistan) were largely Hindus and thus had to be accommodated, being 'sons and daughters of the nation coming home' (Van Schendel 2005: 193). Yet, this perception towards process of cross-border movement gradually changed. Immigrants, no longer directly fleeing as a result of the partition, were presented as illegal infiltrators (Van Schendel 2005: 194; see also discussion in Upadhyaya 2006: 26–29; and Das 2011: 47). This group of immigrants from East Pakistan, later Bangladesh, were often Muslims and were seen as drastically changing the demographic composition of neighbouring provinces (e.g., Tripura, Assam).[47] Such a perception was fuelled by an increasing political sentiment that 'Hindu India was under threat' by Muslims trying to infiltrate into India (Van Schendel 2005: 211).[48] It was particularly the Hindu nationalist party Bharatiya Jana Sangh that raised awareness of the Muslim faith of these migrants (see also discussion Upadhyaya 2006: 26; this party became the Bharatiya Janata Party (BJP) in 1980. But also Jawaharlal Nehru, who led the more centre-left Congress party, took a hard line in 1962 by arguing that 'this infiltration should be stopped and effectively dealt with' (Nehru, quoted in Upadhyaya 2006: 29).

The narrative of 'infiltration' frames these immigrants as intruders trying to steal land from Indian citizens (Van Schendel 2005: 195). It is feared that the immigrants drastically change demographic compositions and local politics, as immigrants are granted voting rights by local politicians in turn for a vote in favour of their party (Van Schendel 2005: 195). Such sentiments particularly thrived in the province of Assam; a province that borders with Bangladesh. In the late 1970s to the mid-1980s, this province experienced xenophobic violence led by the All Assam Students Movement targeting large groups that they identified as Bangladeshi immigrants (Ramachandran 2005: 8; Upadhyaya 2006: 23–24; Puniyani 2012). In reality, the targeted groups were not always Bangladeshi immigrants. They came from the province of West Bengal, or they were Muslims from Assam. The violence in Assam in the summer of 2012, was once again connected to the problem of Bangladeshi immigration (*The Times of India* 2012; see discussion Puniyani 2012). Some have tried to dispute such allegations. An opinion article in the newspaper *Tehelka*, for instance, maintains that attention should be provided to underlying problems, such as a lack of available land and job opportunities (Puniyani 2012; see also McAdam and Saul 2010 on the complexity of such conflicts). Moreover, according this article in *Tehelka*, most of the migration towards Assam has actually taken place prior to the partition, namely in the early twentieth century during a programme under British rule aiming to cope with the overpopulation in the region of Bengal (Puniyani 2012). Despite this, an infiltration narrative towards Bangladeshi immigrants has received much resonance in Indian society and politics

(Van Schendel 2005). In the years following the terrorist attacks of 9/11, Bangladeshi immigration also became connected to the issue of terrorism. At that time the argument was that Bangladesh hosts militant Islamic terrorist groups trying to infiltrate into India (Ramachandran 2005; Upadhyaya 2006: 23–24; McAdam and Saul 2010).

In the light of this infiltration narrative, the Government of India installed a strict border regime. In the early 1990s, under the name of Operation Pushback, India deported hundreds of people that they identified as Bangladeshi immigrants (Van Schendel 2005: 198; Ramachandran 2005; Das 2011), and deportations continue to take place (Van Schendel 2005: 198; Venkatesan 2012; *The Indian Express* 2012). Such operations created dire circumstances for the deportees when Bangladesh did not accept these immigrants. The Bangladesh government argues that there is no illegal immigration from Bangladesh into India, and claims that the deported persons are Bengali-speaking Indians (Ramachandran 2005; Van Schendel 2005: 199–200; Das 2011). As a result, these deportees often ended up in deportation camps in India along the Bangladesh border, in jail in West Bengal, or were once again migrating within India (Van Schendel 2005: 224). Furthermore, India is constructing a fence along the Bangladesh border (large parts of the border have already been fenced). Discussions concerning such a fence already rose in the early 1960s and had officially been approved by the Government of India in 1986 (Van Schendel 2005: 212). Until the late 1990s, the Government of West Bengal, ruled by the Communist Party of India, was sceptical of the strict immigration policy, including the construction of the fence (Van Schendel 2005: 212–213; Oberoi 2006: 116). In 1999, also the Government of West Bengal agreed to fence its border with Bangladesh (Van Schendel 2005: 213). In August 2012, the BJP party argued that more urgent steps need to be taken to complete the fencing of the Bangladesh border to halt illegal migration and to prevent insecurity in Assam (*Daily News* 2012). The Bangladesh border is guarded by the Indian Border Security Force (BSF), which according to Human Rights Watch has abused, tortured, and killed many people crossing the Indian–Bangladesh border (Human Rights Watch 2010).

The described border security measures to halt Bangladeshi immigrants can best be described in terms of confrontation and exceptionality as defined by the Copenhagen School. These border measures do not aim to curb immigration in subtle ways, following the Paris School's logic of security measures that includes practices of profiling, surveillance, and risk management. Instead, the described deportations, shootings, and the construction of a fence represent confrontational, exceptional, defensive types of measures attempting to exclude Bangladeshi immigrants. In that respect, the Government of Bangladesh was highly offended by the construction of the fence 'because it humiliates and belittles us [Bangladesh] before the world' (President Ershad, quoted in Van Schendel 2005: 213). But it is not just the Bangladeshi immigrants who suffer from these measures. Many Indian communities are negatively affected by India's border regime; in terms of trade, family ties, and citizen rights (Van

Schendel 2005). For instance, many Indians were forced to relocate due to the construction of the fence. Based on an agreement between India and Bangladesh regarding the construction of defensive posts along the border, the fence is located 150 yards of the Bangladesh' border on Indian territory (Van Schendel 2005: 213). The area between the fence and the border of Bangladesh encompassed many Indian villages (Van Schendel 2005: 213–214). Even today many Indian farmers have to pass the fence and border guards in order reach their fields, which negatively affects their freedom of movement and access to land (Das 2011: 52).[49]

Despite this defensive approach to Bangladeshi immigration, it has to be noted that there are counter discourses. According to Van Schendel (2005: 223), deportations were frequently accompanied by loud protests claiming that deportations violated human rights. Another counter discourse presents immigration as a process benefitting India's development, as it provides a constant stream of labour supply (see discussion McAdam and Saul 2010). Moreover, many immigrants have been able to enter India (and continue to do so) and to settle down, which suggests that the Government of India has in many respects employed a type of laissez-fair approach towards immigration. Furthermore, the illegal immigrants from East Pakistan who entered India prior to the birth of the nation of Bangladesh in 25 March 1971 have been given the right to stay in India (Van Schendel 2005: 129). In 2014, the Hindu nationalist party BJP party returned to power in the central government, after a long period ruled by the centre-left Congress Party. This is unlikely to improve the situation for Bangladeshi immigrants (Bdnnews24 2014). As argued by Indian Prime Minister Modi, 'illegal Bangladesh migrants in India should pack and leave' (quoted in Bdnews24 2014).

It must also be acknowledged that the problems and concerns experienced by Indian communities that resort to violence, such as in Assam, are real and should be addressed. It is also likely that some Indian groups and communities do appreciate the fence, as they think it could help decrease population density and competition over jobs and lands. It is, however, not necessarily clear that Bangladeshi immigration is amongst the primary causes of such problems (McAdam and Saul 2010; Puniyani 2012), even though it has often been presented in these terms, particularly by the media and right-wing political parties.

Signs of Alternative Securitisation?

Given India's strict immigration policy, there is a risk for the FCO's securitising move on climate migration to further amplify negative perceptions about immigrants and to add to India's policy development of strict border controls. Discussions about cross-border climate migration have risen in Indian society. Greenpeace India released a report arguing that 75 million Bangladeshis may migrate as a consequence of sea level rise of which '[t]he bulk of people from Bangladesh are very likely to immigrate to India' (Rajan 2008: 1). The issue has also been picked up by security-based think tanks, such as the Institute for Defence Studies and Analysis (IDSA) and the Centre for Air Power Studies. For instance, in 2009, IDSA released a report on the security implications of climate change, which included one chapter on climate migration (Gautam 2009). It maintains that 'Even without climate change-related migration, migrants from Nepal and Bangladesh do present a security challenge to India which is likely to exacerbate with climate-related migrations' (Gautam 2009: 101). Even Bangladesh's Prime Minister Sheikh Hasina argued that Bangladesh may experience large-scale climate change-induced displacement that could contribute to 'cross-border problems' (*Daily Star* 2010; McAdam and Saul 2010).

There are, however, no public statements provided by the Government of India that warn of incoming climate migrants from Bangladesh (Boas 2014).[50] Interviewees argued that Bangladeshi immigration is not related to climate change.[51] Instead, their primary message was that these immigration flows are driven by economic factors, and some argued that illegal immigration could to some degree be related to terrorism (even though others were more nuanced about that and argued that terrorism was a separate issue from illegal immigration).[52] The interviewed (both active and retired) immigration officials in the central government did not portray climate migration as an issue at all relevant to their policy making.[53]

Related to that, most interviewees argued that the Indian MOD is not planning for any conflicts or migration caused by climate change;[54] even though water scarcity and related insecurity is identified as a major issue.[55] Unlike many countries of the Global North, India has not experienced a post-Cold War period in which traditional security threats became of lesser concern. India has a tense relationship with its neighbour Pakistan and shares a long, disputed border with China. India may perceive itself as not having the 'luxury' to be concerned with somewhat vague and Western-constructed security issues, such as climate conflict and climate migration. As argued by Chris Evett of the UK's MOD's Development, Concepts and Doctrine Centre:

As far as I can tell, climate change and security are not on the agenda of the Indian MOD. The Indian MOD rather focuses on regional aspects like their defence towards Pakistan and China. Just like we had in the Cold War they are facing an existential threat on their border. So they are focused on traditional security issues at the moment, that is what largely motives them. I could imagine there are a few individuals working on climate change, but nothing more than that. [56]

An important exception here is a speech by A. K. Antony, the Indian Defence Minister from 2006 until May 2014, at the 2012 Asian Security Conference on 'Non-Traditional Security Challenges—Today and Tomorrow'. Here he discussed climate change was as a matter of security, for instance in relation to water scarcity and related conflict (Antony 2012).[57] But also here, no reference to migration was made. Moreover, one senior official mentioned during the interview that cross-border climate migration towards India is gradually being discussed in the government's security establishment, even though it does not represent a widely shared perspective.[58] Despite this, there is no compelling evidence suggesting that the Government of India presently regards cross-border climate migration to be or to become a major issue that it needs to prepare for by means of its border and immigration policy. Moreover, also important from the Copenhagen School's point of view, the Government of India uses no discourse on climate migration to publicly justify border measures. This suggests that the risk for securitising moves on climate migration to become intersected with Indian immigration practices has thus far been less than is often expected.

There is of course a possibility that officials did not want to openly say that they are actually concerned about climate migration. But it rather seemed that the option to deal with climate migration in the context of security (border) policy was just considered odd and not something they actually considered doing. Respondents wondered why I was not engaged with more pressing security issues such as illegal immigration due to economic reasons or with issues of terrorism. This reaction can (partly) be explained by the more rigid institutional governmental structure, and by India's current perspective of climate change as a green and technical issue not related to matters of insecurity and conflict (see previous sections). In this context, climate change and climate migration are not (yet) considered issues of national security and border policy. Unlike in the UK, it seems that the discursive environment in India has not yet developed in such a direction that it allows for climate migration to easily become securitised. Moreover, India has to cope with a myriad of development challenges, such as poverty, communal violence, rural–urban migration, etc. Relatively vague and undefined challenges, such as climate migration, are not on the top of the list. A more politically motivated reason may be that the notion of climate migration is often regarded as a Western discourse (see earlier discussions). This may explain the lack of active engagement with climate migration in the context of India's security policy. Climate migration may be perceived as something 'invented' by the West, and a nothing more than rhetoric based on inclusive scientific evidence. As a result, the Indian security community may not consider it as an issue needing to be put on the top of its agenda.[59]

In short, thus far, there is no compelling evidence that the Government of India is currently using a discourse of climate migration to justify measures of border control management. In the Indian context, the FCO's securitising move therefore largely remained to revolve around the promotion of climate mitigation action.

Concluding Discussion

The macro-level analysis demonstrates the sensitivity of securitising moves on climate migration amongst the emerging developing countries, in particular China, India, and Brazil. In every UN Security Council debate on the topic, they have formed one block opposing the securitising moves. China (together with Russia) even blocked the initiative to have a third formal debate on the climate–security nexus. The macro-level analysis furthermore showed that many of their statements in the UN Security Council debates reflect their positions in the UNFCCC. This suggests that the emerging developing countries were well aware of the strategic intent driving securitising moves on climate migration, seeking to pressurise them to take more action in the UNFCCC. Therefore, these countries actively raised the argument in the UN Security Council debates that industrialised countries are historically responsible for climate change and thus primarily responsible to take action.

The micro-level analysis of India provided more insight into that finding. The FCO's securitising move made the topic of climate migration a political and sensitive issue within the Government of India. As the FCO's arguments on climate migration appeared unbelievable and overdramatic, it fuelled a perception among the Government of India that the FCO was just using these arguments for its own gain and to push India to accept the UK's agenda on climate change. As a result, the Government of India associates notions of climate migration, climate conflict, and even to some degree climate change, with negotiation strategies of the West. The lesson from this case, then, is that alarmist security language tends to politicise climate change and climate migration in a counterproductive manner, as it hinders possibilities for constructive dialogue and collaboration. Interestingly, this confirms some of the Copenhagen School's assumptions, that confrontational and exceptional security language fuels a political environment marked by competition and mistrust.

A question should be raised why insights of the Copenhagen School find a particularly good fit in the Indian context. India is a society that values principles of sovereignty and self-determination (Humphrey and Messner 2006; Vihma 2010; Wagner 2013), and reacts particularly defensively to Western countries trying to impose measures on India or to lecture India on its policy making. In that context, there is a greater likelihood for the FCO's security arguments relying on the Copenhagen School's definition of security (in terms of great danger, exceptionality, otherness) to trigger a defensive and confrontational reaction by the Government of India. The FCO's language on conflict and mass migration by itself has the potential to trigger negative ideas of confrontation, as the Copenhagen School suggests. But this is reinforced and made more likely in the Indian socio-political context (marked by notions of self-determination and scepticism towards Western interference) in which such language is received.

In case of India, it is likely to be more effective if the FCO pursues a narrative which is clear and honest about its economic interests driving its objective to promote climate action and about the economic opportunities the UK hopes to gain from investments in low-carbon technologies. As argued by Samir Saran, Vice President of the Delhi-based Observer Research Foundation: 'If you want policy to be changed you have to tell people, this is the challenge and this is the policy response for it and it has to be believable'.[60] Instead, the framing of climate change (including climate migration) as a matter of great international security is perceived as an attempt by the UK to scare India, to put the blame on India and to delay action on climate change.

Moreover, the review of India's immigration policy showed that there is no simple relation between the securitisation of climate migration and border security policy. Context matters when it comes to understanding the direction in which a securitisation process moves. The Indian government does not yet consider climate migration from Bangladesh to be a threat, nor an issue the security establishment should concern itself with. Instead, India is focussed on other challenges it considers more pressing, and largely perceives the issue of climate migration as a vague and Western construct.

To end, this chapter raises many doubts regarding the effectiveness of securitising moves on climate migration, especially in relation to its objective to promote greater agreement and action on climate change. I will reflect on this question in chapter 6, discussing the outcome of the securitisation process.

Notes

1. Similar to chapter 4, this analysis is based on the discourse network analyser, developed by Leifeld (2013), and the figures are produced by through NetDraw (Borgatti 2002).
2. Telephone interview, FCO Official, 17 November 2011; Interview, UK Government Official, 6 October 2011; Interview, Official of the British High Commission in Delhi, 19 August 2011, Delhi; Interview, FCO Official, the FCO's Climate Change and Energy Department, 23 January 2012.
3. I used some abbreviations to make the figures better readable. I used some abbreviations to make the figures better readable. CC stands for climate change. CM stands for climate migration. Sust. dev. for sustainable development. CBDR for common but differentiated responsibilities. PNG stands for Papua New Guinea, NL for the Netherlands. US for the United States. UK for the United Kingdom. SIDS for Small Island Developing States. NAM for Non-Aligned Movement. G77 for the Group of 77 plus China. CARICOM stands for the Caribbean Community including the Caribbean Common Market. UNSC for the UN Security Council. UNFCCC for the United Nations Framework Convention on Climate Change.
4. Figure 5.3 excludes Bangladesh, because of its weak relation with the opposing coalition. Bangladesh only connected to one of the selected core statements of the opposing coalition (the statement that climate change is a matter of sustainable development).
5. India mainly argued there was no evidence linking climate change and security. Brazil took a more in-between position by arguing that one should be cautious in connecting climate change and security and highlighted that the links are more indirect and highly complex (but it did not say there was no evidence). Russia argued that we should not overdramatise the issue, but did not give specific reasons for that.
6. The statement that 'climate change poses a threat to the SIDS' was only highlighted for those states sceptical of the security framing of climate change, as this was an interesting contradiction in their argument. It was thus not analysed for those states agreeing that climate change is a security issue.
7. This figure is based on the second step of the discourse network analysis I conducted for the UN Security Council debates. As discussed in detail in chapter 4, this

second step zooms in on the core coalition and examines more detailed statements. In the debate of 2007, the core opposing coalition consists of those states that share at least three statements: India, China, Brazil, South Africa, Sudan on behalf of the African Group, Egypt, and Pakistan on behalf of the G77 group.

8. Interview, Official of the British High Commission in Delhi, 19 August 2011, Delhi; and based on interviews held with the FCO's Global Strategic Impacts Team. It was however noted by some interviewees (in the FCO and by the UK's Development, Concepts, and Doctrine Centre) that it was not always possible or easy to get access to the Indian MOD when discussing this topic.

9. Natarajan became the new Environment Minister, when Ramesh became Minister of Rural Development. Her term ended the end of December 2013. Prakash Javadekar is the new Environment Minister.

10. According to Vihma (2011: 78), this notion of differentiated responsibility is in India interpreted as one arguing that Annex I countries (industrialised countries) and non-Annex I countries (developing countries, including India) hold different responsibilities under the convention, meaning that only Annex I countries are required to have binding mitigation targets.

11. In the course of the 2000s, India has taken a more flexible and open stand towards bilateral relations with Western partners. In that light, India's new Prime Minister Modi has in September 2014 visited the US, which may be seen as an attempt to strengthen India–US relations (Sengupta 2014).

12. Documents representing India's views, and interviewees themselves, often refer to the 'West' or to 'industrialised countries' as one actor in the context of climate change negotiations. For that reason, the analysis will frequently use similar terminology to reflect India's perception of, and reaction to, a securitising move on climate migration as promoted by the FCO.

13. Interview, Samir Saran, Senior Fellow and Vice President, Observer Research Foundation, 13 August 2011, Delhi.

14. Interview, Official of the British High Commission in Delhi, 19 August 2011, Delhi.

15. Interview, Kirit Parikh, Member of the Indian Planning Commission until 2009, 20 August 2011, Delhi.

16. Interview, R. R. Rasmi, Joint Secretary on Climate Change, Ministry of Environment and Forests, 19 Augustus 2011, Delhi.

17. This quote is not based on an interview, but was a reply of one of the officers (anonymous) in the Indian MOD in my attempt to arrange for an interview with the Indian MOD. It is not fully clear who this officer was. But since this quote is quite telling, I include it to illustrate thinking in the Government of India. Telephone conversation, 8 July 2011.

18. Interview, R. R. Rasmi, Joint Secretary on Climate Change, Ministry of Environment and Forests, 19 Augustus 2011, Delhi.

19. Interview, Official of the British High Commission in Delhi, 19 August 2011, Delhi. See chapter 6 for more details.

20. This argument builds on my analysis in Boas (2014).

21. Interview, Navroz Dubash, senior researcher at the Centre of Policy Research in Delhi, 23 August 2011, Delhi; see also Gupta and Dutta (2009: 36), and the interview with Samir Saran, Senior Fellow and Vice President, Observer Research Foundation, 13 August 2011, Delhi. The interview with Navroz Dubash has been very central in the development of my argument in this section.

22. Interview, Vijai Sharma, the Secretary of the Ministry of Environment and Forests from 30 June 2008 until 31 December 2010 and in this period part of India's delegation to the UNFCCC, 12 August 2011, Delhi.

23. Such statements in the UN Security Council debates could, arguably, be interpreted as a sign that India tried to desecuritise climate migration. However, except for

these statements, India has not actively been trying to reframe climate migration away from security. India was not driven by a belief or an interest to actively present climate migration in other terms. Instead, as will be clarified in this section, India's reaction was driven by scepticism regarding the UK's agenda on climate change. This scepticism resulted in a tense negotiation environment and represents a situation of backfire.

24. This analysis is also based on an interview with Navroz Dubash, senior researcher at the Centre of Policy Research in Delhi, 23 August 2011, Delhi; and the interview with Samir Saran, Senior Fellow and Vice President, Observer Research Foundation, 13 August 2011, Delhi.

25. Interview, Shyam Saran, Indian Foreign Secretary from 2005–2006, the Indian Prime Minister's Special Envoy on Climate Change from 2007 until March 2010, and in this period India's chief climate change negotiator, 16 August 2011, Delhi.

26. Interview, Shyam Saran, Foreign Secretary from 2005–2006, the Indian Prime Minister's Special Envoy on Climate Change from 2007 until March 2010, and in this period India's chief climate change negotiator, 16 August 2011, Delhi; Interview, Vijai Sharma, the Secretary of the Ministry of Environment and Forests from 30 June 2008 until 31 December 2010 and in this period part of India's delegation to the UNFCCC, 12 August 2011, Delhi; See also interview with Samir Saran, Senior Fellow and Vice President, Observer Research Foundation, 13 August 2011, Delhi.

27. Interview, Samir Saran, Senior Fellow and Vice President, Observer Research Foundation, 13 August 2011, Delhi.

28. Interview, Vijai Sharma, the Secretary of the Ministry of Environment and Forests from 30 June 2008 until 31 December 2010 and in this period part of India's delegation to the UNFCCC, 12 August 2011, Delhi.

29. Interview, Shyam Saran, Foreign Secretary from 2005–2006, the Indian Prime Minister's Special Envoy on Climate Change from 2007 until March 2010, and in this period India's chief climate change negotiator, 16 August 2011, Delhi; this point of analysis is also based on a telephone interview, with Praful Bidwai, journalist and activist, 28 September 2011.

30. Interview, Shyam Saran, Foreign Secretary from 2005–2006, the Indian Prime Minister's Special Envoy on Climate Change from 2007 until March 2010, and in this period India's chief climate change negotiator, 16 August 2011, Delhi.

31. The EU argued in favour of an eight-year commitment, while developing countries (unsuccessfully) insisted on a five-year commitment. The developing countries fear that an eight-year commitment allows industrialised countries to delay mitigation action (Murray 2012).

32. The examined reports are: Ministry of Agriculture 2010; ; Ministry of Environment and Forest 2010a; Ministry of New and Renewable Energy 2010; Ministry of Power 2008; Ministry of Science & Technology 2010a; 2010bMinistry of Urban Development 2010; Ministry of Water Resources 2011.

33. The water mission does actively try to enhance public involvement in water management projects (e.g., through local participative projects with farmers). But the relationship with water scarcity and development is not actively considered.

34. But also these missions are criticised for not taking the needs of the poor sufficiently into account (Byravan and Rajan 2012). For instance, the National Mission on Sustainable Habitat particularly discusses solutions in the realm of energy efficiency, waste water management, urban transport, drinking supply systems, etc., without providing clear proposals that aim to ensure economic and social development of the poor. But, as compared to the other missions, they do more actively discuss matters of human development. This suggests a greater sense of awareness of the linkages between climate change and development.

35. The National Mission for Sustainable Agriculture does once refer to the notion of climate refugees (Ministry of Agriculture 2010: 5). But, it does not explicitly

connect this term to cross-border migration, but refers to the vulnerability of coastal and fishery communities.

36. Here human security is defined as: 'It means, first, safety from such chronic threats as hunger, disease and repression. And second, it means protection from sudden and hurtful disruptions in the patterns of daily life—whether in homes, in jobs or in communities. Such threats can exist at all levels of national income and development' (UNDP 1994: 23).

37. This study is produced by the Indian Network for Climate Change Assessment. This is a network-based programme of the Ministry of Environment and Forests, which consists of over 120 institutions and over 250 scientists country wide. The MOEF, among which its principle scientific advisor, is also one of the authors.

38. Interview, Dr. Subosh Sharma, Principal Scientific Advisor on Climate Change, Ministry of Environment and Forests, 19 August 2011, Delhi.

39. Interview, Dr. Subosh Sharma, Principal Scientific Advisor on Climate Change, Ministry of Environment and Forests, 19 August 2011, Delhi.

40. Interview, Dr. Subosh Sharma, Principal Scientific Advisor on Climate Change, Ministry of Environment and Forests, 19 August 2011, Delhi.

41. This analysis is based on interviews conducted in the Ministry of Environment and Forests held in 2011.

42. The UK's Department for International Development (DFID) has tried to connect the Indian discourse about rural–urban migration to climate change. It funded sterilisation of the Indian rural poor, which was often forced and conducted under inhumane circumstances (Chamberlain 2012; Reid 2014). DFID 'cited the need to fight climate change as one of the key reasons of pressing ahead with such programmes' (Chamberlain 2012; see also Reid 2014). While India is performing such sterilisation acts, it does not appear to have actively adopted a discourse of internal *climate* migration to justify it. In India, development/overpopulation storylines predominantly characterise discourses on internal displacement and sterilisation (Overdorf 2010).

43. Interview, Navroz Dubash, senior researcher at the Centre of Policy Research in Delhi, 23 August 2011, Delhi.

44. Interview, Official of the British High Commission in Delhi, 19 August 2011, Delhi.

45. For other examples, see Campbell et al. 2007: 57; CNA 2007; German Advisory Council on Global Change 2007.

46. However, according to Oberai (2006: 65), the perception of partition refugees from East Pakistan was more negative compared to the perception of refugees from West Pakistan. The refugee stream from East Pakistan (Bengali refugees) was a much longer process that was difficult to put to a full stop, compared to the more short-term refugee crisis in Punjab. This situation led to greater demographic pressures, difficult rehabilitation strategies and worsening relations between India and Pakistan.

47. According to Van Schendel (2005: 195), it was the year of 1962 that the infiltration narrative first appeared in official discourse. Nonetheless, in the provinces of Assam and Tripura, anti-immigrant discourses towards the Bengali population were already active among the community even before the partition (Van Schendel 2005: 194–195).

48. Even though the Muslims immigrants were often targeted by this narrative, Hindus migrating from Bangladesh were also increasingly seen as infiltrators, taking over jobs, land, etc. (Van Schendel 2005: 194–195).

49. Telephone interview, Anurag Danda, Head—Sundarbans Programme & Climate Adaptation, WWF India, 11 July 2011; see also Van Schendel 2005: 216–217.

50. This section builds on, and further elaborates my analysis in Boas (2014).

51. Interview, Senior Official, Government of India, 23 August 2011, Delhi. Interview, Madhukar Gupta, Secretary of the Ministry of Home Affairs from 2007–2009, 14

August 2011, Delhi; Telephone interview, Deb Mukharji, Indian Ambassador to Bangladesh from 1995–2000, 19 September 2011.

52. Some interviewees would argue that some immigration is related to terrorism in the sense that militant groups may attempt to cross the border. But, others, such as Madhukar Gupta (interview, 14 August 2011, Delhi), the former Home Secretary, emphasise that the number of terrorists illegally crossing the border, while being a very serious issue, 'would be miniscule in terms of the absolute number of illegal immigrants'.

53. White (2011: 71) argues in the context of Bangladeshi immigration that 'Indian officials [are] increasingly inclined to cite climate refugees, rather than the Islamist threat, as a concern'. In order to provide evidence for this statement he cites a report by Friedman (2009b), a journalist of the US. Friedman indeed makes such an argument. However, in her article she provides no evidence that actual Indian government officials see climate migration from Bangladesh as a threat.

54. Interview, Military Officer, 15 August 2011, Delhi; Interview, Chris Evett, Futures Team, the UK's Development, Concepts and Doctrine Centre, MOD, 9 November 2011, London; Telephone interview, researcher with the Institute for Defence Studies and Analyses, 7 December 2011; Interview, R.R. Rasmi, Joint Secretary on Climate Change, MOEF, 19 Augustus 2011.

55. Interview, anonymous, London, 2 November 2011, London; see also The Economist (2011) on the sensitivity of water in South Asia.

56. Interview, Chris Evett, Editor, Global Strategic Trends Programme, Futures Team, the UK's Development, Concepts and Doctrine Centre, MOD, 9 November 2011.

57. This indicates that the climate security discourse may become intersected with India's security discourse water (river) sharing with neighbouring countries. This Indian water discourse has, however, not yet actively been connected to the issue of climate change in Indian society, but is largely seen as a problem that has been there for decades.

58. Interview, Senior Official, 18 Augustus 2011, Delhi.

59. To account for the lack of interest in the issue of climate migration by the Indian security community, some colleagues have suggested that the Government of India may fear that an acknowledgement of the climate refugee problem would force India to sign up to binding mitigation targets under the UNFCCC. I however do not expect this to be the reason. Considering India's highly demarcated governmental structure, it is unlikely that the Indian security community would decide not concern itself with climate migration for such a reason.

60. Interview, Samir Saran, Senior Fellow and Vice President, Observer Research Foundation, 13 August 2011, Delhi.

References

Antony, A.K. (2012) *Presidential address at the 14th Asian security conference*. Speech at Institute for Defence Studies and Analyses, New Delhi, 13 February. Available at: http://idsa.in/keyspeeches/DefenceMinisterAKAntony_14ASC (last visit 19 September 2014).

Ashton, J. (2011) *Only diplomacy: hard-headed soft power for a time of risk, scarcity and insecurity*. Speech at Chatham House, London, 21 February 2011. Available at: www.chathamhouse.org/publications/papers/view/109591 (last visit 19 September 2014).

Bdnews24 (Bangladesh News 24) (2014) 'Modi for "good relations" Dhaka', *BDNews24*, 3 May. Available at: http://bdnews24.com/world/2014/05/03/modi-for-good-relations-with-dhaka (last visit 19 September 2014).

Beckett, M. (2006) *Beckett: Berlin speech on climate change and security.* Speech at British Embassy, Berlin, 24 October. Available at: http://ukingermany.fco.gov.uk/en/newsroom/?view=Speech&id=4616005 (last visit 22 March 2013). This speech is no longer available online.

Black, R. (2011) 'Climate talks end with late deal', *BBC*, 11 December. Available at: www.bbc.co.uk/news/science-environment-16124670 (last visit 19 September 2014).

Boas, I. (2012) 'Climate change migration (India)'. In: R. Anderson (gen. ed.), *The encyclopaedia of sustainability: China, India, and East and Southeast Asia: assessing sustainability*, Volume 7. Great Barrington: Berkshire Publishing: 61–6.

Boas, I. (2014) 'Where is the South in security discourse on climate change', *Critical Studies on Security*, 2(2): 148–161.

Borgatti, S. P. (2002) *NetDraw software for network visualization.* Lexington, KY: Analytic Technologies.

Byravan, S. and S .C. Rajan (2012) *An evaluation of India's national action plan on climate change.* Available at: www.preventionweb.net/english/professional/publications/v.php?id=28135 (last visit 19 September 2014).

Campbell, K. M., J. Guiledge, J. R. McNeill, J. Podesta, P. Ogden, I. Fuerth, R. J. Woolsey, T. J. Lennon, J. Smith, R. Weitz, and D. Mix (2007) *The age of consequences: the foreign policy and national security implications of global climate change.* Washington, DC: Center for New American Security and Center for Strategic & International Studies.

Carrington, D. (2010) 'WikiLeaks cables reveal how US manipulated climate accord', *The Guardian*, 3 December. Available at: www.guardian.co.uk/environment/2010/dec/03/wikileaks-us-manipulated-climate-accord (last visit 19 September 2014).

Chamberlain, G. (2012) 'UK aid helps to fund forced sterilisation of India's poor', *The Guardian*, 15 April. Available at: www.theguardian.com/world/2012/apr/15/uk-aid-forced-sterilisation-india (last visit 1 October 2014).

Chaudhuri, P. P. (2012) '4-word principle India's big green victory at Rio', *Hindustan Times*, 21 June. Available at: www.hindustantimes.com/world-news/Americas/4-word-principle-India-s-big-green-victory-at-Rio/Article1-876692.aspx (last visit 19 September 2014).

Cohen, S. (2000) 'India rising', *The Wilson Quarterly*, 24(3): 32–53.

CNA, Military Advisory Board (2007) *National security and the threat of climate change.* Arlington, VA: The CNA Corporation.

Daily News (2012) 'Fence entire Bangladesh border, opposition says', *Daily News*, 8 August. Available at: http://india.nydailynews.com/newsarticle/5022937fc3d4ca7f43000000/fence-entire-bangladesh-border-opposition-says (last visit 3 July 2013).

Daily Star (2010) 'Adopt strategy for food security', *Daily Star*, 22 September. Available at: http://archive.thedailystar.net/newDesign/news-details.php?nid=155466 (last visit 19 September 2014).

Das, S. K. (2011) '"Wrestling with my shadow": the State and the immigrant Muslims in contemporary West Bengal'. In: A. Dasgupta, M. Togawa and A. Barkat (eds.), *Minorities and the state. Changing social and political landscape of Bengal.* New Delhi: Sage: 39–65.

Dasgupta, C. (2008) 'Shifts on climate change—rich countries would like poorer countries to cut emissions', *The Telegraph*, 1 September. Available at: www.telegraphindia.com/1080901/jsp/opinion/story_9755499.jsp (last visit 19 September 2014).

Dastidar, A. G. (2012) 'Cabinet to clear India's tough stand at Doha climate meet', *The Indian Express*, 22 November. Available at: www.indianexpress.com/news/

cabinet-to-clear-india-s-tough-stand-at-doha-climate-meet/1034396/1 (last visit 19 September 2014).

Dubash, N. (2010) 'Copenhagen: climate of mistrust', *Economic & Political Weekly*, 44(52): 8–11.

Dubash, N. (2012a) 'Looking beyond Durban: where to go from here?', *Economic & Political Weekly*, 47(3): 13–17.

Dubash, N. (2012b) 'Climate politics in India: three narratives'. In: N. Dubash (ed.), *Handbook of climate change and India. Development, politics and governance*. New Delhi: Oxford University Press: 197–207.

European Commission (2011) *Common statement by the European Union, Least Developed Countries and the alliance of Small Island States*. Available at: http://ec.europa.eu/commission_2010–2014/hedegaard/headlines/news/2011–12–09_01_en.htm (last visit 19 September 2014).

Friedman L. (2009a) 'A global "national security" issue lurks at Bangladesh border', *The New York Times*, 23 March. Available at: www.nytimes.com/cwire/2009/03/23/23 climatewire-a-global-national-security-issue-lurks-at-ba-10247.html?pagewanted= all (last visit 19 September 2014).

Friedman, L. (2009b) 'How will climate refugees impact national security?', *Scientific American*, 23 March. Available at: www.scientificamerican.com/article.cfm?id=climage-refugees-national-security&page=3 (last visit 19 September 2014).

Foreign and Commonwealth Office (FCO) (2007) *Departmental report. 1 April 2006–31 March 2007*. London: FCO/Crown Copyright.

Foreign and Commonwealth Office (FCO) (2009) *Robin Gwynn: tenacity and a sense of responsibility to power climate change objectives*. Available at the UK web archive: http://webarchive.nationalarchives.gov.uk/20130217073211/http://ukinbangladesh.fco.gov.uk/en/about-us/working-with-bangladesh/climate-change/global-discussion/uk-climate-security-envoy (last visit 19 September 2014).

Gautam, P. K. (2009) 'Climate change and migration'. In: Institute for Defence Studies and Analyses Working Group Report, *Security implications of climate change for India*. New Delhi: Academic Foundation in association with the Institute for Defence Studies and Analyses: 93–103.

German Advisory Council on Global Change (2007) *World in transition: climate change as a security risk*. Berlin: German Advisory Council on Global Change.

Gosh, P. (2012) 'Climate change debate: the rationale of India's position'. In: N. Dubash (ed.), *Handbook of climate change and India. Development, politics and governance*. New Delhi: Oxford University Press: 157–169.

Gosh, P. and C. Dasgupta (2011) 'Smoke 'n mirrors', *The Financial Express*, 14 December. Available at: www.financialexpress.com/news/smoke-n-mirrors/887407 (last visit 19 September 2014).

Government of India (2011) *The constitution of India*. Available at: http://lawmin.nic.in/olwing/coi/coi-english/coi-indexenglish.htm (last visit 19 September 2014).

Gupta, A. and S. Dutta (2009) 'Climate change and security: exploring the link'. In: Institute for Defence Studies and Analyses Working Group Report, *Security implications of climate change for India*. New Delhi: Academic Foundation in association with the Institute for Defence Studies and Analyses: 93–103.

Hartmann, B. (2010) 'Policy arena. Rethinking climate refugees and climate conflict: rhetoric, reality and the process of policy discourse', *Journal of International Development*, 22(2): 233–246.

Human Rights Watch (2010) *"Trigger happy". Excessive use of force by Indian troops at the Bangladesh border*. New York: Human Rights Watch.

Humphrey, J. and D. Messner (2006) 'China and India as emerging global governance actors: challenges for developing and developed countries', *IDS Bulletin*, 36(1): 107–114.

International Energy Agency (IEA) (2011) *CO₂ emissions from fuel combustion. Highlights*. IEA Statistics. OECD/IEA: Paris.

Keeler, C. (2011) 'The end of the Responsibility to Protect?', *The Foreign Policy Journal*, 12 October. Available at: www.foreignpolicyjournal.com/2011/10/12/the-end-of-the-responsibility-to-protect/ (last visit 15 October 2014).

King, E. (2012a) 'EU alliance with small island states vital to success of Doha talks— UK Minister', *Responding to Climate Change (RTCC)*, 4 December. www.rtcc.org/eu-alliance-with-small-island-states-vital-to-success-of-doha-talks-uk-minister/ (last visit 21 September 2014).

King, E. (2012b) 'Hardline Nauru stance risks stalling Doha climate talks', *Responding to Climate Change (RTCC)*, 3 December. Available at: www.rtcc.org/hardline-nauru-stance-risks-stalling-doha-climate-talks/ (last visit 21 September 2014).

King, E. (2013a) 'China and Russia block UN Security Council climate change action', *Responding to Climate Change (RTCC)*, 19 February. Available at: www.rtcc.org/2013/02/18/china-and-russia-block-un-security-council-climate-change-action/ (last visit 30 September 2014).

King, E. (2013b) 'New UN deal could split developing nations: negotiator', *Responding to Climate Change (RTCC)*, 13 June. Available at: www.rtcc.org/2013/06/01/new-un-deal-could-split-developing-nations-negotiator/ (last visit 1 October 2014).

Krause-Jackson, F. (2013) 'Climate change's links to conflict draws UN attention', *Bloomberg*, 15 February. Available at: www.bloomberg.com/news/2013–02–15/climate-change-s-links-to-conflict-draws-un-attention.html (last visit 30 September 2014).

Kumar, M. Group Captain (2011) *Environment change and national security*. New Delhi: Kalpana Shukla Publishers.

Kurtz, G. (2012) 'Securitization of climate change in the United Nations 2007–2010'. In: J. Scheffran, M. Brozska, H. G. Brauch, P. M. Link, and J. Scheilling (eds.), *Climate change, human security and violent conflict*. Hexagon Series on Human and Environmental Security and Peace, Volume 8. Berlin Heidelberg: Springer-Verlag: 669–684.

Leifeld. P. (2013) *Discourse network analyzer*. Available at: https://github.com/leifeld/dna/releases (last visit 27 September 2014).

Lenin, J. (2014) *The UN climate summit reveals India's hypocrisy on saving forests*. Blog hosted by *The Guardian*, 26 September. Available at: www.theguardian.com/environment/india-untamed/2014/sep/26/un-climate-summit-india-hypocrisy-saving-forests (last visit 1 October 2014).

McAdam, J. and B. Saul (2010) *Displacement with dignity: international law and policy responses to climate change migration and security in Bangladesh*. Legal Studies Research Paper, n°10/113. Sydney: Sydney Law School.

McGrath, M. (2014) 'China's per capita carbon emissions overtake EU's', *BBC*, 21 September. Available at: www.bbc.com/news/science-environment-29239194 (last visit 1 October 2014).

Michaelowa, K. and A. Michaelowa (2012) 'India as an emerging power in international climate negotiations', *Climate Policy*, 12(5): 575–590.

Miliband, D. (2009) *David Miliband warns of global threats from climate change*. Speech shown by ITN News. Available at: www.youtube.com/watch?v=dct_ePtqP5k (last visit 22 September 2014).

Ministry of Agriculture (2010) *National mission for sustainable agriculture. Strategies for meeting the challenges of climate change.* Draft, August 2010. Delhi: Government of India.

Ministry of Environment and Forests (MOEF) (2010a) *National mission for a green India.* Draft, 24 May 2010. Delhi: Government of India.

Ministry of Environment and Forests (MOEF) (2010b) *Climate change and India: a 4x4 assessment.* Delhi: MOEF, Government of India.

Ministry of Environment and Forests (MOEF) (2013) *About the ministry. Information setting out the Ministry's key objectives.* Available at: http://envfor.nic.in/about-ministry/about-ministry (last visit 22 September 2014).

Ministry of Environment and Forests (MOEF) (2014) *Climate change division.* Available at: http://moef.nic.in/division/climate_change (last visit 22 September 2014).

Ministry of New and Renewable Energy (2010) *Jawaharlal Nehru national solar mission.* Delhi: Government of India.

Ministry of Power (2008) *National mission for enhanced energy efficiency.* Draft, December 2008. Delhi: Government of India.

Ministry of Science and Technology (2010a) *National mission on strategic knowledge for climate change: under national action plan on climate change.* Delhi: Government of India.

Ministry of Science and Technology (2010b) *National mission for sustaining the Himalayan ecosystem: under national action plan on climate change.* Draft, June 2010. Delhi: Government of India.

Ministry of Urban Development (2010) *National mission on sustainable habitat.* Delhi: Government of India.

Ministry of Water Resources (2011) *National water mission under national action plan on climate change.* Delhi: Government of India.

Muenchow-Pohl, von B. (2012) *India and Europe in a multipolar world.* Washington, DC: Carnegie Endowment for International Peace.

Murray, J. (2012) 'Bonn climate talks: EU plays down talk of Kyoto Protocol rift', *The Guardian*, 16 May. Available at: www.guardian.co.uk/environment/2012/may/16/bonn-climate-talks-eu-kyoto (last visit 22 September 2014).

Narlikar, A. (2006) 'Peculiar chauvinism or strategic calculation? Explaining the negotiating strategy of a rising India', *International Affairs*, 82(1): 59–76.

Narlikar, A. (2011) 'Is India a responsible great power?', *Third World Quarterly*, 32(9): 1607–1621.

Oberoi, P. (2006) *Exile and belonging. Refugees and state policy in South Asia.* Oxford: Oxford University Press.

Overdorf, J. (2010) 'India population: is sterilization the answer?', *Global Post*, 14 July 2010. Available at: www.globalpost.com/dispatch/india/100713/population-growth-sterilization-millennium-development-goals (last visit 15 October 2014).

Pande, V. (2011) 'India at Cancun: the emergence of a confident dealmaker', *Economic & Political Weekly*, 46(4): 14–15.

PBL Netherlands Environmental Assessment Agency (2012) *Trends in global CO_2 emissions. 2012 report.* The Hague: PBL.

PBL Netherlands Environmental Assessment Agency (2013) *Trends in Global CO_2 Emissions. 2013 report.* The Hague: PBL.

Prime Minister (PM)'s Council on Climate Change (2008) *National action plan on climate change.* New Delhi: Government of India.

Prime Minister (PM)'s Strategy Unit (2005) *Investing in prevention. An international strategy to manage risks of instability and improve crisis response*. London: Crown Copyright/PM's Strategy Unit.

Puniyani, R. (2012) 'Assam riots: real issue is development', *Tehelka*, 31 July. Available at: www.tehelka.com/story_main53.asp?filename=Fw310712Assam.asp (last visit 23 September 2014).

Qi, X. (2011) 'The rise of BASIC in UN climate change negotiations', *South African Journal of International Affairs*, 18(3): 295–318.

Rajamani, L. (2009) 'India and climate change: what India wants, needs, and needs to do', *Indian Review*, 8(3): 340–374.

Rajan, S. C. (2008) *Blue alert. Climate migrants in South Asia. Estimates and solutions*. Bangalore, India: Greenpeace.

Ramachandran, S. (2005) *Indifference, impotence and intolerance: transnational Bangladeshis in India*. Global Migration Perspectives, n°42. Geneva: Global Commission on International Migration.

Reid, J. (2014) 'Climate, migration, and sex: the biopolitics of climate-induced migration', *Critical Studies on Security*, 2(2): 196–209.

Roberts, Timmons (2011) 'Multipolarity and the new world (dis)order: US hegemonic decline and the fragmentation of the global climate regime', *Global Environmental Change*, 21(3): 776–784.

Sengupta, S. (2014) 'Narendra Modi outlines goals for India on Eve of a visit with Obama', *The New York Times*, 28 September 2014. Available at: www.nytimes.com/2014/09/29/world/asia/narendra-modi-madison-square-garden-obama.html?_r=0 (last visit 15 October 2014).

Sethi, N. (2012) 'Doha climate talks: India not to enhance its pledge of reducing emissions', *The Times of India*, 4 December. Available at: http://articles.timesofindia.indiatimes.com/2012-12-04/global-warming/35594241_1_doha-climate-talks-funds-and-technologies-doha-round (last visit 23 September 2014).

Smith, K. (2012) 'India's identity and its global aspirations', *Global Society*, 26(3); 369–385.

Stripple, J. (2002) 'Climate change as a security issue'. In: E.A. Page and M. Redclift (eds.), *Human security and the environment. International comparisons*. Cheltenham: Edward Elgar: 105–127.

The Economic Times (2010) 'It's a sell out; cry BJP, Left on India's stand at Cancun', *The Economic Times*, 10 December. Available at: http://articles.economictimes.indiatimes.com/2010-12-10/news/27624379_1_binding-commitments-upa-government-india (last visit 23 September 2014).

The Economic Times (2014) 'India to act on climate change on its own volition: Prakash Javadekar', *The Economic Times*, 24 September. Available at: http://articles.economictimes.indiatimes.com/2014-09-24/news/54279570_1_intended-nationally-determined-contributions-green-climate-fund-prime-minister-narendra-modi (last visit 1 October 2014).

The Economist (2011) 'Unquenchable thirst. A growing rivalry between India, Pakistan and China over the region's great rivers may be threatening South Asia's peace', *The Economist*, 19 November. Available at: www.economist.com/node/21538687?zid=306&ah=1b164dbd43b0cb27ba0d4c3b12a5e227 (last visit 23 September 2014).

The Guardian (2010) 'US embassy cables: EU raises 'creative accounting' with US over climate aid', *The Guardian*, 3 December. Available at: www.guardian.co.uk/world/us-embassy-cables-documents/249185 (last visit 19 September 2014).

The Hindu (2011) 'India not a deal breaker on climate talks: EU', *The Hindu*, 5 December. Available at: www.thehindu.com/news/national/article2689256.ece (last visit 23 September 2014).

The Indian Express (2012) 'Over 250 Bangladeshi immigrants arrested', *The Indian Express*, 7 December. www.indianexpress.com/news/over-250-bangladeshi-immigrants-arrested/1041636 (last visit 23 September 2014).

The Times of India (2011) 'Patkar up in arms against new draft bill on land acquisition', *The Times of India*, 1 August. Available at: http://articles.timesofindia.indiatimes. com/2011–08–01/mumbai/29837705_1_land-acquisition-definition-of-public-purpose-medha-patkar (last visit 23 September 2014).

The Times of India (2012) 'Assam riots: BJP blames Bangladeshi immigrants for violence', *The Times of India*, 28 July. Available at: http://articles.timesofindia.indiatimes. com/2012–07–27/india/32887943_1_assam-violence-assam-riots-bank-politics (last visit 23 September 2014).

Third World Network (2011) *New round of climate talks launched at Durban*. Available at: www.twnside.org.sg/title2/gtrends/gtrends367.htm (last visit 23 September 2014).

Trombetta, M. J. (2014) 'Linking climate-induced migration and security in the EU: insights from the securitization debate', *Critical Studies on Security*, 2(2): 131–147.

United Nations Development Programme (UNDP) (1994) *Human development report 1994*. Oxford: Oxford University Press.

United Nations Framework Convention on Climate Change (UNFCCC) (2012) *Report of the Conference of the Parties on its seventeenth session, held in Durban from 28 November to 11 December 2011*. Available at: http://unfccc.int/resource/docs/2011/ cop17/eng/09a01.pdf (last visit 23 September 2014).

United Nations General Assembly (UNGA) (2009) *Climate change and its possible security implications*. 85th plenary meeting, New York, 3 June.

United Nations Security Council (UNSC) (2007a) *Letter dated 5 April 2007 from the permanent representative of the United Kingdom of Great Britain and Northern Ireland to the United Nations addressed to the president of the Security Council*. Meeting Records. S/PV.5663, 5663rd meeting (Part II), 17 April, New York.

United Nations Security Council (UNSC) (2007b) *Letter dated 5 April 2007 from the permanent representative of the United Kingdom of Great Britain and Northern Ireland to the United Nations addressed to the president of the Security Council*. Meeting records, S/PV.5663, 5663rd meeting (Part I), 17 April, New York.

United Nations Security Council (UNSC) (2011) *Maintenance of international peace and security. Impact of climate change*. Letter dated 1 July 2011 from the permanent representative of Germany to the United Nations addressed to the Secretary-General. Meeting records, S/2011/408, 6587th meeting (Part I), 20 July, New York.

Upadhyaya, P. (2006) 'Securitization matrix in South Asia: Bangladeshi migrants as enemy alien'. In: M. Caballero-Anthony, R. Emmers, and A. Acharya (eds.), *Non-traditional security in Asia. Dilemmas in securitization.* Hampshire: Ashgate Publishing: 13–19.

Van Schendel, W. (2005) *The Bengal borderland. Beyond state and nation in South Asia*. London: Anthem Press.

Venkatesan, J. (2012) 'Committed to deporting illegal migrants, but only lawfully: centre', *The Hindu*, 10 August 2012. Available at: www.thehindu.com/news/national/ article3747019.ece (last visit 24 September 2014).

Vidal, J. and F. Harvey (2011a) 'India dampens Europe's hopes of a new climate change agreement', *The Guardian*, 6 December. Available at: www.guardian.co.uk/environment/2011/dec/06/india-europe-climate-change-agreement (last visit 24 September 2014).

Vidal, J. and F. Harvey (2011b) 'Climate deal salvaged after marathon talks in Durban', *The Guardian*, 11 December. Available at: www.guardian.co.uk/environment/2011/dec/10/un-climate-change-summit-durban (last visit 24 September 2014).

Vidal, J. and F. Harvey (2011c) 'Durban climate deal struck after tense all-night session', *The Guardian*, 11 December. Available at: www.guardian.co.uk/environment/2011/dec/11/durban-climate-deal-struck (last visit 24 September 2014).

Vihma, A. (2010) *Elephant in the room? The new G77 and China dynamics in climate talks*. Briefing paper 6. Helsinki: The Finish Institute of International Affairs.

Vihma, A. (2011) 'India and the global climate governance: between principles and pragmatism', *The Journal of Environment and Development*, 20(1): 69–94.

Wagner, C. (2013) *The EU-India strategic partnership in the field of climate change and sustainable development*. Paper prepared for the Kick-Off Meeting of the EU-India Network on Multi-Level Climate Governance, 10–12 January, Delhi.

White, H. (2011) *Climate change and migration*. Oxford: Oxford University Press.

6 Stage Three

The Outcome of the Securitisation Process on Climate Migration

On the basis of chapter 5, an overall assessment can be made that the FCO's securitising move has not been accepted by the Government of India and failed to resonate in the Indian context. But this finding leaves many questions unaddressed. How did this process affect political relations between the securitiser and its audience in climate change negotiations? Who gained, who lost? How did it affect wider North–South relations in the climate change negotiations and state alliances? And, how did the FCO respond to India's rejection of its securitising move on climate migration; did the FCO change its diplomatic strategy?

To answer such questions, this chapter analyses the outcome of the traced securitisation process on climate migration, according to the framework for analysis as outlined in chapter 3. The first section will examine the wider political consequences in the context of climate change negotiations. The primary picture is that the FCO's securitising move weakened the UK's relations with India on climate change and made India more distrustful of the UK's climate change agenda. The securitisation process did enhance alliances with small island states and the Least Developed Countries, but it is doubtful whether this will help to convince India to commit to ambitious mitigation action under a binding framework. India (together with China) is, however at risk of losing its alliances with other emerging developing countries (in particular, South Africa). This could make India increasingly isolated in the debate. The second section asks in what manner the FCO has responded to the suboptimal outcome of its securitising move on climate migration in the Indian context, and thus whether interaction processes between the FCO and India have affected its diplomatic strategy on climate change. I discuss how the FCO gradually moved away from its alarmist narrative on climate migration and climate conflict. Since 2010, it increasingly relies on an economic prosperity narrative when promoting climate action.

In the analysis, I will give particular attention to India's and the UK's relative positions of power (see chapter 3 for a detailed definition). Has the UK or India been more powerful to determine how the issue of climate migration should be perceived and presented? And has India or the UK been more influential to determine how and by whom climate change should be governed to prevent dangerous levels of climate change? I examine to what extent India has been able to influence the FCO's securitising move and diplomatic strategy on climate change, and whether the UK and/or the Government of India has gained or lost in power in climate change negotiations and therefore in its ability to promote its envisaged approach to mitigation. This analysis focuses on the period of the 2000s until the end of September 2014, and on that basis spells out some trends for future climate change negotiations influenced by the securitisation process.

The Political Consequences for UK–India Relations in Climate Change Negotiations

In this section, I analyse the wider implications of the securitisation process for the UK's and India's position in international climate change negotiations and for their alliances. The main risk is that the FCO's securitising move negatively affects the UK's bargaining position on climate change. The FCO's securitising move provides India with an additional motivation to further increase ties with its like-minded allies in climate change negotiations that are equally sceptical of strict and binding mitigation targets. These allies are the emerging developing countries, organised in the BASIC alliance, consisting of Brazil, South Africa, India, and China (referred to as BASIC). In addition, India represents itself in the group of Like-Minded Developing Countries. This latter group contains several oil/coal-rich countries, such as China, Egypt, India, Iran, Iraq, Saudi Arabia, and Venezuela (Harvey 2013).[1] As discussed in chapter 5, India reacted defensively to the FCO's securitising move on climate migration, and felt attacked by the UK's and the European Union (EU)'s tactic to enhance divisions in the Southern negotiation block (called the G-77 group) through the usage of security narratives on climate change (including climate migration). The FCO's securitising move thus provides India with an additional stimulus to further enhance alliances with like-minded states to counteract strategies by the FCO and the EU in the context of the United Nations Convention on Climate Change (UNFCCC).

In the course of the 2000s, India has already strengthened relationships with other emerging powers in UNFCCC negotiations under the name of the BASIC alliance. Initially, the formation of this alliance was actively supported by the EU (Qi 2011: 301). After the United States (US)'s withdrawal from the Kyoto Protocol in 2001, the EU aimed to create a new multilateral climate change agenda in which the BASIC countries would be encouraged to proactively engage in the UNFCCC negotiations (Qi 2011: 301). To achieve this aim, the EU set up a project called the 'Basic Project'. It aimed to stimulate the BASIC countries to develop common priorities and interests on climate action (Yamin 2007; see discussion Qi 2011: 301–302). But, increasingly, the BASIC group formed an agenda not necessarily benefitting the EU's objectives on climate change (which includes the UK's position on climate change). For instance, the Joint Statement produced at the 13th BASIC Ministerial Meeting on Climate

Change, just prior to the 2012 UNFCCC conference at Doha, reiterated several times that industrialised countries should live up to mitigation pledges, and highlighted their historical responsibility for climate change and the importance of equity. Not once did it mention any type of binding mitigation targets to be adopted by BASIC countries. It commented that:

> The Durban Platform is by no means a process to negotiate a new regime, nor to renegotiate, rewrite or reinterpret the Convention and its principles and provisions. As agreed by all Parties, both the process and the outcome of the Durban Platform are under the Convention, governed by all its principles and provisions, in particular the principles of equity and common but differentiated responsibilities and respective capabilities.
>
> (BASIC 2012)

Moreover, at the Copenhagen UNFCCC conference of 2009, the BASIC countries even side-lined the EU in its leadership role, as the Copenhagen Accord was essentially struck in a last minute negotiation that only included the BASIC countries and the US (BBC 2009; Qi 2011; Michaelowa and Michaelowa 2012: 579).

This shows that EU (including the UK) has been losing in power in international climate change negotiations. It has thus far not been able to convince powerful states to sign up to binding mitigation targets. This relates to the EU's weakening negotiation power more generally in a changing world order where the EU is faced with economic challenges, while large developing countries are on the rise. As argued by Falkner et al. (2010: 275):

> Structural shifts in the international political economy have, if anything, complicated the search for a global deal by strengthening the veto power of certain laggard countries. Whereas during the 1990s the gap between European and American climate policy defined the main fault line in climate politics, more recently the divisions between developed and emerging economies have moved centre stage. This shift manifests itself in climate politics in two principal ways: in the growing share of emerging economies in worldwide emissions; and in the demands that these countries are making for enhanced representation and influence within the established framework of international cooperation.

That geopolitical context has made it easier for (emerging) big powers such as China, India and the US to reject binding and strict obligations under the UNFCCC. It stimulated China and the US to pursue bilateral negotiations on climate change, thereby avoiding binding commitments (Falkner et al. 2010: 257). As another refection of such developments, China and India rejected the term 'commitments' on greenhouse gas (GHG) emission reduction during the Warsaw climate change negotiations of 2013, which was subsequently replaced by 'contributions' (Morales and Krukowska 2013; Morales and

Nicola 2013). The term contributions is intentionally vague to allow for non-binding targets in a new climate agreement aimed to be adopted in 2015. This shows how the major emerging developing countries, China and India, steer away from the EU's and UK's agenda on climate change pushing for binding targets for all state parties.

The described political environment has also made it difficult for the FCO's securitising move to have a profound effect on India's position in the UNFCCC. In the wider geopolitical context, the UK is not in a position to put real pressure on India by other political means (such as through trade restrictions), as this may harm the UK's economic interests that are considered more important than climate change. In such a political environment, the FCO's security narrative on climate migration has to come across as very persuasive and convincing to have any substantive effect.

But the BASIC alliance has been showing some cracks. Together with a range of developing countries, South Africa and Brazil have in recent years become more receptive to the idea of adopting binding mitigation targets (Qi 2011), and so are gradually moving in the EU's and UK's direction. This tension in the BASIC alliance was particular visible during the 2010 climate change negotiations in Cancun, where Brazil and South Africa indicated to support the idea to have binding commitments while this was rejected by India and China (Qi 2011). As argued by the then Indian Environment Minister Jairam Ramesh: 'There are differences within BASIC. India and China are united on this issue. Brazil and South Africa are united' (Ramesh quoted in NDTV 2010 Correspondent). He furthermore stated:

> There is a concerted move by a group of developed countries using developing countries to put pressure on India and China and within BASIC, since South Africa and Brazil are supportive of a legally binding agreement . . .
>
> (Ramesh quoted in NDTV Correspondent 2010)

Moreover, as the analysis in chapters 4 and 5 has shown, South Africa was supportive of securitising moves on climate change and migration performed in the UN Security Council debate of 2011. These developments can empower the UK's position in the negotiations. This could further isolate China and India, and may put them under increasing pressure by both industrialised countries and other developing countries to accept ambitious mitigation targets under a binding framework.

China and India are, however, trying to cope with this. More frequently, they represent themselves in the Like-Minded Developing Countries (LMDCs) group. This group often adopts a firm position against mitigation demands by industrialised countries in the negotiations (Harvey 2013), and thus seeks to obstruct the UK's goal to reach a binding and global mitigation deal. Moreover, in the current geopolitical context, the new powerful economies have a large say as to how international cooperation and multilateralism is developing

(Falkner et al. 2010). China is the most powerful emerging economy, to which India remains closely aligned. Both China and India value principles of non-intervention and sovereignty (Vihma 2010). As a consequence, it may well be that we are moving away from a multilateral approach to climate change, based on binding commitments, that the EU has always been arguing for. We may end up with a new type of global agreement in which values of sovereignty and self-determination prevail.

A counterargument to this analysis is that the FCO's securitising move did succeed in enhancing political ties between the EU, the Least Developed Countries (LDCs), and the Alliance of Small Island States (AOSIS). This may benefit chances to achieve an ambitious and binding global deal on climate change. As discussed in chapters 4 and 5, it is part of the FCO's interest to enhance ties between these groups to strengthen the negotiation block in favour of binding mitigation targets under the UNFCCC. For instance, the FCO created a UK Climate Security Envoy for Vulnerable Countries aimed 'to generate a voice [among vulnerable countries to climate change] that will highlight the impact of climate issues, including to exert more leverage within the UN negotiations' (FCO 2009: 40). The EU–LDC–AOSIS alliance was particularly active in the 2011 Durban UNFCCC conference to push for negotiations towards a new climate deal (Van Schaik 2012). At Durban, the EU, the LDCs, and the AOSIS provided a common statement arguing for urgent mitigation action by the international community (European Commission 2011; for more detail on this alliance, see chapter 5). This alliance risks destabilising the negotiation block of the Global South in the UNFCCC negotiations (often referred to as the group of G-77 countries). It focusses on their differences, for instance, concerning the question whether or not the emerging developing countries need to sign up to binding mitigation targets (see Van Schaik 2012).

While this alliance would enhance pressure on India in climate change negotiations from a wider group of countries, including from the LDCs (see discussion in Van Schaik 2012; see also Vihma 2010), it remains disputable whether this will suffice to convince India to change its negotiation position. This may occur if India is susceptible to the moral argument that it should act as a responsible power to protect vulnerable LDCs or to the idea that a loss in power among some of its Southern allies may harm its interests.

With regards the morality argument, some scholars have asked the question whether India will take on the role as a responsible world and regional power, instead of just being an economic one (Narlikar 2011; Mohan 2010). If so, moral arguments, such as its responsibility for climate action to protect vulnerable states, may become more powerful. As argued by Narlikar (2011), it is still too early to trace such a perception among the Government of India. The Government of India still often acts as a 'veto-player' in multilateral forums on the global commons, including in climate change negotiations (Narlikar 2011). It has not yet built up a reputation as a state willing to give in on its own short-term national interests for the greater good (Narlikar 2011) or to protect other vulnerable states. At least, this does not seem to have been the incentive for India to agree to negotiate 'a protocol, another legal instrument or an agreed outcome with legal force', including all Parties to the convention (UNFCCC 2012; as discussed in chapter 5, this agreement leaves it open to interpretation whether India would be bound to mitigation targets and to what kind of mitigation targets). According to Van Schaik (2012: 1), the alliance between the EU, the LDCs, and the AOSIS serves as 'the reason behind [this] agreement being reached . . . at the Durban Summit of December 2011'. But, India did not sign up to this agreement until the US and China were on board (Van Schaik 2012: 16–17). This suggests that the opinions and decisions of these states are of much greater value to India than those of the LDCs and the AOSIS. There is also no indication that India has moved forward on voluntary mitigation action on a domestic level out of a sense of responsibility to the LDCs. Instead, the rationale guiding its national action on climate change is to prevent loss and damage in India, and primarily (as will be discussed in more detail in the next section) to create co-benefits in terms of energy efficiency and economic growth (PM's Council on Climate Change 2008; see also Planning Commission 2013).

Despite India not (yet) being susceptible to the morality argument, India may consider a split in the G-77 negotiation block to negatively affect its interests. According to Narlikar (2011: 1610), India's role as a coalition leader of developing countries is one of the key reasons why India managed to achieve a relatively powerful position in the General Agreement on Tariffs and Trade and in the World Trade Organisation (WTO). This suggests that India's image as a representative of the Global South functions as an additional asset to India's bargaining power. In the run up to the 2009 Copenhagen UNFCCC conference, *The Times of India* (Sethi 2009) reported that the (former) Environment Minister, Jairam Ramesh, had written to the Indian Prime Minister in a confidential letter (leaked to the press) that India needed to change its reputation of being a deal-breaker and stonewaller in climate change negotiations as its stance is 'disfavoured by the developed countries, small island states and vulnerable countries. It takes away from India's aspirations for permanent membership of the Security Council'. This quote clearly points to India's interest in maintaining good relations with the wider G-77 group to preserve its international reputation and bargaining power (e.g., since it may provide India an entry in the UN Security Council).

However, there are clear signs that India gradually puts less value on its leadership role in the G-77 block, which relates to its position of an emerging economic power. For instance, in the same letter by Ramesh, he argued for India to distance itself from the G-77 group in climate change negotiations (which led to a great deal of commotion in the Indian public square (Mohan 2010: 139). And this is exactly what India has done over the years by putting more emphasis on alternative, small-scale alliances, such as the BASIC group and the Like-Minded Developing Countries, in climate change negotiations (Mohan 2010: 139; Michealowa and Michaelowa 2012: 584). According to Smith (2012: 376–377), since the end of the 1990s many Indian officials felt that India needed to associate itself with a group of more like-minded countries, instead of sticking to an unquestioned solidarity to the Global South and G-77 out of moral principle. They argued that India needed to account for its newly acquired role of an emerging economic power and that such a new and modern attitude would further enhance India's economic growth (Smith 2012: 375–377). Therefore, it is disputable whether further fractures in the Southern block would seriously impact on India's negotiation power on climate change, as the trend suggests that India is already forming new alliances. Furthermore, as discussed in chapter 5, the FCO's strategy that aimed to enhance divisions in the traditional Southern alliances in the UNFCCC negotiations may very well backfire. It can result in a new stalemate between the EU, the LDCs, and the AOSIS on the one hand, and the emerging economies on the other hand.

The relative power of the LDC and EU coalition furthermore depends on the voting rules of the UNFCCC. A proposal has been made by Mexico and Papua New Guinea to allow for decision making to take place on the basis of three-fourth majority vote by the Conference of the Parties in case consensus cannot be reached (Doyle 2011; UNFCCC 2011). In such a scenario, the EU–LDC–AOSIS coalition could become vital in climate change negotiations. There is a total of 48 LDCs (UN-OHRLLS 2014a), and an additional of 29 Small Island Developing States (not listed as LDCs) that can act as UN members in the UNFCCC (UN-OHRLLS 2014b).[2] Together with votes from the EU member states, this coalition could have much voting power in case of majority-ruling (there are a total of 193 UN member states with full voting rights). However, thus far, the UNFCCC's decision-making procedure remains consensus-based (UNFCCC 1992: article 7 and 18). This gives powerful countries such as the US, China, and India a lot of leeway to block proposals that it should sign up to binding mitigation targets.

In sum, the FCO's securitising move on climate migration largely negatively affects political ties between the UK and the Government of India in the realm of climate change negotiations. The FCO's securitising move has compounded a competitive negotiation environment on climate change, instead of smoothing climate change negotiations. This negatively affects the UK's ability (its positional power) to influence the negotiations, as it provides India with an additional reason to more actively engage with like-minded countries sceptical of binding mitigation targets under the UNFCCC. As discussed, China and India managed to replace the term 'commitments' to 'contributions' on GHG emission reductions during the climate talks in Warsaw (Morales and Krukowska 2013; Morales and Nicola 2013). The negotiations on a post-Kyoto framework could therefore develop in such a direction that these emerging economies may not have to commit to legally bounded targets, even when participating in a new global deal (Morales and Krukowska 2013; Morales and Nicola 2013; C2ES 2013).

A counterargument is that the EU (including the UK)–LDC–AOSIS alliance, that partly resulted from the FCO's securitising move, could benefit the UK's interest to put more pressure on India to act. There are, however, significant signs that India has been putting less emphasis on its coalition with the G-77 block, while placing greater value on its alliance with the BASIC group and with coal/oil-rich (developing) countries. Therefore, it is doubtful whether such a strategy by the UK and the EU will be successful. Also, greater divisions in the Southern negotiation block could easily lead to another stalemate in climate change negotiations.

This does not mean that India would by no means change its position in the UNFCCC in such a fashion that it better aligns with that of the UK. Fractures within the BASIC group do put India (and China) under increasing pressure. It makes it more difficult for India to seek strong and stable alliances with other emerging developing countries. Instead, it is forced to collaborate with oil/coal-rich (developing) countries. This is likely to further isolate India and to weaken its moral arguments about the right to development and equity that it often relies on in the negotiations.

While this analysis shows that the securitisation process on climate migration has implications for UK–India relations in climate change politics, it is unlikely to result in greater repercussions for UK–India relations more generally, for instance in the area of trade, traditional security and investment. As discussed, the geopolitical climate is such that it is in the UK's interest to maintain good relationships with India. The UK is unlikely to risk economic relations with India over disagreements on climate change governance.

The FCO's Response: A Shift Towards an Economic Narrative

How did the FCO respond to this situation where its securitising move has suboptimal results? Has the FCO changed its strategy it? If yes, is this new strategy more effective? And is this shift a result of interaction processes with India, or are there other factors at play?

Towards an Economic Prosperity Narrative

Since 2010, the FCO has put more emphasis on the use of economic arguments in its climate change diplomacy, while gradually shifting away from security narratives on climate conflict and climate migration. As briefly mentioned in chapter 4, the economic prosperity rationale represents a second narrative developed by the FCO in the course of the 2000s to promote action on climate change.[3] It has gradually become the FCO's most dominant narrative used in its climate change diplomacy. William Hague, Foreign Secretary from 2010 until July 2014, for instance shifted the attention towards economic and energy-related arguments to promote mitigation action in public speeches (Hague 2010, 2011, 2012). As argued by Hague (2010):

[T]he British Foreign and Commonwealth Office, under my leadership, is a vocal advocate for climate diplomacy. All British Ambassadors carry the argument for a global low carbon transition in their breast pocket or their handbag.

In 2012, this trend was adopted more widely in the FCO. As a reflection of this shift, the Climate Security Team changed its name into the Global Strategic Impacts Team in September 2012. As argued by the Deputy Head of this team:

> The name change reflects an acknowledgement of the wider scope of our team's work. For the best part of the last year we have been working on wider resource security issues and taking a deeper look at the scientific evidence underpinning much of our approach to climate and resource security. The new team name—introduced last September—simply reflects this new reality, which does include an increasing focus on the economic and prosperity aspects of climate change impacts.[4]

The new name and wider remit of the former Climate Security Team allows it to engage with a wider range of narratives, while no longer directly being associated with the notion of climate conflict that has been heavily criticised over the years.

The economic prosperity narrative is based on two related arguments: 1) that of the promotion of economic *opportunities* and, 2) that of raising awareness of economic *risks* associated with climate change. The raising awareness of economic opportunities is a central element of this narrative. It is based on the argument that actors should invest in a low-carbon economy and further pursue recent advances in green technology. It is argued that investment in a low-carbon economy creates new markets, enhances energy efficiency, and thereby lowers energy costs (Beckett 2006; Hague 2010; Ashton 2011; see also Blair 2004; Brown 2009; Cameron 2010).[5] For instance, China has become a key market player in both wind and solar energy (Lacey 2011; Harvey 2012). This is an example of how green technological development opens new markets and creates new opportunities for growth. But, this narrative provides also a sombre (more negatively orientated) message by arguing that climate change creates economic problems in terms of resource scarcity, causing a disruption in energy supplies.[6]

This economic prosperity narrative builds on the message provided by the Stern Review on the Economics of Climate Change, which attempted to highlight the negative economic implications of climate change (Stern 2006; see e.g., Beckett 2006; FCO 2008: 14; and Brown 2009 for such a representation of the Stern Review) and the economic opportunities of early preventive action (Stern 2006; see e.g., FCO 2006: 19, 72). This narrative has been institutionalised in the FCO's climate change diplomacy. As stated in the FCO's 2010–2011 Annual (departmental) Report:

> There is growing international recognition of the approach we have been pioneering in the FCO to strengthen the political conditions for success on

climate. We are now working closely with Germany to replicate this with like-minded partners including the European External Action Service. As part of this effort we have opened a debate with partners in the EU, East Asia, Latin America and elsewhere on the economic benefits, at a time of rising resource stresses, of low carbon growth.

> (FCO 2011; see FCO 2008: 71, on the role
> of business in promoting this narrative)

A notion of security is not eliminated from this narrative. The economic risk–opportunity argument uses a language of risk, resource (in)security,[7] and arguments on energy security (on energy security, see in particular, Hague 2010; 2011). But the concept of security is less explicitly used compared to the security narrative on climate migration, which was linked to alarmist notions of conflict and mass migration. It therefore no longer neatly fits the conceptualisation of security as defined by the Copenhagen School. Even so, some elements of the resource and energy security argument could fit the Copenhagen School's definition of security when used to warn about alarming consequences, such as conflicts over energy security and water. But, by and large, the FCO has attempted to be more subtle in its arguments on resource insecurity. These arguments point to more ordinary risks, such as a decrease in energy access or in economic gain, and at the same time highlight economic opportunities associated with climate action. Such a subtle usage of security does fit the conceptualisation of unease, as provided by the Paris School, and the definition of risk as provided by the Risk School.

In line with the concept of unease as defined by the Paris School, this adapted narrative fuels negative feelings, in a subtle way, of risk, worry, and insecurity among states such as the Government of India (for sake of clarity I focus the discussion here on India). The narrative refers to more regular economic risks and energy problems that may arise, thereby enhancing a sense of worry regarding Indian society's robustness, prosperity, and stability. India is still challenged by multiple problems of human development; ranging from high poverty rates to problems with access to education (*The Hindu* 2011). Therefore, a narrative concentrating on certain weaknesses in India's society, while playing on India's preoccupation with economic growth and energy availability, can fuel worries and feelings of unease in relation to climate change.

Then again, in more positive terms, the narrative concentrates on economic opportunities associated with climate action. The focus of the narrative is on joint efforts to tackle climate change based on shared interests of economic growth, innovation, and foreign investment. In this narrative, the FCO adopts a more collaborative approach to diplomatic negotiations that may come across as attempting to more seriously engage with India's economic interests and needs. Such a perception of this narrative fits the conceptualisation of security as defined by the Risk School, characterised by its focus on dialogue, collaboration, and positive prevention aiming to 'problem-solve' climate risk.

Efforts to enhance economic prosperity do not automatically have these somewhat more positive consequences. If not holistically discussed, such a narrative may only benefit the powerful elite within India and maintain current inequalities in Indian society. According to Amartya Sen (cited in *The Hindu* 2011), India's economic growth has not yet resulted in sufficient reduction of poverty rates and in considerable human development (e.g., by improving access to education, reducing maternal mortality rates, etc.). According to the Human Development Index, India has not substantially been able to improve its human development in the 2000s despite its economic growth (UNDP 2014: 166). As argued by Sen (cited in *The Hindu* 2011) in response to the Human Development Report of 2011: 'The tragedy is that not only China, but even Bangladesh is now doing better on almost every one of these social indicators [such as education, life expectancy, and maternal mortality] than India is doing. . . .' Also in the climate change debate, the Government of India has been accused of 'hiding behind the poor' (Ananthapadmanabhan, Srinivas and Gopal 2007; Chakravarty and Ramana 2012). While arguing internationally that climate action should be based on principles of fairness and equity, internally the Government of India does not itself persuasively live up to these principles. The per capita emissions of India's rural and urban poor are far lower than those of India's urban and rural elite, exemplifying high inequality in economic and consumption behaviour in Indian society (Ananthapadmanabhan, Srinivas and Gopal 2007; Chakravarty and Ramana 2012). Therefore, while acknowledging that economic growth is essential for India's poor to obtain better health care, education, and employment opportunities (Sen 1999), an economic opportunity approach to climate change does not necessarily result in less internal inequalities.

The Level of Contextual Resonance in India

The economic prosperity narrative is likely to find greater resonance in the Indian context. It could therefore be more successful to bolster more ambitious action on the mitigation of climate change by the Government of India.

First of all, the narrative resonates with India's quest for economic growth that characterises its political agenda. Chapter 5 demonstrated that this economic agenda (partly) explains India's hesitance to accept binding mitigation targets under the UNFCCC, out of fear for an economic downturn. In that context, it seems an effective diplomatic strategy for the FCO to demonstrate that climate change action does not equal a decrease in economic growth, but instead may enhance India's economic growth and stability. In this manner, the FCO engages more actively with India's own priorities, interests, and needs (even though it also remains a diplomatic strategy aiming to secure the UK's economic and climate change-related interests). This narrative could ease India's fears about binding mitigation action by showing it can lead to economic opportunities and growth. This could eventually change India's perception of these practices as driven by the Copenhagen School's logic of security measures. It is debatable, however, whether the sombre element of the economic prosperity narrative resonates in India, with its emphasis on economic risks associated with inaction. As discussed, a language of fear does not help to enhance levels of collaboration on climate change. Instead, it adds to feelings of mistrust and provides India with a suspicious perception of the FCO's and the West's interests in climate change negotiations. In similar vein, the sombre element of the economic prosperity narrative plays on feelings of worry by highlighting economic and resource problems caused by climate change. It is doubtful whether the negatively oriented economic prosperity narrative will succeed in enhancing levels of collaboration on climate change between the FCO and the Government of India.

Second, notions of energy security, market mechanisms, technological innovation, and energy efficiency are central to India's National Action Plan on Climate Change (PM's Council on Climate Change 2008). Energy security obtains much attention in Indian society to meet rising energy demands (see Boas 2014 for more details on India's discourse of energy security). Energy security has even become a key objective of India's foreign policy. S. M. Krishna, the Indian Minister of External Affairs from 2009 to October 2012, argued that 'the pursuit of enhanced trade, investment inflows, technology transfers, energy security and other economic imperatives has become an overarching imperative of our foreign policy' (Krishna 2009 quoted in Smith 2012: 376). According to Michaelowa and Michaelowa (2012: 578), the interest in energy security has paved the way for more proactive climate change policies to be developed at the national level as part of India's National Action Plan on Climate Change (see also PM's Council on Climate Change 2008: 13). The National Action Plan on Climate Change argues in favour of a 'market based mechanism to enhance cost effectiveness of improvements in energy efficiency' (PM's Council on Climate Change 2008: 3). Similar to the FCO's economic prosperity narrative, India's NAPCC speaks of 'co-benefits for addressing climate change' (PM's Council on Climate Change). In line with the FCO's argument, the rationale is that India's climate change policy should benefit India's economy and quest for energy security:

> India's development agenda focuses on the need for rapid economic growth as an essential precondition to poverty eradication and improved standards of living. Meeting this agenda, which will also reduce climate-related vulnerability, requires large-scale investment of resources infra-structure, technology and access to energy . . . [D]evelopment of clean energy technologies, though primarily designed to promote energy security, can also generate large benefits in terms of reducing carbon emissions.
> (PM's Council on Climate Change 2008: 13)

The debate on energy security is an area where the UK could potentially gain a lot in its efforts to promote climate action by the Government of India. If India becomes convinced that investment in green and renewable technology (as opposed to the coal industry) is the best way to address its energy deficit, this can have a big positive impact on the environment. Since domestic concerns for energy security have been vital for India to develop a national action plan on climate change, there are opportunities for the FCO to raise further awareness of green energy. It can also be expected that more domestic pressure for investments in green energy will emerge in India, considering that the rise in air pollution in India's urban centres has even outweighed the level of pollution in China's biggest cities between 2008 and 2010 (Chauhan 2012). Therefore, in the context of India's national energy agenda, the FCO's economic prosperity narrative finds greater resonance in the Government of India. It seems a more constructive narrative to promote mitigation action, particularly on the level of India's national climate change action.

Third, in using the economic prosperity narrative, the FCO no longer has to rely on its engagement with the security community to promote action on climate change mitigation. As discussed in chapter 5, the Indian Ministry of Defence is not involved in India's policy making on climate change and the Indian climate change community considers it inappropriate to frame climate change as a matter of national security and defence. As argued by an official of the British High Commission in New Delhi: 'In India there does not seem to be a clear line of communication between the security community and the policy-making on climate change'.[8] Therefore, the strategy to involve the Indian security community in the issue area of climate change does not seem effective to promote climate action. Instead, it seems more logical for the FCO to concentrate its diplomatic engagement on the Indian climate change community, and on economic and energy sectors. With the Indian climate change community it is more effective to use concepts such as energy efficiency, resilience, and development than those related to the alarmist narrative of climate change and security (including the threat of climate migration).[9] These concepts do have affinity, at least on some levels, with the FCO's economic prosperity narrative. This economic prosperity narrative is therefore likely to have a greater fit with the Indian climate change community.

Finally, compared to the securitising move on climate migration, the economic prosperity narrative to a lesser degree comes across a mere rhetorical strategy aiming to promote climate action by the Government of India. For the FCO (and the UK Government as such) mitigation action is about preventing economic and energy losses and about achieving new avenues for economic growth and technological innovation. Its alarmist security narrative on climate migration could not communicate such an understanding of, and interest in, mitigation action (see discussion in chapters 4 and 5). But the economic prosperity narrative does have a clear fit with the FCO's perspective on mitigation. As argued in previous chapters, the FCO's securitising move on climate migration has fuelled the perception among the Government of India that it functions as pure rhetoric. In India's understanding, the alarmist statements on climate migration suggest that the FCO is *demanding* and *enforcing* action in the name of national and international security (see chapter 5). Meanwhile, the economic prosperity narrative represents a diplomatic strategy that attempts (at least to a larger degree) to *engage* with India's economic interests and energy needs, and could appear more honest about the actual economic interests driving the UK's climate change agenda. This could benefit collaboration. Therefore, also from this perspective, the economic prosperity narrative may find greater resonance in the Government of India.

On the basis of this assessment, it can be expected that this narrative provides greater opportunities for the UK and Indian governments to improve collaborative relationships on climate change, and for the FCO to stimulate India to take more ambitious action on climate change mitigation. As a result, the UK would obtain greater influence in climate change negotiations. It is, however, not fully clear how the Government of India will respond to this economic prosperity narrative. Even though, at first glance, the narrative has a greater fit in the Indian context, India may continue to perceive the FCO's endeavours as a sign of UK interference with its policy making. Particularly, if the FCO continues to play on a language of fear and unease by raising awareness of economic and energy risks, it is likely to trigger a defensive reaction by the Government of India rejecting the FCO's efforts.

Explaining the Shift Towards an Economic Narrative

To explain this shift towards an economic narrative, I review two developments that have influenced the FCO's decision to move away from its securitising move on climate migration: its interactions with the Government of India, and domestic developments within the UK Government.

Partly due to the FCO's engagement with the Government of India, the FCO has become aware of the unsuccessful aspects of its securitising move on climate migration. As argued by an FCO official, there is a challenge when a narrative is developed that is not effective with the leading G77 economies, such as China and India, that the FCO aims to target.[10] Partly for this reason, the FCO has started to use the narrative of economic prosperity to bolster greater action on climate change. The FCO is increasingly realising that a narrative needs to be adjusted to its audience: 'For some partners climate security works for others it doesn't'.[11] In relation to India, this also meant that adjustments in the FCO's securitising move were required. As argued by an FCO Official in the Climate Change and Energy Department:

> Telling India that security becomes worse because of climate change is not necessarily the best argument. For India it is all about maintaining growth. So we try to persuade them how they can maintain growth and be green at the same time. Climate change is a problem of the global commons and we all want to maintain growth and some have an overwhelming need to tackle poverty. But our position is that tackling poverty and climate change is not incompatible. So, we try to share our experience and promote energy efficiency, as that may lead to cheaper energy for instance, which is beneficial to the economy.[12]

Along similar lines, an official with the Delhi-based British High Commission argued it was better to use other terms in interactions with the Government of India, such as those on energy efficiency and development.[13] The FCO's perception is that it is important to take emerging powers, such as India, seriously in the present political climate and that greater resonance with their concerns and interests should be achieved to enhance relations on climate change. While the FCO has not fully stopped using its securitising move on climate migration with states such as India, it did realise that these arguments are not necessarily the most effective, and subsequently put more emphasis on the economic prosperity narrative. As argued by the Deputy Head of the FCO's Global Strategic Impacts Team, the prosperity argument has greater resonance in a time of economic difficulties, and also resonates with emerging economies.[14]

This statement by the Deputy Head of the FCO's Global Strategic Impacts Team points to another reason why the FCO moved towards an economic narrative in its climate change diplomacy. It is a narrative that not only finds resonance with some of the FCO's target audiences (such as India), but more importantly, it better reflects priorities set by the UK Coalition Government that started in 2010. Economic growth and economic stability became key policy objectives during the economic recession and with the start of the Coalition Government. The Coalition Government has put high priority on addressing the problems of the UK's economy and currently tries to maintain its renewed growth (Tadeo 2014). Even the UK's national security strategy, produced in the time of the Coalition Government, highlights the economy as one of the key factors guiding its strategic priorities. As stated in the forward of its 2010 Strategic Defence and Security Review:

> The difficult legacy we have inherited has necessitated tough decisions to get our economy back on track. Our national security depends on our economic security and vice versa. So bringing the defence budget back to balance is a vital part of how we tackle the deficit and protect this country's national security.
>
> (Cabinet Office 2010a: 3)

Meanwhile, the promotion of climate action in the UNFCCC obtained a somewhat lower level of priority. For instance, in the 2010 National Security Strategy (NSS) and the 2010 Strategic Defence and Security Review (SDSR), the need for a multilateral deal on climate change mitigation is only mentioned once (Cabinet Office 2010b: 18), and a security narrative on climate migration had not been employed to promote efforts towards such a climate change deal. The 2013 annual report on the UK's national security strategy did not mention climate change at all (Cabinet Office 2013). In contrast, the NSS, in the time of the Labour Government (in Gordon Brown's period as Prime Minister), actively promoted greater action on climate change by the international community. It argued that:

> [Climate change] . . . can be expected to worsen poverty, have a significant impact on global migration patterns, and risk tipping fragile states

into instability, conflict and state failure. From a security perspective, it is important to act now to reduce the scale of climate change by mitigation, such as emissions reduction, and by being able to adapt to climate change that is now already unavoidable.

(Cabinet Office 2009: 8, for a similar quote see p. 40, 52)

Prime Minister David Cameron particularly, and the UK Coalition Government more widely, has in that context been criticised for not providing international leadership on climate change (*The Guardian* 2011).

A narrative that concentrates on investment opportunities, world economic stability, and on achieving better economic relations with emerging powers, resonates with the course taken by the Coalition Government. The use of economic language in climate change negotiations has also explicitly been supported by the UK's Prime Minister David Cameron: 'I passionately believe that by re-casting the argument for action on climate change away from the language of threats and punishments and into positive, profit-making terms, we can have a much wider impact' (Cameron 2010).

To cope with these shifting political priorities, the FCO has reduced its climate diplomacy budget by 39 percent since 2011 (Darby 2014). These budget cuts were approved by former Foreign Secretary William Hague, and the new Foreign Secretary Philip Hammond is expected to approve more budget cuts. As argued by Tom Burke, a former FCO climate change advisor: 'Despite agreeing to the cuts, he[, Mr Hague,] was a reliable supporter of more ambitious efforts on climate change and I don't think Mr Hammond will be' (cited in Darby 2014). The budget cuts not only reflect a decreasing interest in climate change by the Coalition Government, but also a shift in priorities from climate change towards the field of energy and resource security. This is a field that better resonates with the Coalition Government's agenda (see e.g., Cabinet Office 2013 on energy security). As the climate diplomacy budget decreased, the FCO's spending on energy and resource security increased by 11 percent (Darby 2014). The name-change of the FCO's Climate Security Team into the FCO's Global Strategic Impacts Team, including its economic property narrative, resonates with these new interests. In this way, the FCO could maintain its activities in the field of climate diplomacy, while aligning itself with the newly set priorities.

In addition to these political developments, the FCO has received an increasing amount of criticism from other UK Government departments regarding its alarmist security arguments on climate conflict and climate migration. Even though these UK government departments do not represent the FCO's main target audience, this criticism added to a conducive environment in which the FCO was willing to change its diplomatic strategy. Before discussing this, it is important to highlight that inter-ministerial interaction on the topic of climate change, migration, and security has been relatively minor throughout the 2000s. I discussed in chapter 4 that the FCO did collaborate with the Department of Energy and Climate Change and with the Ministry of Defence on some levels. But it was not until recent years (mostly in 2011 and 2012) that the FCO actively tried to seek support for its actions amongst a wider group of UK ministries.[15] Such support became vital as the FCO's endeavours lost the almost-unquestioned support from the Labour Government (see chapter 4 on Blair's activities) when the Coalition Government started.

Different UK ministries have expressed concerns about alarmist security narrative on climate migration. For instance, officials in the UK Department for International Development have been sceptical of the FCO's security narrative on climate migration, mainly for a lack of evidence:

> In terms of insecurity, which is related to migration, we are reluctant to make specific links between climate change and actual wars. We are not convinced that the evidence is really there and thereby not willing to make such assertions. There is a risk of going down that path that we end up measuring our success of climate adaptation in numbers of people who have moved to the UK.[16]

As argued by another DFID Official:

> The FCO is often jumping to conclusions on climate security while DFID thinks we need a more evidence-based approach. The FCO sees climate change as a security risk, it is basically asking itself the question whether the UK has to arm itself against climate wars. While we at DFID think it is not as clear cut as that.[17]

Further scepticism regarding alarmist framings of climate migration rose in response to the publication of the Foresight Report on Migration and Global Environmental Change in October 2011 (The UK Government Office for Science 2011). This report is the result of a Foresight Project on Global Environmental Migration organised by the UK Government Office for Science. The report concentrates on the broader issue of environmental migration, which includes climate migration but also migration due to other environmental impacts, such as natural disasters. It argues against the image of mass climate migration and sets itself apart from securitising moves on the subject by arguing that:

> It is unhelpful to frame the relationship between migration and global environmental change as a security issue; indeed, to do so may undermine efforts to build migration as an adaptation strategy, or to mobilise collaborative action to address environmental change . . .
> (The UK Government Office of Science 2011: 199)

Instead, it emphasises that climate migration is frequently an internal phenomenon or at most a regional one (The UK Government Office for Science 2011: 197). A key message is that environmental migration (including climate migration) should not necessarily be seen as a problem, as something negative. They argue that such migration can also function as an adaptation strategy that can empower local communities in efforts to improve their livelihoods.[18]

Scepticism further rose in the UK's Department of Energy and Climate Change (DECC), one of the departments that did initially support the FCO's securitising move in its negotiations on climate change (see chapter 4):

> The Foresight report shows that environmental migration is a complicated issue—often it is not as simple as 'climate changes and people move'. We need to be accurate in our communication. Obviously if we are creating scare stories and they are completely incredible, it is not going to do you any favours.[19]

In a similar vein, the Ministry of Defence has become increasingly sceptical of alarmist statements on mass climate migration. Throughout the 2000s the MOD tended to support the idea that climate migration is a mass phenomenon affecting the UK's national security, even though this did not result in real policy making.[20] For example, in 2007 the MOD's Development Concepts and Doctrine Centre (DCDC) warned of mass climate migration from Africa (see e.g., DCDC 2007: 29). But DCDC's 2010 Global Strategic Trends Report provided a somewhat more nuanced picture of climate migration. It argued that: 'Such migrants are *likely* to move locally, and then regionally, with a relatively small proportion of them moving internationally' (DCDC 2010: 26, emphasis in the original). Simon Cole, the Assistant Head to the Futures Team at DCDC, commented: 'Our view is that environmental migration occurs locally, then regionally, but with a low probability of international migration'.[21] To explain the change of focus in the DCDC's reports, the Editor argued:

> I think that there is more nervousness about the lack of data, and since the evidence is very little it is difficult to quote climate migration as a trend. In the early 2000s it was an issue that often came up in academia and societal discussions. But now there is more evidence that this figure of 200 million can actually not be substantiated. The Foresight Report provides a good study of environmental migration which will be our starting point. They wrote that this figure of 200 million could not be substantiated.[22]

This rising criticism further contributed to the FCO's mind-set in which it was prepared to acknowledge that some of its narratives were ineffective and not necessarily constructive to promote action on climate change.[23]

In sum, the FCO has increasingly used an economic prosperity narrative in its climate diplomacy, which is likely to find greater resonance in the Government of India. Interaction processes between the FCO and the Government of India have contributed to this change in the FCO's strategy and securitising move. The FCO has become increasingly aware that its securitising move on climate migration can have counterproductive results and does not resonate with some of its key audiences. This suggests that in terms of respective power relations, India at least had some impact on the FCO's decision to change its securitising move.

But the primary reason behind the narrative shift relates to domestic political developments in the UK Government. In the Coalition Government, economic growth and stability have become top priorities, while climate change commands less attention. A narrative on economic prosperity better resonates with these political objectives, and has allowed the FCO to continue its diplomatic work on climate change. A question therefore remains whether the FCO would also have shifted its narrative in case the Labour Government would have remained in power. Has India's influence been sufficiently powerful to cause a narrative shift, or was it just a contributing factor to an already unstable situation?

Despite the examined narrative changes, I do want to emphasise that there has been no totalising shift. The more alarmist securitising moves on climate change and migration have not disappeared. In 2013, Neil Morisetti, as the FCO's interim Special Representative on Climate Change, argued that 'The UK believes that the impacts of a changing climate pose a significant and emerging threat to a country's national security and prosperity. . . . The UK is engaging with our international partners and through international forums to better manage this risk' (quoted King 2013). Moreover, as mentioned in chapter 4, the UK did initiate another debate on climate change in the UN Security Council in 2013. It may well be that the alarmist security narratives on climate change and climate migration will resurrect in a time that the UK political establishment has to start preparing for the high-profile 2015 Conference of the Parties of the UNFCCC in Paris were the international community hopes to salvage a new climate change deal. According to the UK Secretary of State for Energy and Climate Change, Edward Davey, 'The expected impacts of climate change will be integrated into the UK's next strategic defence and security review, expected next summer, just before the Paris conference' (Davey, quoted in The Centre for Climate & Security 2014). In any case, the institutional changes in the FCO's Climate Security Team, the FCO's budget cuts on climate change, and the approach taken by the UK Coalition Government, shows that the securitising move on climate migration has in recent years been subject to significant turbulence, criticism, and change.

Concluding Discussion

This chapter reviewed stage three, the outcome, of the traced securitisation process on climate migration. The most interesting finding is that the FCO decided to more actively use an alternative narrative in its diplomatic endeavours to promote climate action. The economic prosperity narrative has become more prominent in its interactions with the Government of India (and with other emerging powers). As demonstrated in chapter 5, statements on climate migration and climate conflict do not resonate in the Indian context and even triggered a counterproductive response. This provided the FCO with an additional reason to adapt its narrative, to find greater acceptance by its audience. This shows that India at least had some influence (and thus power) on the construction of the FCO's securitising move. But interaction processes between India and the FCO were not the determining factor. A changing political climate within the UK Government itself and related shifting priorities have played a larger and more determining role.

This finding furthermore shows that it is helpful to draw on various insights on securitisation to analyse and understand the dynamic and complex nature of a securitisation process. The economic prosperity narrative represents a shift from the concept of security as defined by the Copenhagen School to a more subtle conceptualisation of security as defined by a mix of the Paris School and Risk School. This economic prosperity narrative has a better fit with the types of mitigation measures the FCO aims to promote, which are equally about more subtle practices of prevention and risk management. This may benefit the FCO's endeavours to promote climate action. Its arguments may seem more genuine and geared towards dialogue, and they better reflect the UK's agenda on climate change.

In terms of positional power in the context of climate change negotiations, the UK Government is mostly negatively affected by the securitisation process on climate migration. The FCO's securitising move has negatively affected political ties between the UK and Indian Governments on climate change and risks to adversely affect the UK's influence in the UNFCCC more widely. The FCO's securitising move triggered a defensive reaction from the Government of India. This creates an additional stimulus for India to enhance ties with other like-minded states in climate change negotiations in order to withstand claims that it needs to sign up to binding and ambitious mitigation targets. Moreover, the FCO has tried to enhance divisions in the G-77 negotiation block by means of its securitising move. It is, however, unlikely that this strategy will succeed in convincing India to change its position on climate change, and it could very well result in new stalemates harming the UK's interest to achieve a solid UNFCCC deal.

This process thus benefits the position of the Government of India. At least in the short-term, it complicates the efforts by the UK seeking to convince India to accept binding mitigation targets. But it is unclear how this will play out in the long-term. The BASIC alliance is already experiencing fractures. South Africa has even shown support of securitising moves on climate migration. As a result, China and India are forging new alliances with oil/coal-rich (developing) countries. China and India thus seem capable to cope with these developments in the present geopolitical context, but it does put them under increasing pressure by industrialised countries, LDCs, and even by other emerging developing countries. It remains to be seen for how long India is able to maintain its defensive negotiation strategy on climate change while becoming increasingly isolated.

Another question is whether any narrative or argument used by the FCO could have convinced India to change its negotiation status in the UNFCCC. In principle, India reacts defensively to the argument that it should accept binding mitigation targets. A similar response can be expected when the FCO uses its economic prosperity narrative. But this latter narrative at least does provide opportunities to bring the UK and India in greater dialogue to discuss shared interests related to energy efficiency and economic trade. This may positively affect the mitigation of climate change; perhaps not immediately on the level of binding mitigation agreements under the UNFCCC, but possibly through greater bilateral collaboration on green energy, and through voluntary contributions to mitigation action under the UNFCCC. The economic prosperity narrative at least does find greater resonance in Indian context.

Notes

1. In a recent submission to the UNFCCC, this group included: Algeria, Argentina, Bolivia, Cuba, China, Democratic Republic of the Congo, Dominica, Ecuador, Egypt, El Salvador, India, Iran, Iraq, Kuwait, Libya, Malaysia, Mali, Nicaragua, Pakistan, Philippines, Qatar, Saudi Arabia, Sri Lanka, Sudan, Syria, and Venezuela (UNFCCC 2014).
2. There is a total of 38 Small Island Developing States that act as UN members, but nine of these are already included in the total number of LDCs.
3. Interview, Official of the British High Commission in Delhi, 19 August 2011, Delhi; Interview, FCO Official, Climate Change and Energy Department, 23 January 2012, London.
4. Email correspondence, Deputy Head of the FCO's Global Strategic Impacts Team (formerly called: Climate Security Team), Climate Change and Energy Department, 6 February 2013.
5. Interview, Official of the British High Commission in Delhi, 19 August 2011, Delhi; Interview, FCO Official, Climate Change and Energy Department, 23 January 2012, London.
6. Telephone interview, Deputy Head of the FCO's Global Strategic Impacts Team (formerly called: Climate Security Team), Climate Change and Energy Department, 24 May 2012 and 1 June 2012.
7. Telephone interview, Deputy Head of the FCO's Global Strategic Impacts Team (formerly called: Climate Security Team), Climate Change and Energy Department, 24 May 2012 and 1 June 2012.
8. Interview, Official of the British High Commission in Delhi, 19 August 2011, Delhi.
9. Interview, Official of the British High Commission in Delhi, 19 August 2011, Delhi.
10. Telephone interview, FCO Official, 17 November 2011.
11. Speech by Deputy Head of the FCO's Global Strategic Impacts Team, Climate Change and Energy Department, 19 October 2012, University of Sussex.
12. Interview, FCO Official, Climate Change and Energy Department, 23 January 2012, London.
13. Interview, Official of the British High Commission in Delhi, 19 August 2011, Delhi.

14. Telephone interview, Deputy Head of the FCO's Global Strategic Impacts Team (formerly called: Climate Security Team), Climate Change and Energy Department, 24 May 2012 and 1 June 2012.
15. Based on interviews conducted in the FCO.
16. Telephone interview, DFID Official, 4 April 2011.
17. Interview, DFID Official, 9 December 2011, London.
18. Such an alternative framing of climate migration is not fully unproblematic either. It remains to be seen whether communities themselves would perceive the need to migrate due to climate change impacts through such a more positive and constructive lens.
19. Telephone interview, DECC Official, and one of DECC's representative in the Project Advisory Group of the Foresight Project on Global Environmental Migration, 20 January 2012.
20. Interview, Edward Ferguson, Head of Defence Strategy and Priorities, Strategy Unit, MOD, 23 January 2011, London, and telephone interview was held 19 February 2013; Telephone interview, MOD Official, formerly with the Sustainable Development Team and currently with the Sustainable Procurement Strategy Division, 5 December 2011.
21. Interview, Simon Cole, Assistant Head Futures Team, Development Concepts and Doctrine Centre (DCDC), MOD, 9 November 2011, Shrivenham.
22. Interview, Chris Evett, Editor, Global Strategic Trends Programme, Futures Team, Development Concepts and Doctrine Centre (DCDC), MOD, 9 November 2011, Shrivenham.
23. Moreover, the choice of the prosperity narrative also related to the fact that it is supported by a greater level of evidence, compared to arguments about climate change being a direct cause of conflict or mass climate migration. Telephone interview, Deputy Head of the FCO's Global Strategic Impacts Team (formerly called: Climate Security Team), Climate Change and Energy Department, 24 May 2012 and 1 June 2012.

References

Ananthapadmanabhan, G., K. Srinivas, and V. Gopal (2007) *Hiding behind the poor: a report on climate injustice*. Bangalore: Greenpeace India.

Ashton, J. (2011) *Only diplomacy: hard-headed soft power for a time of risk, scarcity and insecurity*. Speech at Chatham House, London, 21 February. Available at: www.chathamhouse.org/publications/papers/view/109591 (last visit 19 September 2014).

BASIC (Brazil, South Africa, India, and China) (2012) *Joint statement issued at the conclusion of the 13th BASIC ministerial meeting on climate change*. Beijing, China, 19–20 November 2012. Available at: www.indianembassy.org.cn/newsDetails.aspx?NewsId=381 (last visit 19 September 2014).

BBC (2009) 'Why did Copenhagen fail to deliver a climate deal?', *BBC*, 22 December. Available at: http://news.bbc.co.uk/2/hi/science/nature/8426835.stm (last visit 19 September 2014).

Beckett, M. (2006) *Beckett: Berlin speech on climate change and security*. Speech at British Embassy, Berlin, 24 October. Available at: http://ukingermany.fco.gov.uk/en/newsroom/?view=Speech&id=4616005 (last visit 22 March 2013). This speech is no longer available online.

Blair, T. (2004) 'Full text: Blair's climate change speech', *The Guardian*, 15 September 2004. Available at: www.guardian.co.uk/politics/2004/sep/15/greenpolitics.uk (last visit 3 February 2015).

Boas, I. (2014) 'Where is the South in security discourse on climate change', *Critical Studies on Security*, 2(2): 148–161.

Brown, G. (2009) *Brown: for the planet, there is no plan B*. Speech at Major Economies Forum, 19 October. Available at: www.youtube.com/watch?v=NYnVf33l4mE (last visit 19 September 2014).

Cabinet Office (2009) *Security for the next generation: National Security Strategy Update*. London: Crown Copyright/Cabinet Office.

Cabinet Office (2010a) *Securing Britain in an age of uncertainty. The Strategic Security and Defence Review*. London: Crown Copyright/Cabinet Office.

Cabinet Office (2010b) *A strong Britain in an age of uncertainty. The National Security Strategy*. London: Crown Copyright/Cabinet Office.

Cabinet Office (2013) *Annual report on the National Security Strategy and Strategic Defence and Security Review*. Available at: www.gov.uk/government/uploads/system/uploads/attachment_data/file/267808/Annual-report-on-NSS-and-SDSR.pdf (last visit 2 October 2014).

Cameron, D. (2010) *Use the profit motive to fight climate change*. Statement by Cameron, 7 December. Available at: www.guardian.co.uk/commentisfree/2010/nov/28/david-cameron-climate-change-cancun (last visit 19 September 2014).

Center for Climate and Energy Solutions (C2ES) (2013) *Outcomes of the U.N. climate change conference in Warsaw*. Available at: www.c2es.org/international/negotiations/cop-19/summary (last visit 1 October 2014).

Chakravarty, S. and M. V. Ramana (2012) 'The hiding behind the poor debate: a synthetic overview'. In: N. Dubash (ed.), *Handbook of climate change and India. Development, politics and governance*. New Delhi: Oxford University Press: 218–229.

Chauhan, C. (2012) 'India tops China in air pollution level increase', *Hindustan Times*, 30 November. Available at: www.hindustantimes.com/India-news/NewDelhi/India-tops-China-in-air-pollution-level-increase/Article1–966208.aspx (last visit 19 September 2014).

Darby, M. (2014) 'UK slashes climate change budget', *Responding to Climate Change (RTCC), Guardian Environment Network*, 1 August. Available at: www.theguardian.com/environment/2014/aug/01/uk-slashes-climate-change-diplomacy-budget (last visit 2 October 2014).

Development, Concepts and Doctrine Centre (DCDC) (2007) *The DCDC Global Strategic Trends Programme 2007–2036*. London: Crown Copyright/MOD 2007 (3rd edition).

Development, Concepts and Doctrine Centre (DCDC) (2010) *Strategic Trends Programme. Global strategic trends—out to 2040*. London: MOD (4th edition).

Doyle, A. (2011) 'Call for votes to spur climate talks faces hurdles', *Reuters*, 16 June. Available at: www.reuters.com/article/2011/06/16/us-climate-vote-idUSTRE75F4FP20110616 (last visit 19 September 2014).

European Commission (2011) *Common statement by the European Union, Least Developed Countries and the Alliance of Small Island States*. Available at: http://ec.europa.eu/commission_2010–2014/hedegaard/headlines/news/2011–12–09_01_en.htm (last visit 19 September 2014).

Falkner, R., H. Stephan, and J. Vogler (2010) 'International climate policy after Copenhagen: towards a "building blocks" approach', *Global Policy*, 1(3): 252–262.

Foreign and Commonwealth Office (FCO) (2006) *Departmental report. 1 April 2005–31 March 2006*. London: FCO/Crown Copyright.

Foreign and Commonwealth Office (FCO) (2008) *Departmental report and resource accounts. 1 April 2007–31 March 2008*. Volume 1. London: FCO/Crown Copyright.

Foreign and Commonwealth Office (FCO) (2009) *Robin Gwynn: tenacity and a sense of responsibility to power climate change objectives.* Available at the UK web archive: http://webarchive.nationalarchives.gov.uk/20130217073211/http://ukinbangladesh. fco.gov.uk/en/about-us/working-with-bangladesh/climate-change/global-discussion/ uk-climate-security-envoy (last visit 19 September 2014).

Foreign and Commonwealth Office (FCO) (2011) *Annual report and accounts 2010– 2011 (for the year ended 31 March 2011).* London: FCO/Crown Copyright.

Hague, W. (2010) *The diplomacy of climate change.* Speech at the Council of Foreign Relations, New York, 27 September. Available at: www.gov.uk/government/ speeches/an-effective-response-to-climate-change-underpins-our-security-and-prosperity (last visit 19 September 2014).

Hague, W. (2011) *Climate change "our values, security and prosperity compel us to act".* Speech at the Climate Change and Energy Conference, London, 27 June. Available at: www.gov.uk/government/speeches/climate-change-our-values-security-and-prosperity-compel-us-to-act (last visit 19 September 2014).

Hague, W. (2012) *Foreign policy has to support jobs, growth and prosperity.* Speech to the Confederation of British Industry, London, 16 May. Available at: www.gov. uk/government/speeches/foreign-policy-has-to-support-jobs-and-growth-and-prosperity (last visit 19 September 2014).

Harvey, F. (2012) 'Clean technology: what is the future of green energy?', *The Guardian*, 2 October 2012. Available at: www.guardian.co.uk/sustainable-business/clean-technology-green-energy-future (last visit 19 September 2014).

Harvey, F. (2013) 'As the Warsaw climate talks end, the hard work is just beginning', *The Guardian*, 23 November. Available at: www.theguardian.com/environment/2013/ nov/25/warsaw-climate-talks-end-cop19-2015 (last visit 1 October 2014).

King, E. (2013) 'China and Russia block UN Security Council climate change action', *Responding to Climate Change (RTCC)*, 19 February. Available at: www.rtcc. org/2013/02/18/china-and-russia-block-un-security-council-climate-change-action/ (last visit 30 September 2014).

Lacey, S. (2011) 'How China dominates solar power', *The Guardian*, 12 September. Available at: www.guardian.co.uk/environment/2011/sep/12/how-china-dominates-solar-power (last visit 21 September 2014).

Michaelowa, K. and A. Michaelowa (2012) 'India as an emerging power in international climate negotiations', *Climate Policy*, 12(5): 575–590.

Mohan, R.C. (2010) 'Rising India: partner in shaping the global commons?', *The Washington Quarterly*, 33(3): 133–148.

Morales, A. and E. Krukowska (2013) 'UN climate deal allows countries to make "contributions" on emissions targets, instead of "commitments", *National Post*, 23 November. Available at: http://news.nationalpost.com/2013/11/23/un-climate-deal-allows-countries-to-make-contributions-on-emissions-targets-instead-of-commitments/ (last visit 30 September 2014).

Morales, A. and S. Nicola (2013) Climate talks near impasse as China, India seek changes', *Bloomberg*, 23 November. Available at: www.bloomberg.com/news/ 2013–11–23/china-india-reject-durban-platform-text-at-un-climate-talks.html (last visit 30 September 2014).

Narlikar, A. (2011) 'Is India a responsible great power?', *Third World Quarterly*, 32(9): 1607–1621.

NDTV Correspondent (2010) 'Cancun setback: India, China isolated', *NDTV*, 9 December. Available at: www.ndtv.com/article/india/cancun-setback-india-china-isolated-71437 (last visit 15 October 2014).

Planning Commission, Government of India (2013) *Twelfth five year plan (2012– 2017). Faster, more inclusive and sustainable growth*, Volume 1. New Delhi: Sage Publications India.

Prime Minister (PM)'s Council on Climate Change (2008) *National action plan on climate change*. New Delhi: Government of India.

Qi, X. (2011) 'The rise of BASIC in UN climate change negotiations', *South African Journal of International Affairs*, 18(3): 295–318.

Sen, A. (1999) *Development as freedom*. Oxford: Oxford University Press.

Sethi, N. (2009) 'Jairam for major shift at climate talks', *The Times of India*, 29 October. Available at: http://articles.timesofindia.indiatimes.com/2009–10–19/india/28079441_1_greenhouse-gas-emission-reduction-climate-negotiations-change-negotiations (last visit 23 September 2014).

Smith, K. (2012) 'India's identity and its global aspirations', *Global Society*, 26(3): 369–385.

Stern, N. (2006) *The Stern review on the economics of climate change*. Available at: http://webarchive.nationalarchives.gov.uk/+/http://www.hm-treasury.gov.uk/sternreview_index.htm (last visit 23 September 2014). Published in 2007 in Cambridge, UK, with Cambridge University Press.

Tadeao, M. (2014) 'British economy to surpass pre-recession peak, says BBC', *The Independent*. Available at: www.independent.co.uk/news/business/news/british-economy-to-surpass-prerecession-peak-in-2014-says-bcc-8999713.html# (last visit 15 October 2014).

The Centre for Climate Change & Security (2014) *UK to integrate climate change into military planning*. Available at: http://climateandsecurity.org/2014/10/15/uk-to-integrate-climate-change-into-military-planning/ (last visit 15 October 2014).

The Guardian (2011) 'David Cameron must speak out on climate change, says top scientist', *The Guardian*, 29 June. Available at: www.guardian.co.uk/environment/2011/jun/29/climate-change-david-cameron-king (last visit 19 September 2014).

The Hindu (2011) 'India's human development poor: Sen', *The Hindu*, 16 December. Available at: www.thehindu.com/news/national/article2720812.ece (last visit 23 September 2014).

The UK Government Office for Science (2011) *Foresight: migration and global environmental change. Future challenges and opportunities*. Final Project Report. London: Crown Copyright/The Government Office for Science.

United Nations Development Programme (UNDP) (2014) *Human development report 2014*. New York: UNDP. Available at: http://hdr.undp.org/sites/default/files/hdr14-report-en-1.pdf (last visit 23 September 2014)

United Nations Framework Convention on Climate Change (UNFCCC) (1992) *United Nations Framework Convention on Climate Change*. Available at: http://unfccc.int/resource/docs/convkp/conveng.pdf (last visit 23 September 2014).

United Nations Framework Convention on Climate Change (UNFCCC) (2011) *Revised proposal from Papua New Guinea and Mexico to amend Articles 7 and 18 of the Convention*. Available at: http://unfccc.int/resource/docs/2011/cop17/eng/04r01.pdf (last visit 23 September 2014).

United Nations Framework Convention on Climate Change (UNFCCC) (2012) *Report of the Conference of the Parties on its seventeenth session, held in Durban from*

28 November to 11 December 2011. Available at: http://unfccc.int/resource/docs/2011/cop17/eng/09a01.pdf (last visit 23 September 2014).

United Nations—Office of the High Representative for the Least Developed Countries, Landlocked Developing Countries and Small Island Developing States (UN-OHRLLS) (2014a) *List of Least Developed Countries.* Available at: www.un.org/en/development/desa/policy/cdp/ldc/ldc_list.pdf (last visit 23 September 2014).

United Nations—Office of the High Representative for the Least Developed Countries, Landlocked Developing Countries and Small Island Developing States (UN-OHRLLS) (2014b) *Small Island Developing States. Country profiles.* Available at: http://unohrlls.org/about-sids/country-profiles/ (last visit 23 September 2014).

Van Schaik, L. (2012) *The EU and the progressive alliance negotiating in Durban: saving the climate?* Overseas Development Institute, Working Paper 354. London: Overseas Development Institute and Climate and Development Knowledge Network.

Vihma, A. (2010) *Elephant in the room? The new G77 and China dynamics in climate talks.* Briefing paper 6. Helsinki: The Finish Institute of International Affairs.

Yamin, F. (2007) *The BASIC project final report.* Brighton: Institute of Development Studies. Available at: www.basic-project.net/data/final/BASIC%20Final%20Report%20September%2020071.pdf (last visit 24 September 2014).

7 Conclusion

The aim of the book was to examine the securitisation of climate migration in the context of climate change politics. The issue of climate migration has been played on to spark fears about instability and even violent conflict, to visualise what unabated climate change can do. It is one of the main avenues through which political actors have tried to make their case for urgent climate action. The macro-level analysis of the United Nations (UN) Security Council debates has shown that a range of actors have used such securitising moves, the primary ones being from Europe and from small island states. The micro-level analysis of the securitising move by the United Kingdom (UK)'s Foreign and Commonwealth Office (FCO) revealed that these securitising moves have a strategic character and were carefully crafted by politicians and diplomats.

The emerging developing countries (in particular China, India, and Brazil) have actively opposed securitising moves on climate migration. Even though lower in number (compared to the group of securitisers in the debate), these states are crucial as they function as a key audience to the securitising moves. These countries have come under increasing pressure to commit to binding mitigation action under the UNFCCC, and for that very reason have been targeted by securitising moves on climate migration.

The micro-level analysis zoomed in on India's reaction to the securitising move by the FCO. It showed that the FCO's securitising move on climate migration is not the best strategy in the Indian context. The Government of India has interpreted the FCO's security arguments on climate migration as an inappropriate negotiation tactic seeking to pressure India in the light of climate change negotiations. Moreover, India values principles of self-determination and is an emerging power. The Indian elite therefore considers it warranted that countries such as the UK show more respect to India's interest, needs, and international status. In that context, when the FCO warns of mass climate migration and of climate conflict on India's borders to stimulate greater climate action, it comes across as attempting to scare India, to interfere with its policy making, and as disregarding India's growing power and more pressing concerns. For those reasons, the FCO's securitising move did not add to a greater sense of understanding between India and the UK that collaborative and ambitious steps are necessary to protect the world from dangerous climate change. Neither did the securitising move convince the Government of India that it is in its own best interest to adopt binding mitigation targets to prevent mass immigration flows from Bangladesh. Instead, the securitising move backfired, adding to a difficult negotiation environment that can enhance stalemate and divisions in the UNFCCC.

In the course of the securitisation process, the FCO did adapt its securitising move. It uses a more positively oriented and subtle narrative about economic prosperity, which is likely to be more successful in the Indian context. The India–FCO interaction process was, however, not the main reason for this shift to take place. The change of UK Government in 2010 had a larger impact on the FCO's climate change diplomacy. The UK Coalition Government has shifted priorities away from climate change, and instead focussed its attention on the UK's economy and on questions of resource security. The FCO adapted its diplomatic endeavours in such a way that it would better resonate with these developments in the UK Government.

Given that the micro-level analysis has focussed on the specific study of the FCO–India relations, a question can be raised whether India's reaction would be different in case another industrialised country would use security arguments on climate migration to endorse mitigation action. The UK and India have a special relationship due to their colonial history, which may explain India's sensitive reaction. In that historical context, the FCO can more easily become accused of lecturing India on its policy making and of disrespecting India's right to self-determination and sovereignty. But India's defensive reaction is not limited to the UK's endeavours. Even though India's negative reaction may be somewhat stronger in case of interactions with the UK, interviewees often referred to the 'West' as if being one actor attempting to push India into accepting binding mitigation targets and as interfering with its policy making. Therefore, it can be expected that India would be equally sceptical when other industrialised countries use a security narrative to promote climate action.

The hypothetical argument can be made that India's reaction may be different in case the United States (US) would use a security narrative on climate migration in its climate change diplomacy (as discussed, thus far the US has not actively used securitising moves in such a context). The European Union (EU) (including the UK)'s position in the UNFCCC has become weaker over the years (Falkner et al. 2010; see chapter 6 for details). Meanwhile, large developing countries have becoming increasingly powerful in global politics. In this political environment, emerging developing countries may perceive the US as a more powerful and important actor in climate diplomacy compared to the UK and the EU. Then again, India perceives the US as the key responsible actor on climate change when it comes down to discussions on historical responsibility. Moreover, India's veto in the World Trade Organisation of an agreement to ease trade rules, lobbied for by the US (Brunnstrom and Miles 2014), shows that the Indian Government pursues its 'defensive, nay-saying-strategy' (Narlikar 2006: 60) even when it comes to the US.

The Pragmatic Framework for Analysis on Securitisation

The pragmatic framework for analysis on securitisation, developed in this book, provides insight into the complexity of securitisation processes. The context and the audience are central to this framework to allow for a dynamic and in-depth study of securitisation. It aims to grasp complexity in securitisation processes by engaging with diverging views on security or on security measures that can emerge in different contexts and/or in securitiser–audience interactions. This allows for different theoretical insights on securitisation to be used in the same study and thus to move between the Copenhagen School, the Paris School, Critical Security Studies, and the Risk School.

Studying the contextual environment was particularly helpful to understand why the FCO and the Government of India had certain perceptions, disagreed, acted, or reacted in a particular manner. For instance, by placing the FCO's securitising move in the context of its climate change diplomacy, I was able to understand how and why the FCO attempted to securitise climate migration and in what form. In similar vein, a contextual analysis helped to provide a greater understanding of the sensitivity surrounding securitising moves on climate migration amongst the Government of India. India's sceptical perspective was informed by its negotiation position on climate change and by its view on collaboration with Western countries.

Table 7.1[1] shows how the pragmatic framework for analysis allowed me to draw on various theoretical insights to examine and understand the securitisation process on climate migration. First of all, insights from the Copenhagen School and the Paris School were helpful to understand how securitising moves on climate migration emerged and were promoted (see chapter 4 for details). In line with the Copenhagen School's insights, that underlie the speech act perspective as defined in chapter 3, securitising moves on climate migration were based on high-profile statements and communication strategies by elite actors (e.g., in the UN Security Council debates) aimed to raise awareness of greater climate action. In line with the Paris School, informing the routine–technocratic perspective as defined in chapter 3, the micro-level analysis of the FCO provided insight into the role of the less visible institutional and departmental processes in crafting the securitising move.

A pragmatic analysis of securitisation furthermore helped to demonstrate that the FCO's securitising move was incoherent (see chapters 4 and 5 for details). The FCO conceptualised climate migration through the Copenhagen School's language of exceptionality and great danger, while seeking to promote more mundane and preventive measures of climate change mitigation, as envisaged by the Risk School and the Paris School. This securitising move was easily interpreted as plain rhetoric. In the Government of India, the FCO was seen as trying to deflect attention away from the UK's responsibilities on climate change and as pressuring India by the use of scare stories on climate migration that could not be supported by convincing evidence.

Table 7.1 Applying the Pragmatic Framework for Analysis to FCO–India Interactions in the Securitisation Process on Climate Migration

	Securitising Move		*Audience Response*		*Outcome*
Outcomes of the micro-level analysis	Emergence of the FCO's securitising move	Message of the FCO's securitising move on CM	India's response of backfire	India's non-engagement	The FCO uses an alternative economic narrative
Copenhagen School	×	×	×		
Paris School	×	×			×
Critical Security Studies					
Risk School		×			×
Non-securitisation				×	

Moreover, by allowing for an interplay of the various schools on securitisation, I could provide a more in-depth understanding of India's negative response to the FCO's securitising move (see chapter 5 for details). Most interesting was that India had a different understanding of the FCO's promoted mitigation measures, a perspective that was closer to the Copenhagen School's logic of exceptionality, competition, and confrontation (see next section for a more detailed discussion). This shows that a securitisation process adapts to different contexts, and that it is insufficient to rely on the insights of one school on securitisation to account for complexity and diverse understandings.

Finally, different theoretical insights on securitisation were needed to trace and review the FCO's alternative narrative on economic prosperity (examined in the 'outcome' phase of the securitisation process in chapter 6). This narrative builds on a notion of risk and unease, in line with the Risk School's and Paris School's conceptualisation of security. Such a framing has a better fit with climate measures of risk management and prevention that the FCO aims to promote. It thus better and more genuinely expresses the UK's climate agenda. For that reason, this narrative is expected to face less credibility problems and resistance amongst its audience, and thus may better stimulate collaborative action on climate change by the UK and India.

In the remainder of the conclusion, I will further delve into specific findings of this book and I will review their wider relevance. This section is divided into three discussions. The first discussion focusses on the key question of this book: the connection between climate politics and the securitisation of climate migration. The second discussion centres on the finding that alarmist security language is not necessarily effective to promote climate action. In these two discussions, I relate my findings to the wider securitisation literature on climate change, not necessarily specified to the issue of climate migration. In the third and final discussion, I review the question that has been central to most studies on the securitisation of climate migration: the impact on immigration policy and border security politics.

Securitisation and the Connection With Climate Politics

In informal discussions with students and colleagues, it often sounds counter-intuitive that the securitisation of climate migration is connected to climate change politics. Often the expectation is that the securitisation of climate migration is about border controls and immigration policy. That was also my own initial reaction when hearing that climate migration was framed as a security threat. But as the analysis has shown, the story is more complex than that. The primary context in which the securitisation of climate migration has thus far played out is that of climate change politics. In line with the argument by Methmann and Rothe (2012), the book demonstrates that securitisations in the realm of climate change are promoted through exceptional discourse, while seeking to endorse 'a rather piecemeal and technocratic approach to the management of carbon emissions' (Methmann and Rothe 2012: 324). The examined securitising moves on climate migration did not seek to endorse border security measures to halt climate migrants. Instead, these securitising moves were used to raise the urgency of climate action in the UNFCCC.

Most in-depth accounts of the securitisation of climate change have aimed to understand this relationship between alarmist security language and more subtle practices of risk management by unravelling the structural characteristics (the grammar, underlying contradictions, structural political effects, etc.) of the climate security discourse (see e.g., Trombetta 2008, Corry 2012; Methmann and Rothe 2012; Bettini 2013; Oels 2013). Methmann and Rothe (2012) point towards the paradoxical character of the climate security discourse to explain why alarmist security language leads to the promotion of mundane technocratic measures in the realm of climate governance. They argue that the apocalyptic imagining of climate change is 'articulated as overstraining the capacity of political actors' (Methmann and Rothe 2012: 324). The threat is presented too big and too all-encompassing that we cannot do anything, even something exceptional, to stop it, and therefore our only option is to try and manage it through adaptation and mitigation measures present in the UNFCCC machinery.

My analysis largely explains the discrepancy in the securitisation process through insights on the role of strategy in a securitising move. In support of Floyd's (2010) argument, intentions are crucial in a securitisation process. Because the FCO's securitising move was strategic and instrumental, it used alarmist warning messages to raise the urgency of mitigation measures and not to endorse, consciously at least, exceptional measures in the realm of border controls or in the context of the UN Security Council. This shows how the strategic and calculated usage of a discourse can direct the course of a securitisation process, and make it focussed on promoting particular forms of action. As argued by Brown et al. (2007: 1144): 'Appealing to the hard security concerns of these countries presents another tactic for gathering additional support for a post-Kyoto emissions reduction strategy'. Moreover, precisely the strategic usage of alarmist language has made it unsuccessful amongst its audience. It made India more sceptical of the UK's intentions on climate change and felt pressurised through scare stories that were unfounded. In the words of one interviewee: 'If you want policy to be changed you have to tell people, this is the challenge and this is the policy response for it and it has to be believable'.[2] The lesson from this case, then, is that the framing of the securitiser's message has to be genuine and valid for it to be convincing and thus successful amongst an already sceptical audience.

Moreover, the analysis has shown that securitising moves on climate migration seeking to promote binding mitigation targets can be interpreted by its audience as proposing exceptional action. Scholarly literature on the securitisation of climate change argues that mitigation action to reduce GHG emissions does not resemble the exceptional, competitive, and confrontational logic as outlined by the Copenhagen School (Trombetta 2008; Corry 2012; Methmann and Rothe 2012Oels 2013). Instead, the argument is that such measures are technocratic and more mundane in nature. I agree with this analysis, yet to a limited degree. On the one hand, the FCO and the other securitisers indeed aim to prevent climate change through collaboration on low-carbon economic and technological development. On the other hand, the analysis of India provides a completely different picture. India has increasingly been put under pressure (including through securitisation processes) to sign up to binding mitigation targets under the UN climate convention. India has perceived this as being pushed to undertake extraordinary action. It is largely understood, or at least portrayed, as a confrontational and competitive attempt by industrialised countries seeking to divert attention away from their historical responsibility for climate change, while pressuring India into accepting certain measures that may harm its economy and efforts to alleviate poverty. From this understanding, the promotion of climate change mitigation does not necessarily fit notions of more mundane, piecemeal, risk management, technocratic development, and positive prevention aimed to preserve our current civilisation. Actually, it best corresponds with the Copenhagen School's insights of exceptionality, mistrust, competition, and friend/enemy dichotomies. For that reason, the Copenhagen School's insights do have added value when analysing climate change mitigation in the context of securitisation from the perspective of India.

To further delve into this argument, it is relevant to review Corry's claim that the mitigation of climate change fits the logic of risk management since it governs the '*conditions of possibility*' of danger (Corry 2012: 246, italics in the original). From this perspective, responses to the securitisation of climate change (including climate migration) are about managing the factors that make damaging events possible (these factors being the conditions of possibility), which are the greenhouse gas emissions (GHG). This in contrast to security measures envisaged by the Copenhagen School that according to Corry try to counter 'direct causes of harm' (2012: 246) (e.g., the construction of a fence to stop migrants standing on a country's borders). But this argument seems to overlook that countries such as India actually perceive this governance of the so-called conditions of possibilities of harm (so, the reduction of GHG emissions) as the *direct* cause of harm. From India's perspective, binding mitigation targets actually risk harming India's more pressing concerns, such as poverty alleviation, and discount the wealth aspirations of the Indian population. To reiterate a quote by Samir Saran, Vice-President of the Delhi-based Observer Research Foundation:

> Every Indian who lives in a village who may have a phone and a TV, but other than that little disposable income, still does have dreams. They dream of buying a car one day and other consumer goods. The world spends millions of dollars to tell the rest of the world to consume more through marketing and advertisement, they give people hundreds of possibilities to indulge in activities which contribute to consumption and pollution. And then on the other hand we also hear narratives [in the context of climate change negotiations] that say 'no this is not a good way to live life'. This is a discourse of differentiated lifestyles. One that seeks to limit the aspirations of the developing and emerging world. One that tells the emerging countries that they do not need to live this Western style life, that they can remain deprived, it is not a bad way to live, be happy. That happiness is not about money, not about cars. You can be happy and poor.[3]

Therefore, also from this perspective, climate change mitigation does fit the Copenhagen School's logic of security measures as concerned with more direct threats.

A counter argument can be made that this review of climate change mitigation through the Copenhagen School's insights goes beyond the Copenhagen School's definition of an exceptional measure. Even Buzan et al. (1998) themselves argue that the securitisation of climate change has failed, since it remains focussed on questions of mitigation, which they do not classify as extraordinary. But such an analysis starts from a perception that mitigation is something normal and mundane and seems to ignore how binding mitigation targets are perceived by some actors from the Global South. It also seems to assume that what surpasses the boundary of the normal is equal to all actors, which, as shown in this book, it is not. Therefore, if binding mitigation measures are promoted and actively endorsed, and possibly even become accepted through securitisation tactics, it is relevant to draw on the Copenhagen School's insights when actors perceive such action as something exceptional, confrontational, and competitive.

Nonetheless, it should be noted that this assessment particularly applies to India's perspective of binding mitigation measures in the context of the UNFCCC. India does take actions to improve its domestic energy efficiency, which can add to the mitigation of climate change. It is important to understand that such actions take place on a more voluntary level, for example, on a domestic or bilateral level or through its involvement in international technocratic mechanisms such as the Clean Development Mechanism under the Kyoto Protocol. The sensitivity of the mitigation question relates to India's fear that it may be *bound* to mitigation measures, and strict targets, under a multilateral regime, and therefore become subject to the control and review of industrialised countries (for details, see chapter 5).

The Effectiveness of Fear Appeals to Promote Climate Action

Another important finding is that alarmist security language does not necessarily help to increase the urgency and priority of climate action. I am not the first who argues that a language of threat is not necessarily an effective tool in climate change politics. Several scholars (Moser and Dilling 2004; Ereaut and Segnit 2006; Foust and Murphy 2009; Hulme 2007, 2009; Nisbet 2009; O'Neil and Nicholson-Cole 2009; Bettini 2013) note that apocalyptic language and images risk fuelling disengagement with climate change and enhance a sense of fatalism or scepticism. As argued by O'Neil and Nicholson-Cole (2009: 371), it leads 'to denial of the problem and disengagement with the whole issue in an attempt to avoid the discomfort of contending with it'.

The primary focus of such accounts is on sentiments among the general public. For instance, it is examined how the public responds to alarmist media coverage on climate change or to sensational movies such as *The Day After Tomorrow*. It is analysed whether fear appeals help to convince the public to become more actively engaged with climate change. The main findings are that the dramatic imaging of climate change fuels a sense of scepticism regarding the likelihood of extreme weather impacts, such as severe and sudden sea-level rise (see discussion Lowe et al. 2006; Hulme 2009: 213; Bettini 2013: 69). Furthermore, such fear appeals '. . . drive feelings of helplessness, remoteness, and lack of control'. In other words, the threat is just considered too big and apocalyptic for people to feel able to add anything meaningful to its prevention (Moser and Dilling 2004; Ereaut and Segnit 2006; Foust and Murphy 2009; O'Neil 2009; Bettini 2013).

In building on such findings, this book provides particular insight into the effects of securitising moves among state governments and on governmental cooperation. In the case of India, securitising moves on climate migration only fuelled feelings of mistrust about climate change negotiations and the UK's intentions. The alarmist framing of climate migration was understood as an attempt by industrialised countries to delay action on climate change and to put the blame on India. This shows that fear appeals do not only trigger scepticism about the likelihood of severe climate change, a sense of fatalism or disengagement with the issue, but they also tend to worsen collaborative and constructive political relations and levels of trust needed for climate change action.

Despite this evidence suggesting that fear appeals are ineffective to promote climate action, it cannot be ruled out that a language of threat can help to raise the urgency of action on climate change. The effectiveness depends on the context in which such arguments need to resonate. As discussed, security arguments have contributed to the formation of an alliance between the EU, the Least Developed Countries and the Alliance of Small Island States. These groups of states share the political endeavour to endorse international climate action, and have expressed similar concerns about insecurity caused by climate change. As argued by the representative of Papua New Guinea, on behalf of the Pacific Islands Forum Small Island Developing States, in the UN Security Council:

> The dangers that small islands and their populations face are no less serious than those faced by nations and peoples threatened by guns and bombs. The effects on our populations are as likely to cause massive dislocations of people as past and present wars.
>
> (Mr. Aisi, quoted in UNSC 2007: 28)

It has, however, not been researched in much depth how effective security language has been to forge this coalition, compared to other interests and discourses that bind these actors in the UNFCCC negotiations.

Even though threatening language may find resonance among some actors sharing the political project to promote action on climate change, it does not seem to work effectively with the more powerful emerging developing countries currently unwilling to sign up to ambitious mitigation targets under a binding UNFCCC framework. India does not want to be lectured through scare stories on climate change and wants to be taken seriously. This means that communication with India, and with other emerging powers sharing similar concerns, has to come across as a genuine attempt to create dialogue and collaboration.

Intersection With Immigration Policy

A key theme in the literature on the securitisation of climate *migration* is its intersections with immigration policy (Smith 2007; Hartmann 2010; White 2011; Trombetta 2014). These scholars warn that the securitisation of climate migration adds to the legitimisation of border controls and restrictive immigration politics.

In this research, I found no compelling evidence that the Government of India is currently drawing on the notion of climate migration to justify its restrictive immigration policy. This shows that the Indian context is less susceptible to a discourse on cross-border *climate* migration from Bangladesh than one may expect, at least on the level of India's central government. As discussed in chapter 5, India's security community argues to have other priorities and more urgent issues to deal with (such as its relations with Pakistan and China, and economic migration at the Bangladesh-Indian border) and seems less inclined to put much energy into what they perceive as somewhat vague and so-called Western questions related to the climate change–migration–security nexus.

This finding shows that it is not straightforward that the securitisation of climate migration intersects with immigration policies, also in states other than India. Certainly, there is a risk for such aversive developments (see e.g., the compelling case of Morocco by White 2011), due to the connection between discourses on climate migration and fears expressed in many societies about immigrant groups, such as immigrants from poorer regions who have little economic means to support themselves. But as shown in this analysis, there is no *direct* relation between the securitisation of climate migration and the creation of strict immigration policies. The manner and extent to which the securitisation of climate migration may result in, or justify, restrictive immigration practices depends on the particularities of its receiving context.

To conclude, the securitisation of climate migration deeply intersects with climate change politics. Securitising moves on climate migration work to convince states to do more on the mitigation of GHG emissions. 'Scare' stories are, however, not the best means to convince an already sceptical audience. In fact, it can be counterproductive. This leads to a number of questions that could form the basis of future research on this topic: Does this mean that the securitisation of climate migration ends here or will it continue as a negotiation strategy on climate change? If yes, why? Will European and small island states continue to be the key securitisers? Especially since there is much evidence that this strategy can be counterproductive, it is interesting to research what continues to drive these actors, why their strategies overlap, why they engage in similar narratives, how they communicate, and why they do not (always) acknowledge the counterproductive elements of their narratives. And if it seizes to work as such a strategic narrative, will fears about climate migration linger on, and in the future have more adverse consequences in the field of immigration and security policy?

Notes

1. In Table 7.1, CM stands for climate migration.
2. Interview, Samir Saran, Senior Fellow and Vice President, Observer Research Foundation, 13 August 2011, Delhi.
3. Interview, Samir Saran, Senior Fellow and Vice President, Observer Research Foundation, 13 August 2011, Delhi.

References

Bettini, G. (2013) 'Climate carbarians at the gate? A critique of apocalyptic narratives on "climate refugees"', *Geoforum*, 45(March): 63–72.

Brown, O., A. Hammill, and R. McLeman (2007) 'Climate change as the "new" security threat: implications for Africa', *International Affairs*, 83(6): 1141–1154.

Brunnstrom, D. and T. Miles (2014) 'India's demands block $1 trillion WTO deal on customs rules', *Reuters*, 1 August. Available at: http://in.reuters.com/article/2014/08/01/india-trade-wto-idINKBN0G02GV20140801 (last visit 2 October 2014).

Buzan, B., O. Wæver, and J. de Wilde (1998) *Security: a new framework for analysis*. Boulder, CO: Lynne Rienner.

Corry, O. (2012) 'Securitisation and "riskification": second-order security and the politics of climate change', *Millennium: Journal of International Studies*, 40(2): 235–258.

Ereaut, S. and N. Segnit (2006) *Warm words. How are we telling the climate story and can we tell it better?* London: Institute for Public Policy Research.

Falkner, R., H. Stephan, and J. Vogler (2010) 'International climate policy after Copenhagen: towards a "building blocks" approach', *Global Policy*, 1(3): 252–262.

Floyd, R. (2010) *Security and the environment. Securitisation and theory and US environmental security policy*. Cambridge: Cambridge University Press.

Foust, C. R. and W. O. Murphy (2009) 'Revealing and reframing apocalyptic tragedy in global warming discourse', *Environmental Communication: A Journal of Nature and Culture*, 3(2): 151–167.

Hartmann, B. (2010) 'Policy arena. Rethinking climate refugees and climate conflict: rhetoric, reality and the process of policy discourse', *Journal of International Development*, 22(2): 233–246.

Hulme, M. (2007) 'Newspaper scare headlines can be counter-productive', *Nature*, 445(7120): 818.

Hulme, M. (2009) *Why we disagree about climate change*. Cambridge: Cambridge University Press.

Lowe, T., K. Brown, S. Dessai, M. Doria, K. Haynes and K. Vincet (2006) 'Does tomorrow ever come? Disaster narrative and public perceptions of climate change', *Public Understanding of Science*, 15(4): 435–457.

Methmann, C. and D. Rothe (2012) 'Politics for the day after tomorrow: the political effect of apocalyptic imageries in global climate governance', *Security Dialogue*, 43(4): 323–344.

Moser, S. C. and L. Dilling (2004) 'Making Climate HOT. Communicating the Urgency and Challenge of Global Climate Change', *Environment*, 46(10): 33–46.

Narlikar, A. (2006) 'Peculiar chauvinism or strategic calculation? Explaining the negotiating strategy of a rising India', *International Affairs*, 82(1): 59–76.

Nisbet, M. C. (2009) 'Communicating climate change: why frames matter for public engagement', *Environment: Science and Policy for Sustainable Development*, 51(2): 12–23.

Oels, A. (2013) 'Rendering climate change governable by risk: from probability to contingency', *Geoforum*, 56(1): 17–29.

O'Neil, S. and S. Nicholson-Cole (2009) '"Fear won't do it". Promoting positive engagement with climate change through visual and iconic representations', *Science Communications*, 30(3): 355–379.

Smith, P. J. (2007) 'Climate change, mass migration and the military response', *Orbis*, 51(4): 617–633.

Trombetta, M. J. (2008) 'Environmental security and climate change: analysing the discourse', *Cambridge Review of International Affairs*, 21(4): 585–602.

Trombetta, M. J. (2014) 'Linking climate-induced migration and security in the EU: insights from the securitization debate', *Critical Studies on Security*, 2(2): 131–147.

United Nations Security Council (UNSC) (2007) *Letter dated 5 April 2007 from the permanent representative of the United Kingdom of Great Britain and Northern Ireland to the United Nations addressed to the president of the Security Council*. Meeting records, S/PV.5663, 5663rd meeting (Part 1), 17 April, New York.

White, H. (2011) *Climate change and migration*. Oxford: Oxford University Press.

Appendix
List of Interviews

This appendix provides a record of the interviews conducted. Not all details are provided for every interviewee, as some requested their identity to be protected. The occupation of the interviewees provided below represents their occupation at the time of the interview.

Table A.1a List of Interviews Relevant to the Analysis of the FCO/UK Government

Interviews with Officials in the Foreign & Commonwealth Office (FCO), name/ occupation	*Date of the Interview*
Corinne Kitsell, Deputy Director, the FCO's Migration Directorate	18 November 2011, telephone interview
John Ashton, the FCO's Special Representative for Climate Change (from June 2006–June 2012) and Head of the former FCO's Environmental Policy Department	31 January 2012, and 24 May 2012, telephone interview
Sarah Cullum, Head of the FCO's Global Strategic Impacts Team (formerly called Climate Security Team), the FCO's Climate Change and Energy Department	8 March 2011, London (final email communication, 8 February 2013)
Joel Watson, Deputy Head of the FCO's Global Strategic Impacts Team (formerly called Climate Security Team), the FCO's Climate Change and Energy Department	31 October 2011, London; 19 October 2012, University of Sussex; a telephone interview on 24 May 2012 and 1 June 2012 (final email communication February 2013)
FCO Official	24 March 2011, telephone interview
FCO Official, the FCO's Climate Change and Energy Department	23 January 2012, London
FCO Official	7 November 2011 London; a telephone interview on 17 November 2011
Former FCO Official (worked in various departments until late 2000s)	9 May 2012, Canterbury
Official of the British High Commission in Delhi (India)	19 August 2011, Delhi

(*Continued*)

Table A.1a (Continued)

Interviews with Officials in the Foreign & Commonwealth Office (FCO), name/occupation	Date of the Interview
Haimanti Poddar, Senior Regional Adviser, Climate Change and Energy Unit, British Deputy High Commission, Calcutta (India)	30 September 2011, telephone interview
Margaret Beckett, MP Labour Party; Secretary of State for Environment, Food and Rural Affairs 2001–2006; Foreign Secretary 2006–2007	23 November 2011, London

Interviews with Officials of the Department of Energy and Climate Change (DECC), name/occupation	Date of the Interview
DECC Official	31 January 2012, telephone interview
DECC Official; a DECC representative in the Project Advisory Group of the Foresight Project on Global Environmental Migration	20 January 2012, telephone interview

Interviews with Officials of the Department for International Development (DFID), name/occupation	Date of the Interview
Lizzy Whitehead, Natural Resource Advisor, Growth and Resilience Department—Policy Division, DFID	1 June 2012, telephone interview
Peter Gordon, Policy Division and Research and Evidence Division, DFID. Previously with DFID's Migration Team	9 December 2011, London
Izabella Koziel, Climate and Environment Adviser, Climate and Environment Research Team, Research and Evidence Division, DFID	30 November 2011, telephone interview
DFID Official, Humanitarian & Disaster Risk Policy Group, DFID	23 January 2012, London
DFID Official (Official, Department for International Development)	4 April 2011, telephone interview
DFID Official	9 December 2011, London

Interviews with Officials of the Home Office, name/occupation	Date of the Interview
Chris Attwood, the Home Office lead to the Foresight Project on Global Environmental Migration, Home Office Science: Migration and Border Analysis, part of the Home Office's Migration Knowledge Management Network	11 November 2011, London

(*Continued*)

Table A.1a (Continued)

Interviews with Officials of the Ministry of Defence (MOD), name/occupation	Date of the Interview
Edward Ferguson, Head of Defence Strategy and Priorities, Strategy Unit, MOD	23 January 2011, London; a telephone interview on 19 February 2013
MOD Official, formerly with the Sustainable Development Team and currently with the Sustainable Procurement Strategy Division, MOD	5 December 2011, telephone interview
Simon Cole, Assistant Head Futures Team, Development Concepts and Doctrine Centre (DCDC), MOD	9 November 2011, Shrivenham (the interview was held together with Chris Evett and Richard Pethybridge)
Richard Pethybridge, Global Strategic Trends Programme, Futures Team, DCDC, MOD	9 November 2011, Shrivenham (the interview was held together with Simon Cole and Chris Evett)
Chris Evett, Editor, Global Strategic Trends Programme, Futures Team, DCDC, MOD	9 November 2011, Shrivenham (part of the interview was held together with Simon Cole and Richard Pethybridge; the second part was held separately)
Gregory Hammond, Global Strategic Trends Programme, Futures Team, DCDC, MOD	1 December 2011, telephone interview
Maurice Dixon, Group Captain, MOD	9 December 2011, London

Interviews with Officials of the UK Government Stabilisation Unit, name/occupation	Date of the Interview
Sharon Harvey, Head Lessons Team, Stabilisation Unit	19 July 2012, telephone interview
Matthew Waterfield, Stabilisation Unit	20 August 2012, telephone interview

Interviews with Officials of the UK Government (anonymous/or interviewees with an overarching role), name/occupation	Date of the Interview
Rear Admiral Neil Morisetti, the UK's Climate and Energy Security Envoy (until the end of 2012) (in 2013, the FCO's Special Representative for Climate Change)	27 October 2011, London
UK Government Official	6 October 2011, London

Think Tanks, name/occupation	Date of the Interview
Nick Mabey, Chief Executive, E3G (think tank); former senior advisor PM's Strategy Unit; former FCO Official	14 November 2011, London
Shane Tomlinson, E3G, Director of Development	14 November 2011, London
Research Analyst, Climate Change and Security Programme. Royal United Services Institute for Defence and Security Studies.	14 October 2011, London

(*Continued*)

Table A.1a (Continued)

Think Tanks, name/occupation	Date of the Interview
James de Waal, Visiting Fellow, International Security Programme, Chatham House, and UK Government Official	11 November 2011, London

NGOs, name/occupation	Date of the Interview
Hannah Smith, Project Manager, Climate Outreach and Information Network, Coordinator of the UK Climate Change and Migration Coalition	23 November 2011, London
Tory Timms, Campaigner, Environmental Justice Foundation	11 November 2011, London
Janani Vivekananda, Climate Change and Conflict Adviser.International Alert	2 November 2011, London; and a telephone interview on 27 June 2011

Researchers, name/occupation	Date of the Interview
Prof. Andrew Watkinson, Director Living with Environmental Change (LWEC), School of Environmental Sciences, University of East Anglia; member of the High Level Stakeholder Group of the Foresight Project on Global Environmental Migration	28 October 2011, telephone interview
Prof. Ronald Skeldon, Research Fellow with DFID from June 2009–March 2011, Professor at the Department of Geography, University of Sussex	28 November 2011, Brighton, University of Sussex
Corinne Schoch, Climate Change Group, International Institute for Environment and Development	6 October 2011, London
Katie Harris, Overseas Development Institute	27 October 2011, London
Dr. Tim Forsyth, London School of Economics and Political Science	24 November 2011, telephone interview

Table A.1b Interviews Relevant to the Analysis of India

Interviews with Officials in the Ministry of Environment and Forests (MOEF), name/occupation	Date of the Interview
Vijai Sharma, the Secretary of the MOEF from 30 June 2008 until 31 December 2010 and in this period part of India's delegation to the UNFCCC (retired)	12 August 2011, Delhi
R.R. Rasmi, Joint Secretary on Climate Change, MOEF	19 Augustus 2011, Delhi
Dr. Subosh Sharma, MOEF's principal Scientific Advisor on Climate Change	19 August 2011, Delhi
Dr. Nalini Bath, Head, Division of Impact Assessment, MOEF	19 Augustus 2011, Delhi

(Continued)

Table A.1b (Continued)

Interviews with Officials in the Ministry of Home Affairs, name/occupation	Date of the Interview
Madhukar Gupta, Secretary of the Ministry of Home Affairs from 2007–2009 (retired)	14 August 2011, Delhi
Santosh Kumar, Professor and Head of Policy, Planning and Cross Cutting Issues Division, National Institute for Disaster Management, Ministry of Home Affairs	17 August 2011, Delhi
Lt. Col. P. K. Pathak, Consultant, National Institute for Disaster Management, Ministry of Home Affairs	17 August 2011, Delhi

Interviews with Officials in the Ministry of External Affairs, name/occupation	Date of the Interview
Deb Mukharji, Indian Ambassador to Bangladesh from 1995–2000 (retired)	19 September 2011, telephone interview
Dr. Arvind Gupta, Additional Secretary in the Ministry of External Affairs (MEA, retired in 2013), and until August 2014 on deputation as the Director-General of Institute for Defence Studies and Analyses, Secretary of the National Security Council Secretariat (NSCS) from 1999–2007	18 August 2011, Delhi

Interviews with Officials in the Ministry of Rural Development, name/occupation	Date of the Interview
Indu Sharma, Project Director MGNREGA (Mahatma Gandhi National Rural Employment Guarantee Act), Ministry of Rural Affairs	19 August 2011, Delhi

Interviews with Officials, Office of the Principal Scientific Adviser to the Government of India, name/occupation	Date of the Interview
Neeraj Sinha, Scientist 'F'/Senior Director	17 August 2011, Delhi

Interviews with Officials in the Ministry of Science & Technology, name/occupation	Date of the Interview
Dr. Akhilesh Gupta, Adviser/Scientist-G & Coordinator—Climate Change Programme Department of Science & Technology	26 August 2011, Delhi

Interviews with Officials in the Ministry of Defence, name/occupation	Date of the Interview
Military Officer	15 August 2011, Delhi

Interview with Officials of the Planning Commission	Date of the Interview
Kirit Parikh, Member of the Indian Planning Commission until 2009 (retired)	20 August 2011, Delhi

(*Continued*)

Table A.1b (Continued)

Interviews, in the Government of India (anonymous or interviewees with an overarching role), name/occupation	Date of the Interview
Shyam Saran, Indian Foreign Secretary from 2005–2006, the Indian Prime Minister's Special Envoy on Climate Change from 2007 until March 2010, and in this period India's chief climate change negotiator (retired)	16 August 2011, Delhi

Interviews, in the Government of India (anonymous or interviewees with an overarching role), name/occupation	Date of the Interview
Chandrashekar Dasgupta, Member of the Prime Minister's Council on Climate Change	22 November 2011, telephone interview
Nitin Desai, Member of the Prime Minister's Council on Climate Change	25 August 2011, Delhi
Sunita Narain, Member of the Prime Minister's Council on Climate Change, and Director General of the Centre for Science and Environment	1 November 2011, telephone interview
Senior Official	23 August 2011, Delhi
Senior Official	18 Augustus 2011, Delhi

Interview, with Officials in the Government of West Bengal, name/occupation	Date of the Interview
Debal Ray, Chief Environmental Officer, Department of Environment, the Government of West Bengal	19 August 2011, Calcutta (Kolkata)
S. C. Acharyya, Jt. Project Director, Sundarban Development Board, Sundarban Affairs Department, Govt. of West Bengal	27 August 2011, Calcutta (Kolkata)

International Organisations, name/occupation	Date of the Interview
Ritu Bharadwaj, Climate Change and Energy Unit, DFID India	12 August 2011, Delhi

International Organisations, name/occupation	Date of the Interview
Anita Jawadurovna Wadud, Project Development and Programme Coordinator, International Organisation for Migration (IOM), Dhaka, Bangladesh	12 October 2011, telephone interview
Rabab Fatima, Regional Representative for South Asia, IOM, Dhaka, Bangladesh	13 October 2011, telephone interview

(Continued)

Table A.1b (Continued)

International Organisations, name/ occupation	Date of the Interview
G. Padmanabhan, Disaster Risk Management and Recovery, UNDP	12 August 2011, Delhi
Sarabjit Singh, Emergency Specialist, UNICEF	20 August 2011, Delhi

Think Tanks, name/occupation	Date of the Interview
Samir Saran, Senior Fellow and Vice President, Observer Research Foundation	13 August 2011, Delhi
Sarang Shidore and Sanya Mahajan, Strategic trends Programme 2050, Institute for Defence Studies and Analyses	7 December 2011, telephone interview
Namrata Goswami, Research Fellow, IDSA	23 August 2011, Delhi
Col. Pradeep Gautam, Research Fellow, IDSA (formerly with the MOD)	23 August 2011, Delhi

Researchers, name/occupation	Date of the Interview
Navroz Dubash, Senior Researcher, the Centre of Policy Research in Delhi	23 August 2011, Delhi
Katha Kartiki, Research Associate, the Climate Initiative, the Centre of Policy Research in Delhi	23 August 2011, Delhi
Researcher, TERI (The Energy and Research Institute)	11 August 2011, Delhi

Researchers, name/occupation	Date of the Interview
Samir Das, Professor of Political Science, University of Calcutta	29 August 2011, Calcutta (Kolkata)
Sujatha Byravan, Senior Fellow at Centre for Development Finance	26 September 2011, telephone interview
Sudir Chella Rajan, Professor and Head Humanities and Social Sciences	11 July 2011, telephone interview
Prof. Sanoy Hazarika, Centre for North East Studies & Policy Research (also columnist)	16 August 2011, Delhi
Praful Bidwai, Research Journalist/ Columnist and Activist	28 September 2011, telephone interview
Sunjadeep Banarjee, ICIMOD (International Centre for Integrated Mountain Development, Nepal)	28 July 2011, telephone interview

NGO, name/occupation	Date of the Interview
Anurag Danda, Head—Sundarbans Programme & Climate Adaptation, WWF India	11 July 2011, telephone interview
Siddharth Patthak, Policy Officer— Climate and Energy, Greenpeace India	10 August 2011, Delhi
Ravi Nair, South Asia Human Rights Documentation Centre	24 August 2011, Delhi

Index

Lightning Source UK Ltd.
Milton Keynes UK
UKHW011058140621
385488UK00010B/2402